CONSULTATION: PRACTICE AND PRACTITIONER

JONELL KIRBY, Ed.D.

Counseling and Guidance Department
West Virginia College of Graduate Studies
Institute, West Virginia

Contributors: Don Bubenzer, Ph.D.
William C. Childers, Ph.D.
William H. Culp, Ph.D.
Ernest Husson, M.A.
John West, Ed.D.
Terry Berkeley, Ed.D.

ACCELERATED DEVELOPMENT INC.

Publisher

Muncie,   Indiana

CONSULTATION: PRACTICE AND PRACTITIONER

Library of Congress Number: 84-70095

International Standard Book Number: 0-915202-48-4

Technical Development: Michelle Crowe
                          Tanya Dalton
                          Judy McWilliams
                          Sheila Sheward

Order additional copies from

Accelerated Development Inc.
Publishers   Tel (317) 284-7511
3400 Kilgore Avenue, Muncie, Indiana 47304

DEDICATION

To Joe

FOREWORD

This is a magnificent book. It will be frequently used by a variety of professionals in the wide range of disciplines in which members increasingly describe their work as "consulting." Each of us is a consultant—whatever our professional titles. Any lay person or professional who reads this book will find himself or herself building relationships that are voluntary, that are outside of the formal authority structure, that focus upon role responsibility, and that define the consulting person as having expertise in the area of consultation. Professor Kirby, helpfully, describes these four conditions as definitive of the consulting role.

This is a very useful book. It is sound in both theory and practice. Dr. Kirby presents a sound and clear discussion of the Facilitative-Directive Process Model. She gives precise and specific illustrations of how the useful model may be applied to a wide range of fields such as hospitals, community agencies, educational institutions, and business organizations. Professions will want to keep the book in a personal professional library so as to constantly refer to the wealth of detail about techniques, group exercises, scales, process tables, and stages that are integrated into each chapter. These details will be useful to the professional consultant and "trainer," but will also be useful to managers, police, ministers, adult educators, parents, administrators and anyone who gives assistance in some form.

Five successful consultants have been invited to present individual chapters that present in rich detail the specific "what" and "how" of consulting in both one-on-one relationships and group settings. Thus the reader can see how styles differ, precisely how a given theory might be interpreted, what a consultant might do in a given agency or business situation, how a consultant might handle an angry client, what different persons might do at various "stages" of the consulting process.

Kirby and her collaborators write very well. They achieve a fortunate blending of abstract theory and concrete cases. They give enough theory to provide context and structure, and enough specific detail to tell both the novice and the expert consultant what is happening. Both the novice and the expert will find the book delightful and stimulating.

I predict that this book will be discussed a great deal and widely read. The school principal and the hospital administrator will see how a perceptual restructuring of the duties of the job will be greatly enriched by seeing the significance of the consulting relationship. The parent can be more effective when he or she "consults" with the child. The effective teacher builds a consulting relationship with the co-learners in the classroom. Consulting relationships enrich the Community Mental Health Center. This book, which says so many things so well, will be a part of the healthful societal role changes that are happening in our culture. Kirby does an excellent job of clarifying the changing role of the consultant in a changing culture. The effective consultant deals with the relationship universals: informal and non-hierarchical power, the volunteer relationship, and the catalytic and facilitative relationships that form the structure of our changing culture. Our emerging culture is fast becoming a consultative and information-processing society in which the consultant is the prototype person. This book is a welcome part of this societal transformation.

Jack R. Gibb
La Jolla, California

PREFACE

Consultation is a helping modality that is being given priority by more and more practitioners in the Health and Human Services fields. Consultation is replacing referrals for comprehensive treatment and services. Previously, highly specialized practitioners tried to stay within narrowly defined areas of expertise and as client needs were identified outside those limits, the client was referred. For both the specialist and the client, this relaying of responsibility was frustrating and often resulted in inadequate services. The Service Receiver as a person, in a holistic sense, got lost in the process, and the Service Provider, as a caring professional, experienced a loss of control and worried about the outcomes for the individual.

Even though appreciation for specialized expertise has continued to increase, so has dissatisfaction with service fragmentation. Given the limitations of human capabilities and the rapidly exploding information environment, the answer clearly is not to go back to an earlier concept of the general practitioner, neither does continuing to refer clients seem tolerable. A viable alternative that is finding much favor and acceptance among professionals is to incorporate consultation as a major component of the Service Providers role and responsibility.

Consultation as a practice found its way into the health and human services fields before the activity was clearly articulated and certainly before the role and function were systematically taught. This book reflects my own evolving interest in consultation, the practice and the practitioner, and its contents represent my definitions and approach to skill development. Several successful practitioners, whose consultative work in a variety of settings was known to the author, were invited to share their experiences in case specific examples. These writers show how various techniques and strategies that emerge from their individual philosophical position are applied to the consulting process. Experiences of these writers will help differentiate between the practice of consultation and other roles the Service Provider might assume. This writer's view is that the conditions of health and human services delivery argue for consultation to become a *common activity that cuts across all professional fields.* If this becomes a reality, *consulting will be a cohesive force that discourages feelings of isolation and encourages professional identity and responsibility.* Consistent with expectations of the times, Service Providers are seeking help in developing expertise in performing this role. Requests from practitioners for clarification of the consulting role, questions about appropriate group and individual intervention techniques and strategies, and expressed concern about ways to think about helping in a consulting context caused this book to be written.

A book is never an individual affair, and this one is less so than most. Several years ago a call from a group of hospital social workers for help in consulting with patients and their families piqued my interest in the topic. Since that time both practitioners and graduate students, many of whom are fully employed professionals, have engaged in dialogue with me, asked penetrating questions that stimulated new ideas, read and reacted to numerous drafts of this book, took risks and tried out consulting models, and tested techniques and strategies. They gave feedback and through their involvement kept my motivation high. Thus, learning and teaching has been synonymous, and the writing has been a parallel activity. My appreciation to all of these people is deeply felt and my hope is that they, individually and collectively, will personalize this seemingly categorical reference. Unknowingly to them, perhaps, they have shaped this book.

Producing a book requires many kinds of assistance and support, both tangible and intangible. I would like to acknowledge and thank the members of the West Virginia Board of Regents and the faculty and administrators at the West Virginia College of Graduate Studies for granting me a sabbatical, and numerous other kinds of support, that made sustained and continuous attention to this writing possible. Truly, the production of a book is a joint effort between a writer and publisher. My gratitude is extended to the editors of Accelerated Development for their expert assistance in the preparation of the manuscript and to the publishers for their commitment to my professional development.

Much of the content of the book reflects my personal development as a consulting practitioner and many of the examples are drawn from that practice. A colleague who has been involved with me in numerous consultative activities and whose insight and sensitivity have been invaluable in my own growth is also my husband. My special thanks are extended to him, Joe Kirby, for his professional as well as personal support.

Obviously the several authors, whose chapters are included, have made major contributions to this book. Because these writers are recognized as scholars and successful practitioners in their respective fields and as consultants, their views are especially appreciated and valued. Working with them has added immeasurably to my own growth.

No word of appreciation would be complete without acknowledging the very real help provided by those who typed and retyped portions of this book and did so in a pleasant and timely manner. Making a difficult task enjoyable were Ruth Craigo, Anne Foley, Diana Saylers, and Barbara Burford. My special thanks are extended to them.

Jonell Kirby

January 1985

CONTENTS

5 CONSULTATION IN HOSPITALS: DEVELOPMENT OF A TRAIN-THE-TRAINER PROGRAM 145

6 CASE CONSULTATION: THE COMMUNITY MENTAL .... 197 HEALTH CENTER'S ENTREE TO THE SCHOOL SYSTEM

7 ORGANIZATIONAL CONSULTATION: A CASE STUDY 235

LIST OF FIGURES

LIST OF TABLES

LIST OF ACTIVITIES

LIST OF READER INVOLVEMENT ACTIVITIES

LIST OF CONSULTEES ACTIVITIES

LIST OF TECHNIQUES

CONSULTATION: DEFINITIONS AND MODEL

Jonell H. Kirby, Ed.D.

CONSULTATION: DEFINITIONS AND MODEL

Jonell H. Kirby, Ed.D.

Consulting, advising, instructing, directing, guiding—all of these words have meaning to educators, parents, and most Human and Health service providers. Most professionals view consulting as a legitimate and helpful role. Consulting seems to imply more expertise but less authority than advising, instructing, directing, or guiding. A consultant's help generally is sought at times when those in authority, such as teachers or parents, feel stymied in their legally defined authoritative roles and ineffective or frustrated in their efforts to influence the behavior of others for whom they are responsible. *In a sense, a consultant is a catalytic agent in that the consultant sets into motion changes between persons and/or among social forces without appreciable changes occurring in the person of the consultant nor in the relationship role of the consultant to the social system.*

Consulting generally is seen as offering a professional service to another professional resulting in an impact on some other individual. Dinkmeyer and Carlson (1975) defined consulting as "a process by which administrators, teachers, parents, pupil personnel specialists, and other significant adults in the life of a client communicate *about* him" (p. 1).

A consultant's advice or help is sought because he/she is viewed as an expert. This person with expertise may be a person who is external to the group or system seeking help, and indeed this request would be the usual situation, but the consultant also may be a person who is part of the group. When the individual serving as a consultant is a member of the group, the consultative service is performed as a psychological outsider. That is, the consultant has no vested interest in, nor administrative responsibility for, the decisions made by the group.

A minister who is consulted about a teenage daughter who is pregnant and unmarried would be an example of an *external consultant*. A family member who is seen as successful in the academic world might be consulted about potential school and college referrals for a son. In this case, a family member is asked to become a consultant. In both instances, *the choice of the consultant reflects the values of those seeking help and offers a clue concerning their hoped for outcomes.* The question which will have to be confronted in both cases is, "What does the daughter or son want?" The youth might be called the *primary,* albeit invisible, *client* who is to receive an indirect service; the parents are the consultees. Perhaps these parents are the only ones who want to see some change effected. Also, these parent's choice of consultant may reflect their values and may not be those of the "primary client."

RELATIONSHIP DEFINITIONS

Lippitt (1975) offered the observation that "consultation, like supervision, or love, is a general label for many variations of relationships" (p. 42). An examination of the literature and observations of professionals prove Lippitt correct. As a way to seek clarification, consultation is herein defined in terms of relationship conditions.

CONDITION 1: CONSULTANT-CONSULTEE RELATIONSHIP IS VOLUNTARY

Problems arise in meeting this criterion when consultative services are secured by one person for someone else as suggested previously. When this happens, consultation shifts from the contact person being the consultee to the consultee's *client* becoming the consultee. The definition criterion for consultation must still be met, i.e., the consultee's client must *volunteer* to work with the consultant. When the term *Initiator* is used hereafter, the intent is to communicate that the contact person secured the services of the consultant to work with another person or group.

CONDITION 2: THE FOCUS OF CONSULTATION INTERVENTION IS ON A WORK SITUATION OR ROLE OF RESPONSIBILITY OF THE CONSULTEE

The situation may relate to a role responsibility, such as parent, or to a work responsibility, such as administrator. The consultee's perception of the nature of his/her responsibility, rather than their adequacy in those roles, is the focus of attention.

CONDITION 3: THE CONSULTANT IS FUNCTIONING OUTSIDE THE STRUCTURAL HIERARCHY

In the role of consultant an individual has no authority or power over the consultee and is not responsible for outcomes of decisions made by the consultee. The removal of even perceptions of power is a rather

persuasive argument for securing external consultants, even when expertise is available within the system.

CONDITION 4: THE CONSULTANT IS
PERCEIVED AS AN EXPERT IN THE AREA IN
WHICH CONSULTATION IS OFFERED

Power based on expertise is the only legitimate source of power for
the consultant. This power base may be developed slowly within the context of the consultative process, or the consultant may bring a reputation
of expertise to the group.

A consultant functions as a catalyst or facilitator. This means the
consultant offers information when needed, structure for the problem
exploration process when appropriate, suggestions and alternatives when
helpful, and encouragement and support when useful. Nevertheless, the
consultant's role is to stimulate action rather than control the action; the
consultant manages the decision-making process but is not responsible
for the choices of the consultee nor outcomes those choices precipitate.

Consultation is a role appropriate for individuals of various professions. Skills and understanding needed to function effectively as a consultant are those possessed by numerous individuals. However, the application of personal and professional skills in problem situations as a
consultant is identifiably different from the application of the same skills
in other role functions, such as that of counselor, minister, social
worker, administrator, and so forth.

Example Situations

Some examples of consultative experiences of the author are
presented in Figure 1.1. The purpose of the figure is to show some
diverse requests that meet the relationship conditions articulated earlier.
When the consultee's goal was to involve the consultant in working
directly with the consultee's client i.e., the person(s) in the consultee's
work hierarchy, the term *Initiator* is used. When the consultant accepts
the request to provide direct services to the consultee's client then the
client becomes the consultee.

(Initiator) Consultee	Stated Need or Perceived Problem	Impact Group (Primary Client)
A. SCHOOL SETTING		
Committee Chairperson (Initiator)	Which site to choose and how to organize for early, middle, and secondary educators	School community, Bus drivers, Faculty
Principal (Initiator)	Teachers are too authoritarian with students and too dependent on the principal for leadership.	Teacher and Administration, Students
High School Principal (Initiator)	Low morale, unidentified hostility, and problems	80 Faculty, Staff, and Administrators indirectly
Teacher (Consultee)	Children are generally disruptive and irresponsible	Students
Teacher Aide Supervisor (Initiator)	Teachers and teachers aides are somewhat suspicious of each other and do not work together effectively	25 Teachers 25 Aides
Faculty Members (Consultees)	The administrator is not responsive to our needs and personal problems	Administrators
B. FAMILY SETTING		
Parents (Consultee)	We are into a second marriage and childen are involved. How can we survive the disruption?	Children, Parents, Grand-parents, Step-grand-parents
Wife (Consultee)	My husband just will not work. We have a child and I can't. How can I make him see that he has responsibility?	Wife, Husband, Children
Husband (Consultee)	My wife refuses to stop work even though the children are having problems. Why won't she stay home and be a wife and mother?	Husband, Wife, Children

Figure 1.1. Examples of consultative issues.

(Initiator) Consultee	Stated Need or Perceived Problem	Impact Group (Primary Client)

C. COMMUNITY OR PROFESSIONAL SETTING

Lawyer (Initiator)	Younger members of the firm are not treated equally and personal growth is stymied.	25 to 30 Professional lawyers
Member Professional Staff Chamber of Commerce (Initiator)	Advisory council needs help in setting long term goals for C of C, establishing priorities and allocating resources.	Professional staff, Advisory Council
Hospital Social Workers (Initiator)	Need help in working with families with children confined to the hospital	10 to 15 Social workers, Visitors and Staff
Minister (Initiator)	Fragmented services due to youth workers, teachers, and leaders not following church policy	Staff members, Youths, Parents, Church officials
Administrator Social Worker (Initiator)	Social system unresponsive to needs and problems of foster parents	10 Professional staff, 8 to 10 Foster parents

Figure 1.1. Continued.

Implicit in these examples is the notion that *a consultative relationship is suggested when an individual seeks help to bring about a change in the system (work or role related), and the change will have an impact on one or more other persons.*

Operational Definition

Operationally defined, a consultative relationship meets the following relationship conditions:

1. the relationship is voluntary,

2. the focus of attention is on the problem situation as articulated by the consultee(s),

3. the consultant is not functioning as a part of the structural hierarchy, and

4. the power that resides in consultant's expertise is sufficient to facilitate change.

Issues involving the problem, the client, potential barriers, and expected outcomes need to be addressed before a consultant agrees to initiate a consultative relationship through an Initiator. These issues and related questions are as follows:

1. THE PROBLEM

    a. What is the problem?

    b. What is the intended outcome or product from the viewpoint of the Initiator?

    c. How was the problem identified?

    d. Is the problem perceived by the Initiator only?

    e. Who owns the problem?

    f. Does the problem have meaning to the person or people who will receive help?

2. CLIENTS

    a. Who will be involved in the relationship?

    b. What are their similarities?

    c. What are their differences?

    d. How do they feel about being involved?

    e. What fears will they bring to the group?

3. BARRIERS

    a. What are the initial barriers which I, as a consultant, will face?

    b. To what concerns must I as the consultant respond in order to initiate involvement of the primary client(s)?

    c. How would relationships be different if the people involved in the consultative relationship did not know each other?

    d. How does my professional role affect my consultative contact?

4. OBJECTIVES OR OUTCOMES

    a. Why did the Initiator seek my help—as opposed to someone else?

    b. What are expected outcomes from the viewpoint of the Initiator?

    c. Who will benefit from the experience?

PROCESS MODEL OF GROUP CONSULTATION

When a consultant works with groups, he/she is quite often requested to do so by an individual, referred to previously as the Initiator, who is in a position of responsibility for the work performance of that group. For the consultant, making the transition from working with the Initiator to consulting with the group is most difficult. If the consultant is ineffective at this point, then ineffective consultation will result. Questions of motives—of the consultant's as well as the initiator's—tend to loom large with the client group; motivation of the group is often a factor partly because these group members were not the ones who requested the consultation. Other issues of concern are organizational constraints which can present real problems or they can be used as convincing excuses to sabotage the consultative process. Therefore, the initial contact with the client group is a critical point if workable relationships with the group and the consultant are to evolve.

Consultation is a *process*. It is a process whereby the consultant helps the consultees achieve their goals. Thus, the consultant facilitates the consultees' problem-solving process and, at times, guides, leads, or directs consultees as they use the consultant's expertise in their goal-seeking behavior. In the next section is offered a model useful to consultants who work from the process perspective. A variety of techniques and strategies are appropriately applied within this plan.

FACILITATIVE-DIRECTIVE PROCESS MODEL

In the Facilitative-Directive Process Model of consultation, as the name implies, the initiating role of the consultant is perceived as being essentially facilitative. Once a problem is identified, the consultant moves into a more directive or guiding role. Conceptually this approach is similar to the one outlined by Lippitt (1975). Both the Facilitative-Directive Process Model and the one suggested by Lippitt (1975) identified seven phases or stages. At each stage, a new level of integration is experienced and the problem situation is viewed by the consultee in a qualitatively different way.

In the Facilitative-Directive Process Model, the seven stages are defined in terms of the consultant's orientation that responds to the consultees' attitudes. Additionally, the consultant's function at each stage is differentiated, and, in general terms, outcomes or movement indicators for each stage are specified. Stages as they relate to the consultant's intervention style are as follows:

FACILITATIVE—Phase I (Member Involvement)

Stage 1—Initial (definition and awareness)

Stage 2—Tentative task commitment

Stage 3—Problem clarification

DIRECTIVE—Phase II (Problem Solving)

Stage 4—Alternative exploration

Stage 5—Action

Stage 6—Stabilization

TERMINATION—Phase III

Stage 7—Projection/Termination

A description and summary of the Facilitative-Directive Process Consultative Model is provided in Figure 1.2. Essentially, the model is a means for *operationalizing, sequencing, pacing,* and *attending.* Thus, the consultative model, beginning with the initiating activity and ending with assessment, is a structured guide. As a guide, techniques and procedures which are to be used at each stage are not part of the model, but the description of the model includes how group techniques, such as ones discussed in subsequent chapters, can be used in the context of consulting.

As indicated previously, the Facilitative-Directive Process Model is applied to a group setting, however, the model is applicable with little modification when working with individuals.

STAGE CONCEPT

The Facilitative-Directive Process Model depicts changes of consultee's attitude through seven discernable stages. Functions of the consultant at each stage suggest techniques and strategies appropriate to short term process goals. Note that the consultant's orientation at each stage is in response to the consultee's attitude: The "Movement Indicators" are cues the consultant uses to mark the end of one stage and readiness for a new focus of attention. How the consultant responds to the consultees' attitude is described sequentially.

Stage 1

Initially (Stage 1), the consultant is concerned with responding to consultees who are, understandably, ambivalent about being involved. Thus the *consultee's attitude* is one of questioning the reason for the contact, the role the consultant will serve and his/her own role in the group. The *function* of the consultant at Stage 1 is to establish a helpful relationship by responding to consultees' concerns. The *consultant's orientation* is open, accepting, and congruent. The consultant demonstrates an *acceptance* of the individuals' feelings and *respect* for their individual uniqueness.

Resources and techniques which are applied at Stage 1 are those which generally are thought of as representing a client-centered (Rogers, 1951) or facilitative attitude. A high level of communication skills are needed (Carkhuff, 1969a; 1969b). This means facilitative conditions (i.e., empathy and respect) are necessary for change to occur.

Stage 2

Stage 2 is reached when group members make a decision that the task of the group seems appropriate and that he/she is part of the group. At Stage 2, a shift occurs in the personal concern from "What is the group about?" to "What is my role in the group?" The *consultee's attitude* then is related to self in the change process. In response, the consultant's *function* is to explore the relationship of sub-systems to the functioning of the group and the impact the interdependent sub-system has on the individual.

FACTORS	PHASE I — FACILITATIVE		
	STAGE 1	STAGE 2	STAGE 3
	Initial (Definitional & Awareness)	Tentative Task Commitment	Problem Clarification
FUNCTION	Establish rapport; discuss purpose of consultation and source of referral	Explore relationship of sub-parts of system; clarify consultant's role; define participants' role; establish ground rules	a) Surface concerns; b) dialogue issues; c) prioritize
CONSULTANT ORIENTATION	Facilitative; open, trust, respect, congruence . . . . . Basically client centered	Client and task centered; group leader	Facilitative; task-centered structured procedure
CONSULTEE'S ATTITUDE	Questioning: a) concerning problem b) concerning roles and expectations	Questions own role in process; recognizes need for change; makes decision to participate	Active participant; open; revealing; trusting
MOVEMENT INDICATORS	Tentative trust and agreement with importance of issues; expressed hope	Verbal "contract" with each participant to work on problem	Prioritized list of concerns; Problem defined & issues clarified

Figure 1.2 Facilitative-directive process model.

PHASE 2 — DIRECTIVE			
STAGE 4	STAGE 5	STAGE 6	STAGE 7
Alternative Exploration	Action	Stabilization	Projection/ Termination
Generate alternatives; evaluate these; solve problems	Plan "next" step / short range goal(s)	Report on first try of "plan;" provide feedback; reassess	Predict effectiveness of plans; identify sources of strengths; plan for "check-up"
Instructing; active; structured (consultant-trainer)	Guiding; questioning; assisting; introducing new materials, resources	Facilitative; raises issues; checks out individual commitment — reaches consensus	Reflective; facilitative; summarizing; supporting
Exploring alternatives; risking; high trust	Making tentative choices; checking out data; committing to action	Seeking group support; evaluating self; committing to group goal	Involved; supportive; committed
Alternatives identified; values explored; clarification of options	Statement of next step: what, when, how, who	Plan of action a) individual b) group	Follow-up plan and feedback system

Figure 1.2 Continued

Again, the consultant relates as a facilitator whose concern is to understand the consultee. After a reasonable level of comfort is reached in terms of the purpose and value of the group, the consultant helps the group establish ground rules.

This stage terminates when agreement is reached that each individual is committed to the work of the group and concensus has been reached concerning how the group will function.

Stage 3

The *consultee's attitude* is to move into the work of the group, but the specifics of the task have not been articulated. This *function* must receive attention from the consultant. The consultant structures the task (such as identifying issues, defining problems, etc.) while continuing to respond to the open, trusting, psychologically revealing behavior of the consultee. This stage is completed when the group has defined their problems, surfaced their individual and group concerns and reached a consensus concerning the importance of issues that were generated.

Basic responses the consultant makes at this stage are still essentially facilitative. However, the task is structured at this stage so that the attention of the group is on common concerns. The consultant can use any number of strategies of group leadership to help the group articulate those concerns. Numerous group techniques are described in other chapters that can be applied at this stage.

From the author's point of view, this stage represents the appropriate time to initiate the first step of the VISUAL method of problem solving. (See Chapter 2 for a discussion of the VISUAL Model and Chapter 3 for example applications.) Conceptually, problem definition is the task. Thus, the first step of the VISUAL method, i.e., "VERBALIZE ABOUT THE PROBLEM UNTIL A CLEAR PROBLEM CAN BE STATED," is an appropriate tool or technique (Kirby, 1979).

Phases I and II

Stages 1 through 3 comprise the first phase, Phase I, (Member Involvement), which is the FACILITATIVE dimension of the process. Following Phase I the approach shifts to a far more DIRECTIVE style. Until this point, completion of Stage 3, the consultant has been interested in helping the group articulate their concerns, helping them establish a trusting relationship with each other and obtaining a commitment, individually and collectively, to the work of the group. Sometimes the consultant's role ends here—but that would have been made clear in the beginning, i.e., when objectives were stated and agreed upon. At any rate, the consultative process moves into a new phase, Phase II (Problem Solving), where a shift occurs from facilitating the group to a more active leadership or structuring role. If the consultant's work ends with Phase I, responsibility for developing and implementing a response to identified concerns is someone elses. If the consultant is committed to the group to help them deal with problems which have been identified, then the consultant shifts to a new type of interaction and new techniques and strategies are required to help the group progress toward termination.

Stage 4

By the start of Stage 4, the problem has been defined and the group is ready to explore alternatives. Because trust in the group has been developed, *consultees' attitude* reveals willingness to take risks and cooperate. The consultant's *function* is to help the group amplify their problems, explore alternatives and potential options, weigh those options against the potential cost, and predict the ultimate outcomes for each possible course of action. The consultant's orientation is more instructing or assigning than reflecting and facilitating. Nevertheless, this shift in emphasis does not negate a person-centered attitude. Again, the VISUAL method, mentioned previously, offers a tool which is useful at this stage. Stage 4 is a natural progression following the work of Stage 3 (problem clarification stage) and provides the basic information which will be needed in Stage 5, the Action stage.

Stage 5

The consultees are ready to make a tentative choice or choices. Their choices will be based on ideas they generated in the previous Stage that helped them clarify changes they wanted to occur or objectives they wanted to reach. The *consultee's attitude* then is commitment to action. The *function* of the consultant is to help the group develop an individual, or more likely, a common plan of action. The "next steps" are enumerated in rather specific terms (see VISUAL method, Chapter 2). Group members can make important contributions to each other as each member shares one's goals and objectives, gets clarifications from the group, and makes explicit steps which one will take to initiate the proposed plan of action.

The consultant helps the group establish a plan to follow-up their individual and group efforts. Stage 5 ends with an agreement that each member will implement his/her plans, observe outcomes, and report back to the group at the agreed time.

Usually Stage 5 ends with a high note of excitement and optimistic attitudes. In a sense, for the consultant a plateau is reached, and consultees move to a period of stabilization.

Stage 6

The consultee meets the group with an awareness of shared experiences and commitment. The *consultees' attitude* reflects self evaluation and concern for the group. The *function* of the consultant is to help group members assess their progress, develop new directions, and, where appropriate, support individual differences and common needs. The consultant's orientation is a mixture of the facilitative and directive: the task is structured and the consultant maintains a task attending posture; yet, the needs of the individual and the developmental dimension of the group require concern for the relationships among group members. This dimension ends with a new commitment to a plan of action. This commitment may be to the initial plan, a modified plan, or an entirely new plan. Ways to follow progress and make additional change/corrections are developed. Approval from the consultant is communicated.

Stage 7—Phase III

Stage 7 is the termination stage (Phase III). The consultative process has run its course, and like a maturing child the help of this stronger person (expert) is less often needed and continued help may be seen as an intrusion and may be resented. The *consultees' attitude* has moved to one of confidence and acceptance; therefore, the group is facilitative and supportive with their peers. Strength is demonstrated as the consultees reflect feelings of others and show acceptance for individual uniqueness. The consultant has modeled the skills of being facilitative and has taught steps in problem resolution. The *function* of the consultant at Stage 7 is to respond to strengths of the group and point ways the group can maintain growth through planned "check-ups." In an emotional context, the consultant removes himself/herself from an ongoing process. Stage 7 ends with the group commitment to their own growth and expressions of comfort in receiving feedback and planning for change.

Summary

The Facilitative-Directive Process Model has been presented as a way to map the strategies and techniques of consultation. In consultation, the relationship between the consultant and consultee is differentiated from other helper-helpee relationships in that the consultant:

1. invites, but does not control, participation;

2. focuses attention on work or role responsibility of the consultee;

3. communicates cooperation and equality; and

4. works outside the structural hierarchy.

CONSULTATION—A ROLE FUNCTION

Other writers have addressed the issue of consultation, and several authors have advanced conceptual frameworks for the practice of consultation. Almost all writers have mentioned the confusion associated with the word consultation. Perhaps confusion relates to the fact that consultation is a role performed by many professionals. Generally, consultation is not viewed as a profession *per se*. Nevertheless, to differentiate the role of consultation from other roles is important. Just as "teaching" is a *role* practiced by many professionals and parents, teaching is not the only way to address concerns and developmental issues—"to teach" implies a different response from such things as "to supervise" or "to counsel." When the role is confused in the mind of the practitioner, appropriate role behaviors are not maintained and the usual outcome is frustration and feelings of inadequacy.

The contributed Chapters 3 through 7 can be utilized to help differentiate between consultation and other professional roles. Several articles, published elsewhere, have focused on the nature, training, and application of consulting as a change agent process. Together these authors bring a sense of identity to the practice of consultation and to the practitioner. A brief review of these approaches to consultation suggested by the several authors is offered. These writers, while representing many and diverse professional fields and areas of expertise, hold many common attitudes about the consultative relationships, yet enrich the practice by offering a variety of techniques and strategies.

DIRECT—A CONSULTATION SKILLS TRAINING MODEL

DIRECT Model—A Consultation Skills Training Model by Stum (1982) is reviewed first because the skills articulated therein are so similar to those suggested as needed by the consultant using the Facilitative-Directive Process Model. Additionally, skills are fitted into a two-way process model that includes seven steps and four levels. The author noted the model was developed as a response to the "collective anxiety" of former students in consultation process courses. They were anxious because they felt they needed to know, "What are you supposed to do in a consulting interview, and *how* are you supposed to do it?" (p. 296).

Consistent with the Facilitative-Directive Process Model, the DIRECT Model assumes the consultant recognizes the immediate goal for each stage and uses... "responses" or leads to structure each step. The consultant progresses through four levels at each stage, i.e., *enter, initiate, educate,* and *evaluate.* Since DIRECT Model was offered as a skills training model, Stum (1982) proposed an evaluation scale he identified as TREC—The Technique and Relationship Evaluation Chart (Figure 1.3).

As explained by Stum (1982), "The Seven Steps are shown down the side of TREC and the Four Levels are diagrammed across the chart. Under each level, 'Cue' words are given as aides in remembering the behavior and leads indicated for that level" (p. 298).

Obviously a wide range of group techniques would fit under the "cue" words. In addition to its intended purpose, this model could be used to devise a filing system for techniques and strategies of consultation.

Direct Steps	1	2	3	4	Possible	Score
—A— Establish Consulting Relationship	Situation is . . .	consult . . . problem solving	steps together	work together? . . . move to problem	(10)	___
—B— Identify, Clarify Problem	history . . . . . . position	summarize . . . . . . theme	feelings . . . . problem scope	problem defined? . . . move to goals	(10)	___
—C— Determine Desired Outcome	goal setting	goal summary	measure progress	goals set? . . . move to developing ideas	(10)	___
—D— Develop Ideas and Strategies	previous ideas	"brainstorm"	add ideas . . . . support change	ideas developed? . . . move to planning	(10)	___
—E— Develop a Plan	choose, link ideas	consultee behavior	state plan	plan developed? . . . move to specify plan	(10)	___
—F— Specify Plan	steps in plan	time-frame	evaluation	plan specified? . . . move to confirm relationship	(10)	___
—G— Confirm Consulting Relationship	follow-up	confidence	summary . . . . relationship	work completed? . . . move to future contact	(10)	___
POSSIBLE	(7)	(14)	(21)	(28)	(70)	

PROCESS/CONTENT/RELATIONSHIP SUMMARY

TOTAL SCORE ___

Figure 1.3 Technique & relationship evaluation chart (TREC) lead response levels.

CONSULCUBE—A SYSTEMATIC FRAMEWORK

While consulting is not explicitly defined in most of the articles and works on the topic, the commonality of practice is implied in Blake and Mouton's (1976) conceptualization which they refer to as the "Consulcube" (Blake & Mouton, 1976, p. 7). The Consulcube is a three-dimensional figure comprised of 100 cells (5 units of change x 5 types of intervention x 4 kinds of focal issues), and can be used by consultants in analyzing, classifying, and explaining the process and procedures they use in consultation. Conceptually, the Consulcube is broad enough to encompass a wide range of approaches to consultation, including the Facilitative-Directive Process Model. A consultant can use the Consulcube to help expand one's range of interventions, force one into an analysis of the unit of change, and help one define issues in ways that suggest techniques for change. This writer believes a coding system derived from the consulcube could serve as a helpful tool for filing materials relevant to consultation.

Apparently Blake and Mouton (1976) are rather pragmatic in their definition of consultation. They leave relationship criteria and role differentiation somewhat to the practitioner. They recognize Lippitt's (1959) definition of consultation, but conclude that the consultative role is expanding so much that a precise identification of the consultant as presently designated is probably not possible.

CAPLAN'S MODEL—MENTAL HEALTH CONSULTATION

Professionals with expertise in the mental health fields generally are involved in clinical practice. Skills used by a clinician are those that facilitate clients to explore their personal lives, feelings, and individual issues. Mental health consultation requires the application of significantly different skills: (1) The consultant's orientation is changed from the clinician working with "patients" to one of a professional work with a "colleague" and (2) the focus of concern is no longer the personal lives of the helpee but the work problems of the consultee.

Because Caplan (1970) has so clearly delineated the roles of the mental health professional working as a therapist to that of working as a consultant, his model should be studied and his distinctions considered as one tries to devise a role definition for a consultant in any setting.

In his book, Caplan (1970) restricts the use of the word consultation

> to denote a process of interaction between two professional persons—the consultant, who is the specialist, and the consultee, who invokes the consultant's help in regard to a current work problem with which he is having some difficulty and which he has decided is within the other's area of specialized competence. The work problem involves the management or treatment of one or more clients of the consultee, or the planning or implementation of a program to cater to such elements. (p. 19)

Caplan (1970) discussed the need for the consultant to have a plan, or "conceptual map," for consultation so that one can quickly choose appropriate responses and set limits on one's role. As a definition of consultation, Caplan's (1970) work deserves special attention. As a model of consultation, especially for the professional working within a professional relationship, the model deserves repeated study and assimilation.

In the lead article of a special issue on consultation, the Journal writers noted: "At this stage of development in the field of consultation, most writers and practitioners tend to define consultation through the actual process, vis a' vis what the consultant actually does" (Kurpius & Robinson, 1978, p. 321). This definition is still typically the case. Caplan (1970) is one of the few to articulate the salient features of consultation and distinguish the consultant's role from other professional roles.

CASE CONSULTATION—A COMMUNITY MENTAL HEALTH CENTER (CMHC) TEAM APPROACH

Case Consultation, the model proposed by West and Berkeley (Chapter 6, this publication), offers the strength that comes from interdisciplinary corroboration and the financial efficiency that comes from interagency cooperation. Case Consultation is the suggested approach for the Community Mental Health Center (CMHC) Team to apply in assuming a role as external consultant to the school system.

Case Consultation, according to these authors (West & Berkeley) has evolved, partially at least, from the demands from citizens for more services, less delay, and quicker results. West and Berkeley view the schools as being in a potentially powerful position to respond to the demands emanating from the community but may lack the expertise and other resources necessary to effectuate change. The needed expertise can be brought by the CMHC Team to bear on the school related problems through the consultative process.

These authors articulate the role and function of the CMHC Team as consultants to the school system and suggest procedures for entering and leaving the relationship. While they describe a process model paralleling closely the Facilitative-Directive Process Model (Kirby) suggested previously, there are some important preliminary steps to entering the consultant-consultee relationship. These involve administrative relationship development and contract negotiations. While the Community Mental Health Center and the School System are the two systems described as interfacing in the Case Conference process, other agencies will find the model and techniques useful and applicable.

A particularly important aspect of the West and Berkeley presentation is the example situation described along with illustrations of specific probes and responses the consultant might use to enhance problem conceptualization and resolution. Their approach recognizes the importance of diverse issues that are brought to bear on the problem solving activity that forms the focus for Case Consultation. Maintaining the partnership attitude between the consultant (i.e., the CMHC Team) and the Consultee is a central theme in these authors' presentation.

The Case Conference approach suggests the importance of high level group leadership skills and sensitivity to group process dynamics. The CMHC Team works as a group and interacts, most often, with a group. Thus the Case Conference Consultant is a group leader and facilitator. Group skills and attitudes of effective leadership form the backdrop for successful implementation of this interdisciplinary team model.

STRATEGIC SYSTEMIC CONSULTATION PROCESS

A consultant looking for a rationale for consultation using system theory and group dynamic intervention strategies will find the model proposed by Bubenzer (Chapter 4) attractive. Referring to his approach as the Strategic Systemic Consultation Process (SSCP), Bubenzer described an interrelated sequence of seven steps that takes the consultant through the following processes:

1. problem identification,

2. generating objectives,

3. assessing the climate for change,

4. specifying resources,

5. developing change strategies,

6. change implementation, and

7. evaluation.

The dynamics of an interrelated system is the continuing focus for the consultant using the SSCP approach. Thus, in addition to group leadership skills, the consultant applying this model must possess expertise in three general areas. These are

1. problem solving/planning appropriate for community agencies,

2. facilitative skills to bring about attitudinal changes, and

3. role flexibility that allows the consultant to respond to the identified consultees and their assessment of problems and shifts in concerns.

Bubenzer contributed more than a model to the understanding of consultation. Using the SSCP approach, Bubenzer showed how an individual can apply these steps of the process when working within a community agency setting. Additionally, and perhaps more importantly, he then illustrated the application of the SSCP Model wherein the consultative function is performed by a seven person interdisciplinary team (MDT) in a community agency context. Thus, a complex situation is reduced to operationally simple components. Bubenzer walks the reader through two applied cases: one in which a consultative team (MDT) works with an individual case in a community agency, and a second one in which an individual consults with an agency as consultee.

CONSULTANT AS TRAINER

The Internal Consultant as Trainer

As an insider, serving as a consultant to colleagues and others who know him/her well, Husson (Chapter 3) suggested that working from the assumption that participating agencies, as consultees, bring three major concerns to the consultative relationship:

1. the consultant's *credibility;*

2. the agency *resources* that will be allocated to this consultative activity; and

3. the outcomes, as they pertain to the agency's sense of *accountability.*

While these three aspects of consultation are important, regardless of the context, Husson sensitized us to the fact that without a reputation as an effective facilitator and good problem solver in the discharge of his/her professional duties, the insider, even if recruited as a consultant to work with a peer group or agency within the human service system, would not gain the cooperation and commitment needed to be an effective leader or trainer.

On the other hand, a practitioner with recognized skills as a helper is likely to be requested to serve as a consultant. Husson implied that part of the credibility dimension, for the insider, depends on using those very strategies and techniques that, by reputation, colleagues have come to expect. Working from this point of view Husson seemed to suggest that the successful practitioner can "package" a set of techniques and strategies to be utilized when the individual serves as a consultant to train other service providers. The consultant, as an insider, is in a position somewhat like the singer who has a hit tune: the audience wants and expects to hear the artist's most popular song and will feel cheated if they do not—even if the singer has moved on to other music and styles and has tired of the tune that made the individual famous.

Husson's articulation of the competencies to be addressed in the consultative relationship with service providers, whose professional role requires them to perform under life threatening conditions, is a useful conceptualization. If the consultee accepts the notion that the consultant is addressing a *specific* and *limited* set of competencies important to the work of the consultee, but not comprising the professional expertise identified as those most useful in crisis situations, the consultee will be more accepting of the peer as consultant and more open to trying out new behaviors. This element of the process appears to be closely allied to the concept of individual and agency credibility.

External Consultant as Trainer

Reflecting a personal philosophy that helping skills are of utmost importance in providing adequate care in a hospital setting, Childers (Chapter 5) proposes a Train-the-Trainer Consultative Model that promises rapid diffusion of skills and knowledge. Gaining acceptance by the hospital staff is an initial barrier for the external consultant, especially if the consultant's professional role is not within the health care service area. Nevertheless, with attention to credibility concerns and careful differentiation between the technical and nontechnical concerns of the health care provider, the consultant with expertise in human relations training can find hospital staffs receptive to both the training program and to the person of the consultant. Once initial credibility is established and the first cadre of workers is prepared to implement the training program in their respective hospital, the requests for similar programs seem to multiply. Credibility, accountability, and resource allocation for the training program are important common themes voiced by Childers and Husson (Chapters 5 and 3 respectively) for both external and internal consultants serving as trainers.

As a trainer, Childers seemed to suggest that a consultant's success with cooperating agencies is far more likely if the guidelines are followed:

1. Cultivate a relationship that allows enough interaction for the agency personnel to develop an awareness that training is needed, and acceptance of the proposed program is expressed.

2. Begin with interested "volunteers," thus making the program a "grass roots" effort and responsibility.

3. Initiate the concept that the consultant will move to the tertiary level (providing support and assistance) once individuals are trained to assume the consultative role.

4. Follow-up with maintenance support and professional development assistance on a continuing basis.

ORGANIZATIONAL CONSULTATION

Writing from a small organization case study perspective, Culp (Chapter 7) stresses the personality factors of the practitioner as constituting the critical element in consultation. While Culp uses the Facilitative-Directive Process Model in an organizational development context, he made it clear that the personal agenda of the practitioner is the potential weak link. To Culp the model and the strategies used by the consultant are important, but the style of the consultant will still determine whether or not procedures will be effective. Culp, who has participated in the TORI Internship program with Jack Gibb (1978), implied that Trust (the T of the TORI process), on the part of the consultant, is the foundation upon which all other elements are dependent.

Culp presented a case study of a consultative process. He included activities in the case report to help the reader take the mental position of the practitioner, thus giving some practice in role-playing. Nevertheless, Culp made the point that one can never develop the self-assurance, self-Trust, needed to be an effective consultant by just reading about it. Practice is mandatory. Practice, under the tutorage of a competent consultant, is, of course, desirable.

Culp assumed the trainer-consultant role as he moved from working with the individual company owner-manager to staff development. As a trainer, Culp applied a *Want-Think-Feel-Do* workshop model to help participants articulate their individual and group needs and establish common goals. Throughout both case reports Culp showed the importance of compatibility between the consultant's personal philosophy and strategies used to implement changes within the organization.

SUMMARY

Most writers agree that consulting is an identifiable role that requires *application* of various skills and knowledge that defines what the consultant can do and say.

In some instances, at least as the consultative process is described in the literature, a consultant works with the consultee's client (such as a teacher's student); thus, offering a *direct* service to the client. This service leaves the consultant-consultee relationship unclear. When the consultant works with the consultee's client, then the relationship is questionable as to being consultative. In an effort to bring a sharper operational definition, this writer has used identifying terminology to show changes in relationships that occur. A restatement of terms and the context of those uses are provided as follows:

1. A consultative relationship is established when the consultant works with an individual:

   a. concerning a role responsibility or work situation;

   b. the relation is, and remains, voluntary;

   c. the consultant has power based on expertise; and

   d. the consultant is *not* a part of the structural hierarchy.

2. A consultant works with a consultee about a situation that has an impact on another individual or group. This person or group is the consultee's client and is therefore referred to as the "primary client" in the consultative process. The "primary client" is *not* generally seen by the consultant in the absence of the consultee, except perhaps to secure information about the primary client for diagnostic purposes.

3. When the consultee asks the consultant to work with the "primary client(s)," with or without the consultee being present, the consultee's role changes to *initiator,* and the "primary client" assumes the role of consultee. If the relationship is to be consultative with the new consultee (the ones

receiving direct service of the consultant) the conditions of the consultative relationship, as specified in Item 1 previously, must be met. If the four conditions of a consultative relationship are not met, then those services received by the "primary client" are something other than consultation.

If the conditions of the consultative relationship are met, the consultant can work with the consultee from such positions as trainer, change agent, or facilitator. Techniques and strategies that are useful for accomplishing consultative goals are discussed elsewhere.

REFERENCES

Blake, R. R., & Mouton, J. S. (1976). *Consultation*. Reading, MA: Addison-Wesley.

Caplan, G. (1970). *The theory and practice of mental health consultation*. New York: Basic Books.

Carkhuff, R. R. (1969a). *Helping and human relations: A primer for lay and professional helpers*. Vol. 1: Selection and Training. New York: Holt, Rinehart and Winston.

Carkhuff, R. R. (1969b). *Helping and human relations: A primer for lay and professional helpers*. Vol. 2: *Practice and Research*. New York: Holt, Rinehart and Winston.

Dinkmeyer, D., & Carlson, J. (Eds.). (1975). *Consultation: A book of readings*. New York: John Wiley.

Gibb, J. (1978). *TRUST: A new view of personal and organizational development*. Los Angeles: Guild of Tutors Press.

Kirby, J. (1979). *Second marriage*. Muncie, IN: Accelerated Development.

Kurpius, D., & Robinson, S.E. (1978). An overview of consultation. *Personnel and Guidance Journal, 56*(6), 321-323.

Lippitt, R. (1975). Dimensions of the consultant's job. In D. Dinkmeyer & J. Carlson (Eds.). *Consultation—A book of readings*. New York: John Wiley. pp.42-50.

Lippitt, R. (1959). Dimensions of the consultant's job. *Journal of Social Issues*, 5-12.

Rogers, C. R. (1951). *Client-centered therapy*. Boston: Houghton Mifflin.

Stum, D. L. (1982). DIRECT—A consultation skills training model. *Personnel and Guidance Journal, 60* (5), 196-301.

APPLICATION OF FACILITATIVE-DIRECTIVE PROCESS MODEL

Jonell H. Kirby, Ed.D.

APPLICATION OF FACILITATIVE-DIRECTIVE PROCESS MODEL

Jonell H. Kirby, Ed.D.

Models of consultation help establish the behavioral parameters for the consultant and offer a guide for picking and choosing strategies and techniques to accomplish relationship goals. In Chapter 1 were introduced the Facilitative-Directive Process Model and presented a brief overview of other models and operational definitions of consultation. This chapter is concerned with the application of the Facilitative-Directive Process Model to a group setting.

The assumption is made, for purposes of discussing this model, that an Initiator has secured the services of the consultant to work with a group. Group members are ambivalent about working with the consultant. The consultant approaches this group with the knowledge that they, individually as well as collectively, may not wish to be there; they may not wish to work with this consultant; they may not perceive a problem or issue that needs their attention. Obviously, the initial contact is critical!

Without a conceptual map, to use Caplan's (1970) term, the consultant is likely to fall into the trap of relying on his/her most comfortable or usual professional role. For example, a supervisor, in the position of consultant, is likely to use the role of structural power as a controlling technique. A novice consultant is likely to try to rush the group process and try to reach agreement to work together prematurely. Without a consultative plan, the likelihood exists that the consultant will not maintain role consistency. When roles are diffused, consultees become confused and anxious, and they tend to vocalize unhappiness with the consultant and lack of interest in the work to be done. The Facilitative-Directive Process Model offers a conceptual map whereby the consultant can organize and monitor his/her behavior to assure appropriate focus and movement. With a well developed plan, the consultant can proceed with a self-confidence that is likely to be translated into success. Because the consultant is self-confident, consultees will perceive the experience as successful also.

In this chapter the Facilitative-Directive Process Model is presented stage by stage and techniques and strategies appropriate to each stage are identified. Those techniques presented are described in great enough detail to be used by the consultant. When worksheets are recommended, a facsimile is included and may be reproduced as needed to implement the activity.

A wide range of group techniques could be applied at several stages of the consultative process. Those illustrative examples that are given are suggestive and no effort has been made to be comprehensive. The expectation is that the user is well grounded in personality theory and group practice. If this is true, these representative approaches will stimulate the reader to create new techniques and adapt these to fit unique situations.

By definition, the four relationship criteria characterizing consultation (see Chapter 1) must be established and maintained throughout the consultative process. The consultant's initial goal is to develop a relationship with the group that meets the conditions identified as consultative. Even when the consultant takes the Directive stance, it is with the permission of consultees that the consultant assumes that posture.

STAGE 1: INITIAL DEFINITION
AND AWARENESS

The consultees approach the initial session with minimal commitment to the process. They want to know the purpose of the group, what is expected of them, what is expected of others, and what role the consultant is to play. Obviously, opening the session is a crucial point. To develop trust and common agreement concerning the value of the group working together is important. The consultant responds to the group, individually and collectively, with acceptance, trust, and respect.

Developing Rapport (Modeling Openness)

Because ambivalence is the pervasive attitude of the consultees, the consultant can initiate trust and openness by making a clear but brief statement about the purpose of the group, the role of the consultant, and the expected outcomes. Because motivations of those involved are usually questioned, the consultant that "puts his/her cards on the table" will find fewer misgivings on the part of consultees and in a reciprocal fashion less defensiveness on the part of the consultant. This writer initiates the consultative relationship by being very explicit about the following points:

1. why I am here, i.e., who requested help and the problem as stated by the Initiator, my interest or identity with the Initiator, and my knowledge of the problem situation;

2. my expectations for the group in terms of the outcomes; and

3. my perceptions about the expected role of group members.

Warm-up

After the introductory remarks a warm-up activity designed to get the group involved in the process and initiate identification of the problem is used. Three techniques appropriate for three very different groups are given to illustrate the rapport-building aspect of the process.

Example 1 for Stage 1
Parent Education Group

This group is comprised of approximately 15 parents (mostly mothers) who joined the group because they are concerned about being "good" parents and have experienced difficulties in performing their role. Some have been referred to this group by counselors, but all are voluntary participants. In addition to opening the group to discussion, the warm-up activity for the parents is designed to communicate the belief that:

1. all behavior is purposeful,

2. all behavior makes sense in the context of the family group interaction, and

3. every individual is influenced by every other member of the family.

The "French Scene Family Group Technique" (Kirby, 1981) is a technique especially useful as a warm-up activity with these parents because it addresses their own behavior, beliefs, and attitudes from the vantage point of their early experiences in their respective family of origin. This approach is less threatening than focusing immediately on their parenting concerns. A description of the French Scene Family Group Technique follows.

TECHNIQUE 2.1: FRENCH SCENE FAMILY GROUP TECHNIQUE (KIRBY, 1981)

Purpose

To examine ways one's beliefs, attitudes, and values are developed and maintained through family communication patterns and interactions.

Assumptions

One's concept of self is essentially a reflection of impressions of one's role in one's family of origin.

Techniques: Procedures and Process

1. Present Worksheet I, Figure 2.1, French Scene Family Group Technique. Read the brief explanation of the technique aloud while the group members read silently. Point out example and explain shorthand notations: F (father); M (mother); S (sister); me, i.e., self, that person's position in the family; GM (grandmother); dotted line shows individual not in the same household, "—-F"; SS (step-sister), etc.

2. Allow participants about 15 minutes to diagram their own family group constellations using the "French Scene" concept. Begin with the constellation one was born into (family of origin) and record important changes—additions and deletions—ending with one's present family constellation.

3. After participants have depicted their several family systems, using Worksheet II, Figure 2.2, as a guide, ask them to examine each family constellation and for each one consider and make notes about the following questions:

   a. What value(s) were important to the family?

   b. Who was the most powerful person in the family?

   c. Who was least powerful?

   d. How did you find your place? Describe the role you played such as "pleaser," "conformer," "problem solver," etc.

   e. Who did you most try to please?

   f. How has this changed over time?

   g. Who, in your family of origin, are you most like?

   h. Do the adjectives you used to describe yourself reveal anything about the influence your family had on your beliefs about yourself?

i. Is there a differentiation between behaviors which are appropriate or expected of males and females: Has this expectation influenced your view of yourself? Has it had an effect on your choice of a spouse or special friends?

4. Discuss information generated by this activity. Allow participants to share ideas and impressions and raise questions as they feel comfortable doing so. Do not pressure an individual to reveal personal information, but accept and recognize each contribution.

Other Questions for Participants' Consideration

• How much has your family membership changed over time?

• Who influenced the values in the family?

• How did you find your place in your family of origin? Has it changed over time? How did you relate to the "Most Powerful" person? Has this changed?

• Who was most opposite when you were growing up? If married, does your spouse also fit the description of being "most opposite" i.e., like your sibling?

• Who gave you permission to behave as you do? Who can give you permission to change?

• If one person in the family changes, what happens to the family? Why is change difficult?

• When membership in the family changed, what happened?

Effective Elements of the Technique

• Generates personal information about the individual which can be used to discuss concepts of needs, values, attitudes.

• Helps members of a family see and understand how their individual perceptions are similar and different.

- Offers a common experience as a reference for discussion.

- Describes rather than diagnoses—does not place blame.

- Defines problems and concerns in terms of communication patterns and expectations, and offers hope for change, in the context of the family.

- Grants individuals permission to view their world in a subjective manner and permission to use this information as a basis for making personal statements and/or assessments.

Other Applications of this Group Technique

The exercise can be used effectively as a "warm-up" exercise in multiple family group work. Begin as indicated previously. Then have individuals in a group pair off and share what they have learned about themselves from the exercise. After a few minutes, have each individual introduce his/her partner by telling something about his/her family memberships and the roles he/she played in the family systems.

This exercise also can be presented to large groups to provide a reference point for questions and answers. After individual work is completed, a panel comprised of five or six of the participants might be used to initiate the sharing experience. Each panel member can share what they learned about themselves by doing this activity. After five or six have presented their personal impression, others usually are willing and even anxious to share also.

Discussion of Outcomes
for Example 1

Upon completion of this task, group members feel they have a common attitude and share a common cultural experience. That is, they have all lived in families and the way they are now is greatly influenced by that family of origin. They experience awareness that individual behavior is, to a large extent, a product of family interactions.

This group was concerned with parenting skills and the behavior of their children. Following this activity, these parents had sufficient generalized information to initiate discussion concerning the work of the group and ground rules. This information was useful at Stage 2 of

WORKSHEET I FOR "FRENCH SCENE" FAMILY GROUP TECHNIQUE

The name of this technique is derived from drama. In drama, a French Scene is created when a character enters/leaves the stage. Beginning with your early life, depict changes in your family constellation by using the French Scene concept. Use shorthand notations to identify various family relationships and your own place in the family. An example follows:

"French Scene" Family Group Technique

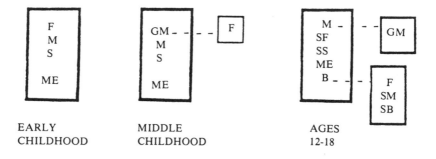

| EARLY
CHILDHOOD | MIDDLE
CHILDHOOD | AGES
12-18 |

YOUR NOTES: (Use back if needed)

Figure 2.1. Worksheet I for French scene family group technique.

WORKSHEET II FOR FAMILY VALUES AND CHANGES

1. Review your French Scene Family Groups. For each representation, consider the following questions:

   Make notes on Worksheet I

   a. What did your family (each French Scene) value most?
   b. Who was the most powerful person in the family?
   c. Who was the least powerful?
   d. How did you find your place in the family?
   e. Who did you try most to please?

2. After answering the previous questions, describe yourself.

   _____

   _____

   _____

3. Also consider:

   a. How has your role changed over time?
   b. Who in your family of origin are you most like?
   c. How influential was your family in shaping your concept of what you "should" be like?
   d. How similar are you to other members of the same sex of you family of origin?

Figure 2.2. Worksheet II for family values and changes.

Facilitative-Directive Consultative Model. This group was anxious to proceed once they had shared the information generated from the application of the French Scene Family Group Technique.

Example 2 for Stage 1
Chamber of Commerce Advisory Board

This group was comprised of approximately thirty men who were appointed to this important board because they were successful and influential. It is the task of the Advisory Board to offer guidance and supervision to the professional staff that work for the Verdent Hills Chamber of Commerce. These men have limited time to spend in the discharge of this duty. Therefore, they used a (Friday evening—all day Saturday) "planning conference" format to develop a five-year plan for the Chamber of Commerce. The Advisory Board was able to formulate their goals, prioritize those goals, and articulate role expectations for the professional staff during the fifteen working hours of the conference. It was the consultant's responsibility to structure the meeting and manage the process in such a fashion that the members would work together effectively and efficiently.

Obviously the warm-up activity used with this group had to be carefully selected to match the participants value system, i.e., it had to be task-oriented, dignified, and have face validity. An activity was devised that allowed participants to introduce themselves and at the same time indicate their areas of special interest concerning the city. Additionally, the activity allowed room for a wide range of participation—from very minimal to intense. This warm-up activity, as used with the Verdent Hills Chamber of Commerce Advisory Board, is identified as "Technique 2.2: Theme Development" and is described in the technique that follows.

TECHNIQUE 2.2: THEME DEVELOPMENT

Purposes

To allow participants to make individual decisions and express self interest.

Procedures

1. Give each participant a 3 x 5 card on which the following has been written:

    (On Side 1) Your name and the firm or company you represent

    (On Side 2) If you had unlimited resources, what *one* thing would you do for the greater Verdent Hills area? Assume favorable conditions for your project.

2. After a few minutes, begin the introductions and sharing of ideas. Be sure to start the procedure with someone who volunteers to begin.

3. After the first person has shared his/her information, proceed "round robin" until all have introduced themselves and told what they would like to do (for Verdent Hills). Each suggestion is accepted and acknowledged by the consultant and, when appropriate, the consultant emphasizes similarities and differences among the "dreams" and the concerns these represent. This "pairing" technique helps develop cohesiveness and working relationships.

**Discussion of Outcome
for Example 2**

As a warm-up activity, the "Theme Development" technique served its purpose. Cohesiveness was developed and some ideas were introduced that were useful to the group as they moved into the next stage of the consultative process. For the next stage, the consultant used the *themes* that emerged from the "fantasies" to assign individuals to task groups. Because individuals were placed in task groups with others of common philosophies, little time was needed to develop a working relationship among members of task groups, thus production was maximized.

**Example 3 for Stage 1
Womens Career Exploration Group**

This group was comprised of eight women who had never worked outside the house or who had been only temporarily employed but wanted to enter the work force with the ultimate goal of earning a respectable living and pursuing a career. Their ages ranged from 28 to 42 and all had been or were married and all but two had one or more children. The purpose of the group was to provide self-awareness experiences and build self-confidence. Individually and as a group, the women feared change and the loss of security they believed would occur when/if they embarked on a career. A warm-up activity was chosen that would help the women see the similarities in their developmental histories and identify common interests. A "time line" technique was used. A description of the technique follows:

TECHNIQUE 2.3: TIME LINE

Purposes

1. For Part A the purposes are

   a. to enable participants to experience a sense of shared development and

   b. to have participants to begin to own and accept who they are with an appreciation for change.

2. For Part B the purposes are

   a. to provide incidents of humorous relief and

   b. to have participants become more comfortable with change as a necessity.

PART A: PAST

Procedures

1. Prepare long narrow slips of paper folded in sections and labeled to represent decades of life. (Because the oldest person in this example was in her fourth decade, the time line extends through five decades beginning with the present as indicated below:)

2. Ask each person to take the strip of paper and list the highlights of their lives for each decade—those things they are willing to share. They are allowed 10 to 15 minutes to develop their time lines. The consultant also develops a personal time line historical record.

3. Upon completion, tape the records to the wall and refer to them as members introduce themselves to the group. Begin with the consultant, sharing only those aspects of one's life one feels comfortable sharing.

4. Leave the records on display during the entire session and refer to them often throughout the groups' time together.

PART B: FUTURE

The past is important, but so is the future. The past might influence what will happen next but it does not control it.

Procedures

1. As a way of introducing this idea and stimulating the group to share their ideas about what would or could happen in the next few decades, present them with a "time line of the future" and ask participants to consider the next five decades.

Ask them to consider what life will be like in general and to record their ideas on the "time line of the future."

Year	What will you be doing?	Who will be involved?
1980		
1990		
2000		
2010		
2020		

2. Display the time line records for each individual.

3. Have the group share what they have written as was done in Part A. During this sharing period, the leader points out similarities and differences and the group discusses their future projections.

**Discussion of Outcomes
for Example 3**

The "Time Line" technique was a useful activity for the group. As these women examined their histories (Part A: Past), they experienced a sense of shared development and experiential constraints. As they processed the meaning "marker events" had on their lives, they began to own and accept who they were and appreciate their need to face change. The projections of the future (Part B: Future) provided incidents of humorous relief and a range of safe topics (since they were "fantasies") for discussion. With insight, the women became more comfortable with the notion that change is constant and inevitable and even a reason for optimism. The activity instigated enough self-exploration to commit members to continuing work as a group. Thus, consultees were ready to work at Stage 2 following the application of the "Time Line" technique.

STAGE 2: TENTATIVE TASK COMMITMENT

Stage theory conceptualizes growth or change occurring when one reassesses one's experiences and arrives at an assumption or explanation that is qualitatively different from the assumption or view previously held. A state of cognitive disequilibrium or dissonance is apparently created when views one holds no longer seem adequate to explain all of one's personal impression; thus, reframing occurs. Movement from one stage to the next represents a reframing of one's point of view.

When a consultant effectively establishes rapport and addresses Stage I concerns, i.e., questioning the motives of the consultant and In-itiatior, these issues begin to seem unimportant and lose relevance for consultees. The individual at Stage 2 is concerned with group membership, i.e., "Do I belong in this group?", and for the collective body the issues are goal development and work procedures including normative behavior and "ground rules." Group norms are in the process of development and will stabilize at this stage.

A consultant's role at Stage 2 can be characterized as group "leader" or group "facilitator." *The consultant's primary role at this stage is to manage the interpersonal relationship development.* Group process theory typically represents the personal relationships within a group moving along a continuum comprised of four stages:

Stage 1 Introductory

Stage 2 Conflict

Stage 3 Work or deliberation

Stage 4 Conclusion or termination

The groups' interpersonal relationship stage can be assessed by topics that are discussed and the "comfort" zone or level of risk indicated through those topics. Very briefly, the *Introductory* stage is represented by unsure communication—"a kind of 'chicken dancing' in which participants identify members' attitudes and feelings toward certain objects and events" (Applbaum, Bodaken, Sereno, & Anatol, 1979, p. 193). Essentially, "chicken-dancing" occurred at Stage 1 of the Facilitative—Directive Process Model.

Conflict is recognized when the group questions the leader's style, the procedures proposed, the administrative details and similar "safe" topics that indicate defensiveness, discomfort, or resistance. The group leader welcomes this level of interactions because it represents movement. The work done at the conflict stage of group process moves groups through the disquieting experiences of group membership questions. The conflict stage coincides with Stage 2 of the Facilitative-Directive Process Model. Thus, the consultant focuses on techniques that are effective under conditions of resistance and can accomplish task objectives.

Stages of group development and Facilitative-Directive Process Stages are correlated in a predictable fashion. This relationship is depicted in Figure 2.3.

Using group process theory as a conceptual map, a consultant will use the seemingly low production period of Stage 2 to establish group norms of openness, trust, and respect. Individual anxieties will be effectively redirected from personal relevant concerns to task relevant concerns. Unfinished business at this group process developmental level will

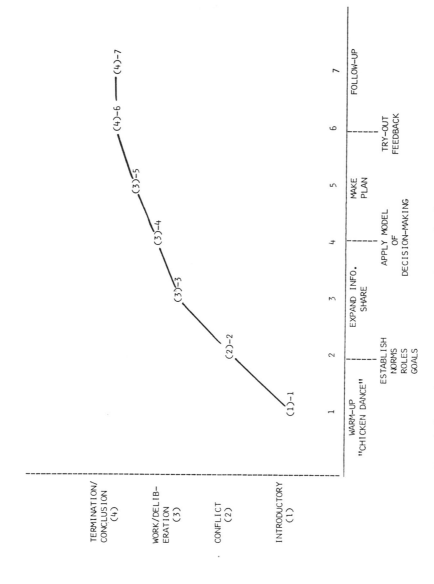

Figure 2.3. Correlation of group process and consultation stages.

only surface later as personal hidden agenda and other dysfunctional behaviors. Therefore, the process is not to be rushed or forced, rather it is to be managed.

Group techniques that can be used to facilitate the groups' movement at this Stage include such well known techniques as *brainstorming, buzz groups,* and *posting.* These techniques are described and the directions for using them are given. However, because the use of these techniques tend to evolve from the topic being considered and basically are spontaneous responses, only one example (i.e., the application of Buzz groups to an inservice program for teachers) is included for illustrative purposes.

TECHNIQUE 2.4: BRAINSTORMING

Purposes

1. To encourage creativity;

2. To give every person, even the most timid, an opportunity to share ideas freely without making public one's personal thoughts (Quantity—as opposed to quality—is encouraged.); and

3. To have small group production rather than individual production.

Procedures

1. Provide the following instructions to the group:

   a. Think of both ideas and solution; piggyback on other's ideas.

   b. Strive for quantity, do not evaluate, "the more the better."

   c. Welcome, encourage, reinforce all ideas, no matter how wild.

   d. Do not criticize, evaluate, or limit any contributions.

2. Divide large groups into small groups, eight individuals each.

3. Appoint (or ask the group to choose) a leader, to enforce the four basic previous rules as provided in Step 1.

4. Appoint (or ask the group to choose) a secretary to record all ideas.

5. Set a time limit.

6. State clearly the topic or questions to be discussed.

7. Develop a composite list of ideas from the work of these several sub-groups.

TECHNIQUE 2.5: BUZZ GROUPS

The buzz group is especially useful when information has been provided to a large group, and immediate and more or less spontaneous reactions are desirable.

Purpose

To encourage each person to be *active* in a discussion, yet preserves anonymity.

Procedures

1. Divide the group of participants, or audience into small sub-groups (from 3 to 12).

2. Appoint, or have the group elect, a chairperson.

3. Instruct the group to discuss an issue relevant to some aspects of the topic under consideration.

4. Have the chairperson report the information generated by the sub-group and/or a consensus reached by the sub-group to the large group.

Example for Stage 2
Teachers Concerns about Discipline

Teachers are sometimes reluctant to discuss professional concerns about issues such as discipline quite possibly because they make an assumption that they should be experts and "know what is best," or correct, or expected. Thus, a structured group assignment is useful to help break through their professional resistance.

The Buzz Group Technique was used with a group of veteran teachers who were meeting to discuss problems of discipline. While they seemed interested in the topic, they appeared satisfied to let the consultant "give" them advice. In an effort to shift the expectations from passive listening to active participation, the consultant divided the large group into sub-groups of five to eight members each. A "saying" relevant to the issue was given to each group to discuss. The saying was
"SPARE THE ROD AND SPOIL THE CHILD"
Members of the sub-groups were asked to respond to the following points:

- What does the saying mean?

- Why has it survived as a saying?

- Individually, how do you react to the underlying philosophy?

- Develop a group consensus: Do you agree? Why or why not?

Upon completion of the buzz group task (approximately 20 minutes) a panel, comprised of one member from each buzz group, discussed the topic by (1) sharing the information generated in the previous buzz group; (2) the group's conclusions; and (3) personal views of participants. After each presenter had spoken, the discussion was opened for comments from the "audience." This generated much lively discussion, divergent viewpoints, and interest.

Other Applications of Buzz Group Technique

The Buzz Group Technique is especially effective when one has reason to believe that divergent views are present, but that the group is reluctant to share those views. For example, this consultant has used a modification of this technique to help teachers understand their role in career education. For that purpose, eight sentences or beliefs about how one makes career choices were used. Each buzz group was given a different statement to discuss. Because all of the sentences were presented to the group through the panel discussion, participants heard quite a variety of views and they also surfaced some of their own beliefs.

High school and elementary age students also enjoy reacting in this fashion to ideas, philosophy, theory, and situations; almost all topics of interest to parents can be offered in this way.

TECHNIQUE 2.6: POSTING

While the procedures are as simple as those of brainstorming, the skills of the chairperson of the sub-groups are important elements requiring careful application of this technique.

Purposes

1. To help a group clarify individual perceptions, biases, and points-of-view.

2. To enable group members to understand better common concerns and expectations of a group.

Procedures

1. As consultant or group leader state when posting will be conducted (before, during, or after a presentation).

2. Form small groups (comprised of about 6 to 12) to discuss and list all questions or ideas they have about the issue as stated.

3. Have each small group clarify ideas and questions within the group. Ask them to record these into understandable forms. (This could be a potential problem if a chairperson is seen as judgmental or critical.)

4. Have the small group members display and share ideas and questions with the entire group.

Strengths of Posting

Confusion and divergence can be exposed, and cohesiveness among the group, even with real differences, can be developed through the discussion that follows.

Weakness of Posting

A potential weakness is the time required for adequately listing questions and ideas and then addressing these in some meaningful manner.

Termination of Stage 2

Termination of Stage 2 occurs when the group, individually and collectively, agrees to work with the consultant on a task they believe to be appropriate. This agreement, or "contract," may be secured by having the group restate their problem and summarize their expectations of the consultant.

In family group consultation, a consultant would likely ask each family member individually about willingness to work with the consultant. The contract is verified in the following manner:

First, the consultant reframes the presenting problems to encompass the short term goal for the group and inquires directly, "Is this goal the one on which you are ready to work?" After each person in the group has made such an agreement, they are ready to proceed to Stage 3 of the Facilitative-Directive Process Model.

If the consultant brings a high level of skill in communicating "unconditional positive regard," to use Carl Roger's (1961) term, then the procedures recommended as useful at this stage will be effectively implemented. Without this skill, failure can be predicted. If training in communicating the facilitative conditions i.e., empathy, warmth, and respect, is needed, some excellent materials are readily available. For example, Carkhuff (1969) suggested a procedure for selection and training professional and non-professionals alike. Gazda, Asbury, Blazer, Childers, Desselle, and Walters (1977) developed a manual that is especially helpful for training educators. Another one for the training health providers was developed by Gazda, Walters, and Childers (1975).

Similarly, the consultant will find the literature on group leadership and group techniques are replete with helpful suggestions for procedures that are primarily facilitative and therefore applicable to Stage 2 of the Facilitative-Directive Process Model.

STAGE 3: PROBLEM CLARIFICATION

As a facilitator, a consultant is concerned with structuring the situation so that the consultees' group continues to specify and articulate common issues as time unfolds. *Pacing* is important so that participants move from intense task-oriented activities to experiential activities which accommodate divergent levels of self-disclosure, risk, and commitment.

After a group has become committed to a group task and the work rules have been established, the group moves into a stage (Stage 3) that requires the use of techniques that tap into the informational resources and opinions of participants. While the consultant wishes to motivate information giving and data gathering, anonymity is often the preferred mode so that individual contributions will not be discounted or undue weight be given to the ideas because of the personal influence of the contributor. The work of the group must continue in such a way that individual issues, thoughts, needs, and values can be surfaced without judgments (positive or negative) from others in the group.

Failure to apply appropriate techniques at this stage will result in the most powerful members of a group speaking for the group and the less powerful leaving the group with no one the wiser about his/her beliefs, feelings, and attitudes. *Recognize the importance of every person presenting his/her "views" before consensus is reached. Therefore, discussions alone will not be adequate because this procedure fails to get information from the easily intimidated and reluctant speakers, and the most vocal and/or otherwise powerful individuals control the group's considerations.*

Two examples will be used to show the application of techniques that are useful for purposes just discussed. The examples are taken from:

The Chamber of Commerce Advisory Board Planning Conference. (This conference also was discussed in terms of Stage 1.)

A school facing low morale among the faculty. (The principal was the initiator, teachers were consultees.)

Example 1 for Stage 3
Chamber of Commerce Advisory
Board Planning Conference

Picking up on the information already shared about this group (see Example 2 for Stage 1), in this section is described the procedure used at Stage 3 with this group. The consultant wished to encourage each member of the board to share his concerns independently and express his views concerning the importance of each problem without fear of reprisal from supervisors or from more influential members. In other words, anonymity was an important step at this time. The sequence of steps followed in generating role statements for the Chamber of Commerce is outlined as "Technique 2.7: Goal-Role Statements"

TECHNIQUE 2.7: GOAL-ROLE STATEMENTS

The Goal-Role Statements are developed through a series of sequential steps. Examples used to clarify the sequences are from the work of the Chamber of Commerce Advisory Board Planning Conference described previously under Technique 2.2.

Purposes

1. To encourage each person to share his/her concerns independently, and

2. To have each person express his/her views concerning the importance of each problem without fear of reprisal.

Procedures

1. Divide the large group into small (6 to 8) task groups. (Using impressions gained from the fantasy warm-up exercise, see

Technique 2.2, the Advisory Board members were assigned to groups according to similarities in interest and philosophy. For example, one group was comprised of men whose fantasies indicated a special concern about "transportation" and another was comprised of men concerned with "culture.")

2. Ask the task groups to discuss their concerns that relate to the work of the conference. (In this example, the Verdent Hills Community and work of the Chamber of Commerce were the concerns.) Ask them to record issues and questions, one a page, on newsprint. They are to continue this activity until all of their concerns have been identified (approximately one hour).

3. Hang the pages containing the issues on the wall around the room so that the entire group can review them.

4. Reconvene the large group and read aloud issues and questions (round robin fashion).

5. Remove from the wall the sheets containing the issues.

6. As the consultant, evenly and randomly assign the sheets from Step 5 to the task groups. Ask each group to develop a goal statement for each issue statement assigned to them. Thus, the group that generated the issue may not be the ones to develop the goal statement from it. (This will require about 2 hours.)

7. After the task groups have completed goal statements, ask them to assume that they wish to respond to each goal statement. Ask them to develop a "Role" statement for each goal. In this example the role statement tells what the Chamber of Commerce will do to reach the stated goal.

An example of sequential activities from the Chamber of Commerce Planning Conference includes the following:

ISSUE: "Many of the people in business in Verdent Hills are not involved in the work of the Chamber of

Commerce and seem unaware of the concerns," an original "issue" statement.

GOAL: "City of Verdent Hills will seek to enhance the understanding of its constituents on issues that are germane to the business and professional community."

ROLE: "The Chamber of Commerce shall sponsor seminars and forums, and encourage communications through the news media on said issues."

8. After the work of the task groups are completed, develop a composite of goal/role statements and provide a copy for each participant.

9. Ask each person to work independently and to assign a number, using weight from 0 to 20, to each role statement to represent the relative importance they view the role to be. Instruct participants to consider each item separately. For those statements they feel are most important assign higher numbers, and those of lesser importance, lower numbers. Participants are told that they can assign any number as often as they wish. For example, if they feel that five items are of extremely high importance, they can assign 20 to each of the five, if they feel five are unimportant, all five might receive one.

10. Upon completion of assigning weights, collect all papers.

11. Identify a "reader" who will shuffle the collected papers so identities cannot be known, and then the reader will read aloud the numbers from each sheet.

12. Record the numbers from Step 11 on the chalkboard and then sum.

Example: The assigned weight for one item from 10 people might look like this:

$$12 + 3 + 5 + 10 + 2 + 20 + 9 + 8 + 3 + 10 = 82$$

13. Upon completion of Step 12, prioritize these role statements based upon assigned weights which reveal their relative importance to the group.

Discussion of Weighting Procedure

While obviously not everyone of the 10 people agreed on the relative importance of this example item, an overall agreement was reached by summing the individual scores. In most cases, the top ten items will be agreed upon as most important by almost, if not all, participants. If one examines those weights indicated in the example, one will notice that one person assigned a weight of 20 (of major importance) and another assigned it a low number of two (which represented little importance). However, most weights were not so extreme with most people perceiving it as of some, but not extreme importance. Thus, the advantage of displaying all of the weights—the individual items can be discussed in the general framework of the relative weights which are assigned. If, in the example of Step 12, the person who assigned a 20 had a vested interest in the issue, the vote is understandable, but anonymity is respected. Additionally, a powerful member cannot intimidate a less powerful one, nor can he/she sway the votes his/her way because personal positions are confidential. Thus, the group can terminate with a prioritized list of goals with positive feelings about the group. Also, they will own decisions as belonging to the group and thus they will see the group as responsible for the choice.

Application of Role-Goal Statements Technique

This technique has many applications. Some example applications follow:

1. To identify and prioritize topics for classroom discussion at all grade levels.

2. To assess community action plans similar to the one described.

3. To determine topics of concern for inservice workshops, seminars, and so forth.

4. To assess strengths/weaknesses of potential employees, consultants, and so forth.

5. To help family groups make decisions.

Example 2 for Stage 3
School Problem Identification Process

River Port High School administrators recognized that problems existed and that the faculty morale was low. However, these administrators were unable to articulate the problems. A pervasive fear among the faculty was that if they discussed their problems with administrators, the faculty would either be considered troublemakers by the central office or they would be seen as disloyal by their peers. Thus, the request for an outside consultant to "identify" and "assess areas of concern."

The procedures this consultant used to secure and summarize the requested information is presented as "Technique 2.8: Problem Identification." Obviously, if the consultative contract ends with the report, the relationship terminates at Stage 3. This is not unusual. The experience of this consultant has been that the consultative relationship often ends with the identification of problems or issues, but this is understood at the beginning of the process and is specified in the "contractual" verbal or written agreement between the consultant and the consultee. Similarly, a consultative process may begin at the Directive Phase (Stage 4). For example, when a consultant is brought in as a "trainer," the process essentially begins at Stage 4. The assumption is that the Facilitative Phase (Stages 1 through 3) has been completed, committees have articulated their problem, and the help of a consultant is needed or desired.

"Technique 2.8: Problem Identification" as outlined traces the consultant's contact with the consultee's clients and is conceptualized as a "diagnostic" process. The consultee, in this case, is the principal and not the teachers.

TECHNIQUE 2.8: PROBLEM IDENTIFICATION

Purposes

1. To help a group identify problems.

2. To enable the group to prioritize problems, once identified, so as to determine which ones are of major importance.

Procedures

1. Secure the information (group meeting)

   a. As consultant, explain the purpose of the meeting (i.e., to help the administrators identify problems and concerns of the faculty and possible causes of low morale).

   b. Outline procedures that will be followed in identifying the group's concerns, and answer their questions about the procedures. As the consultant be sure to be *clear, concise,* and *totally honest* throughout the procedure.

   c. Ask each person to write his/her personal concerns and perceptions of problems (as they pertain to River Port High School). Lists are to be anonymous. The group members are free to list as many problems as they wish in whatever fashion they choose. This activity will require about 20 minutes.

   d. After completing the listing, ask participants to hand in their lists. At this point, there is no additional discussion.

2. Develop a problem checklist and a Problem Rating Sheet

   a. As consultant, develop a checklist of concerns from problem statements as provided by participants. The checklist includes all of the stated problems, even if only one person listed the problem. Problems are categorized under subheadings such as "administrative," "teacher-teacher relationships," and so forth.

   b. Develop the checklist into a Problem Rating Sheet for participants to indicate their perception of *each* stated problem (i.e., major, minor, or average) and to assign weights to be used in prioritizing. (Figure 2.4 is an illustration and is excerpted from the "Problem Rating Sheet" developed for River Port High School.)

	Check one (x)			0-20
PROBLEM RATING SHEET RIVER PORT HIGH SCHOOL	MAJOR	MINOR	AVERAGE	WEIGHTS
A. Administrative Area 1. The administration does not support faculty (the faculty feels cut off and without power in many situations).				
2. The principal seems to favor students in situations of conflict with teachers.				
B. Teacher Area 1. Teachers do not know what is going on, so they are suspicious and unhappy.				

Figure 2.4. Excerpt from Problem Rating Sheet developed for River Port High School.

3. Obtain ratings on the identified problems

    a. Send a cover letter and the Problem Rating Sheet to all participants. The cover letter reviews the procedures used to gain information from the group, provides instructions for completing the Rating Sheet, and reminds group members of the purpose and proposed use of the information.

    b. Request that the Problem Rating Sheets are to be returned to you completed.

4. Summarize data

a. Summarize the information to show the percentage of faculty rating each problem in each category as major, minor, average.

b. Develop a prioritized list of problems, based on weights assigned.

5. Provide feedback

a. Develop a report containing the information summarized from Step 4.

b. Send a copy to each participant.

Discussion of Outcomes for Example 2

This process is an adaption of the one described under the topic of the Chamber of Commerce. Again, its application is similar to ones listed previously. However, this technique has an additional advantage in that the consultant can obtain data with limited contact with participants. Of course, trust in the consultant is necessary before the group will share information, even in this form.

Applied to the River Port High School, this approach was most effective. The three items receiving the first, second, and third highest percentage of ratings as major concerns also received the first, second, and third rankings by weighting; thus, both responses yielded the same information for the top three concerns. For the next seven concerns, there were differences in ranking by percentages and weighting, but the same seven items emerged in the top ten by both procedures. Thus, needs of the school were adequately served. The administration could see problems and how intense they appeared to the faculty. At the same time, perceptions of the individual were kept anonymous and confidentiality was maintained.

STAGE 4: ALTERNATIVE EXPLORATION

How can the consultant assume a directive stance without becoming a part of the structural hierarchy? Group leadership skills are uniquely applicable at Stage 4. Suggesting, teaching, leading, without coercing; this is the objective. The developmental stage at which a group is functioning is the critical element. A cohesive group should be functioning at the "work stage"; thus, hidden agenda should be at a minimum; the work norms should have been established. Techniques used at Stage 4 of the Facilitative-Directive Process Model presupposes an interdependent level of group functioning has been reached.

Assuming the group is at the work level, the consultant is free to focus primary attention on task, as opposed to relationships, and can use the group norms to enhance goal-seeking behaviors. Stage 4 initiates the "Directive" phase of the process model. Assuming a consultant-consultee relationship exists, it is appropriate for the consultant to present decision-making models at Stage 4 and let the group decide on the one to apply. Or the consultant may simply instruct the group on the procedure or model of decision making to be used at this stage. This latter approach assumes the consultant has the groups' implied, if not explicit, permission to choose the method to be used.

The approach at Stage 4 is DIRECTIVE, and this implies that the consultant structures the decision-making process. Two techniques that have potential for wide application are presented in the following content. One of these techniques is the VISUAL method developed by Kirby (1979) and the other is adopted from the Rational Manager model proposed by Kepner and Tregoe (1965).

Example 1 for Stage 4
Visual Method

The VISUAL method is so named because (1) it displays, in writing, a range of alternatives along with the positive and negative aspects of each, and (2) it is an acronym derived from the summary steps in the decision-making process. The six steps of problem solving using the VISUAL method are presented in Figure 2.5.

Only one example of the application of the VISUAL approach will be offered at this time because Husson (Chapter 3) suggested ways to train consultees to use the approach and discusses its importance. The VISUAL method was used in a problem-solving situation with nine high

Step	Activities for VISUAL Method of Problem-Solving
1	Verbalize: Discuss problems and state clearly.
2	Identify alternatives: Prepare exhaustive list of ideas.
3	Survey advantages and disadvantages for each alternative.
4	Underline those advantages and disadvantages which are of major importance to persons involved.
5	Accept one alternative—choose the "best" one.
6	List what, how, and when to accomplish the accepted alternative.

Figure 2.5. Activities for VISUAL Method of problem-solving.

NOTE: From *Second Marriage* (p. 48) by Jonell Kirby, 1979. Muncie, IN: Accelerated Development. Copyright 1979 by Accelerated Development. Reprinted by permission.

school principals. Their basic concern as articulated by them facilitated by the consultant was finally stated as follows:

(V)—What to do about our summer school program: It is expensive, not quality education, and encourages early graduation.

Clearly stating the problem was not an easy task. Their initial statement was, "Should we discontinue summer school?" Participants working through this problem were obviously impressed with the range of options they generated and the quality of their decisions. Even this part of the model helped them enhance their professional skills. A copy of their report is presented in Figures 2.6 and 2.7.

Example 2 of Stage 4
Rational Management Model

A rational management model has been advanced by Kepner and Tregoe (1965). In their book, *The Rational Manager,* these authors set forth a process of analyzing problems comprised of seven steps, and a process of decision making also comprised of seven steps. The consultant searching for strategies and techniques to use at the fourth stage of the Facilitative-Directive Process Model will find the "Rational Management" model a highly useful one.

The following example, application of this model to decision making, is excerpted from the work of a *committee* serving in a consultative role. This committee, comprised of faculty members, were appointed by their president to study the organizational structure and administrative services of their college. The president believed that many problems within the college were grounded in the nature of the organization and implementation of roles and functions at several levels of administrative leadership. Members of the consultative committee were members of the system with whom they were consulting, but in the role of committee member they were serving outside the structural hierarchy. For discussion purposes the committee shall hereafter be identified as the "Internal Consultation Team" or ICT Committee and the college shall be referred to as PERSONS College, a fictitious name to preserve privacy.

1. <u>V</u>

WHAT TO DO ABOUT OUR SUMMER SCHOOL PROGRAM:
IT IS EXPENSIVE, NOT QUALITY EDUCATION,
AND ENCOURAGES EARLY GRADUATION.

2. <u>I</u>	(1) Discontinue Summer School	(2) Limit Summer School for Make-up Only
3. <u>S</u>	Advantages:	Advantages:
4. <u>U</u>	*No expense entailed. *Early graduation not possible. *No mess, no fuss, no bother!	*Slow student could graduate "on time." *Reduce cost. *Quality less an issue. *Remediation possible.
	Disadvantages:	Disadvantages:
	*Parents (taxpayers) expect Summer School. *No opportunity for slow students to graduate on time. *Some advanced students need option. *Students want option. *Teachers desire option. *Tradition--present system built on expectation. *County office plan accommodates Summer School.	*Smacks of "poor" quality. *Teachers reluctant to teach in program. *Gives student "an out" when they don't want to work during regular session. *More discipline problems.

5. <u>A</u>   Accept options 3 and 5.

6. <u>L</u>   List next steps. (See separate sheet.)

Figure 2.6. Report of nine school principals using the VISUAL method for problem solving.

(3) Validate Quality	(4) Keep Summer School As Is	(5) Eliminate Need--Scheduling
Advantages:	Advantages:	Advantages:
*Gives assurance that program is same quality regular school. *Gives good students an option for early graduation. *Gives parents flexibility in educating children. *Gives failing students chance to "catch up." *Does not give students "an out" for quality work. *Meets community expectations.	*Acceptable to many. *Gets "problem" students through "on time." *Students who take Summer School work assume responsibility for choice (if not quality). *Less likely to draw attention of parents.	*Less expensive. *More options for all students.
Disadvantages:	Disadvantages:	Disadvantages:
*Requires systematic study and effort on part of staff. *More curriculum study needed. *Necessary to change students expectations. *Some teachers will be nonsupportive.	*Too expensive for quality. *Accountability questionable. *Unfair to all students.	*Difficult to accommodate. *Probably create a period of disruption. *Teacher's resistance. *Eliminating school-related but non-academic options. *Resistance from parents.

Figure 2.6. Continued.

WHAT	HOW	WHEN
Validate quality	Appoint a curriculum committee to determine criteria.	First week School term
	Survey school records to determine extent of need for Summer School.	Initiate survey at First grading period
	Form Parent-Student Advisory Committee to provide inputs for Summer School needs.	
	Form Committee to examine other school systems to determine their Summer School needs and responses.	

- -

Eliminate need for Summer School through regular school-year scheduling to accomplish remediation and acceleration.

Figure 2.7. Step 6 in VISUAL method with outcomes as identified from Figure 2.6.

In the application of the Rational Manager Model (Kepner & Tregoe, 1965) problems are viewed as deviations from a standard. Expressing those deviations was the work of the ICT Committee as they progressed through Stages 1, 2, and 3 of the Facilitative-Directive Process Model. This example of their work at Stage 4, i.e., the point of generating and evaluating objectives, illustrates the application of the seven steps of the "Rational" decision making steps. These steps are outlined in Figure 2.8.

---

1. State the objectives that will be considered to address the problem.

2. Classify objectives as (a) "musts"—necessary requirements—and (b) "wants." The "wants" are weighed and ranked.

3. Generate possible alternative ways of attaining the objectives.

4. Examine alternatives in relation to "must" and "want" criteria.

5. Tentatively choose an alternative or several alternatives in combinations that responds closest to objectives.

6. Explore all potential adverse consequences that *might* occur if each alterative was implemented.

7. Make final choice with attention to

    a. specific actions to be taken to implement decisions,

    b. offensive actions to take to minimize adverse actions, and

    c. ways to insure that decisions are operationalized.

Figure 2.8 Steps used for "Rational" decision making by ICT committee at Persons College.

For purposes of recommending action to the president, the ICT Committee limited their attention to five problems they considered to be of major importance. Two of these problems, along with the committee's objectives and their "must" and "want" criteria are displayed in Figure 2.9.

Problem Statement:

The roles and functions of administrative and academic units in the Persons College organization are not clearly defined.

Overall Objective:

To recommend an action plan which will result in clearly written definitions of roles and functions of administrative and academic units as well as administrators.

"Must" Objectives:

1. The president and his administrators must be involved and committed to the process.
2. Action steps must involve the effected individuals.
3. The process must result in written organizational role definitions that consider the elements of ambiguity, conflict, overload (quantity and quality), and decision-making authority.
4. The process must result in a mechanism for updating definitions of roles and functions.
5. The overall objective must be achieved within six months.

"Want" Objectives:

1. The action plan has broad acceptance among academic and administrative unit heads.
2. The action plan can be implemented quickly.
3. The action plan does not require a major commitment of faculty time.

Problem Statement:

There is no established structure for nurturing innovative ideas at Persons College.

Overall Objective:

To recommend an action plan for the ongoing development and implementation of innovative ideas at Persons College.

"Must" Objectives

1. Approaches to innovations are encouraged through strategies for recognizing, supporting, and rewarding contributions.
2. Administration commitment to innovations is reflected in role and function statements.

"Want" Objectives:

1. Faculty is oriented toward innovative goals and creative management.
2. Annual performance reviews stress focus on innovative ideas contributed during the year.

Figure 2.9. Example of application of "Rational" model by ICT Committee at Persons College.

The ICT Committee generated a number of alternative ways to obtain their objectives (Step 3 of the "Rational" decision-making process), examined alternatives in relation to the "must" and "want" criteria (Step 4) and made a recommendation to the president for action. In Figure 2.10 the "action plan" recommended by the ICT Committee to address the first major concern, i.e., "the role and function of administrative and academic units in the Persons College organization are not clearly defined."

Objective:

The action plan will result in clearly written definitions of roles and functions of administrators, and administrative and academic units.

Recommendation:

The President appoints an advisory team to

1. develop a participatory process for role analysis.
2. use the process, beginning with the advisory team and the members' collective and individual responsibilities, to develop written definitions of roles and functions of the administrative and academic units necessary to accomplish the mission of the College.
3. identify an internal consultant to be involved in the process.
4. utilize the participatory process for needed role revisions.
5. initiate the development of the process and of written role descriptions by (date).

Figure 2.10. Action Plan (Step 7) recommended by ICT Committee to Persons College.

STAGE 5: ACTION

Stage 5 is actually a continuation of the process initiated by Stage 4. It is concerned with *immediacy,* and *specificity* in terms of what to do, how to do it, when to do it, and other dimensions. In the VISUAL approach it is Step 6 (i.e., List what, how, and when to accomplish the accepted alternative); in the Rational Manager Modél (Kepner & Tregore, 1965) it culminates with the completion of Step 7.

Stage 5 is identifiable in that the individual consultees are no longer in the "theoretically possible" dimension. At this stage they have personalized their decisions and have assumed, or in some cases perhaps assigned, responsibility for carrying out a plan of action.

A level of independence as well as interdependence has been reached by the time Stage 4 is completed in terms of group process. The group that has reached and worked at a mature level of functioning is now ready for Stage 5 where they will feel somewhat independent of the consultant. Throughout activities in Stage 5 a noticeable rise will occur in self-confidence in individuals and an appreciation of others within the group. This is as it should be as individuals seek work (or role) related help from a consultant and at the same time retain the option of applying their newly gained understanding and expertise in other relevant situations. In other words, the consultee has increased his/her capacity to master future problems of a similar type. Caplan (1970) listed this as a characteristic descriptive of the consulting relationship.

The action steps of the decision-making process are those that represent this consultative stage. Examples specific to Stage 5 will be foregone since examples presented under the discussion of Stage 4 are applicable.

STAGE 6: STABILIZATION

Stage 6 is really the feedback loop in the process. As a consultant one must recognize that consultees may not proceed with an evaluation of the impact their choices and actions have on the system if there is not follow-up by the consultant. Part of the problem people have in making adequate decisions is their willingness to assign to fate those occurrences that are under one's control but are unanticipated. Through activities in Stage 6 accountability is taught and the aspect of control one can have or does not have over one's life is stressed.

Additionally, many people *need* group support in order to proceed with their plan. Feedback from consultant and from peers provide impetus to maintain and resolve under trying even if anticipated circumstances.

Finally, many individuals are so structured and concrete that they may not be able to modify and to adapt their plan even though confronted with an obvious need to do so. This stage offers structure yet accommodates recommendation and suggests flexibility.

STAGE 7: PROJECTION/TERMINATION

Stage 7 may not even involve the consultant's presence, a telephone call or note might suffice. The purpose of Stage 7 is to have "markers" or points of "celebration" so that the group can experience a shared feeling of success and movement. Progress will be made and change will occur over time. With change new pressures will occur perhaps. Some members of a group need to reassess their choices, share their feelings, and receive reinforcement and validation. The consultant, if effective, has helped the group gain expertise in their work role or responsibilities. Feedback at Stage 7 reinforces personal performance and reaffirms common concerns of the group. With families, this might be called the "well family" check up.

REFERENCES

Applbaum, R. L., Bodaken, E. M., Sereno, K. K., & Anatol, K. W. E. (1979). *The process of group communication.* Chicago: Science Research Associates.

Caplan, G. (1970). *The theory and practice of mental health consultation.* New York: Basic Books.

Carkhuff, R. R. (1969). *Helping and human relations: A primer for lay and professional helpers.* Vol. 2: *Practice and research.* New York: Holt, Reinhart and Winston.

Gazda, G. M., Asbury, F. R., Blazer, F. J., Childers, W. C., Desselle, R. E., & Walters, R. P. (1977). *Human relations development: A manual for educators* (2nd ed.). Boston: Allyn & Bacon.

Gazda, G. M., Walters, R. P., & Childers, W. C. (1975). *Human relations development: A manual for health services.* Boston: Allyn & Bacon.

Kepner, C. H., & Tregoe, B. B. (1965). *The rational manager.* New York: McGraw-Hill.

Kirby, J. (1981). Relationship building in second marriages and merged families. *Journal of Specialists in Group Work,* 6(1), 35-41.

Kirby, J. (1979). *Second marriage.* Muncie, IN: Accelerated Development.

Rogers, C. R. (1961). *On becoming a person.* Boston: Houghton-Mifflin.

CONSULTING WITH COMMUNITY AGENCIES AND EMERGENCY SERVICE PROVIDERS

Ernest C. Husson, M.A.

Ernest C. Husson, M.A.

Ernest C. Husson, who holds an undergraduate degree in Math and Science Education and advanced degrees in both Education Administration and Counseling, is principal of Carver Vocational-Technical Center at Malden, West Virginia and Adjunct Professor of Counseling at West Virginia College of Graduate Studies. Mr. Husson's expertise as a practical problem solver with a humanistic orientation has led to his demand as an internal consultant within the educational community and as a trainer-consultant for emergency personnel such as hospital workers and police officers. Mr. Husson combines consultation theory and practice through the delivery of on-site courses for master's level students who are involved in providing health and human services in various community-based agencies. Presently Mr. Husson is involved with the training of correctional counselors and administrators at Huttonsville State Prison.

CONSULTING WITH COMMUNITY AGENCIES AND EMERGENCY SERVICE PROVIDERS

Ernest C. Husson, M.A.

When a consultant assumes the role of trainer for a service agency, several problems are imminent. First is the problem of credibility: what skill does the consultant possess that is desired or needed by that agency? Second is the problem of resources: how does one justify the allocation of resources to this activity? Third is the problem of accountability: how can the expectations be made clear and understood by participants?

In this chapter are offered a rationale for becoming involved as a trainer for service based personnel and a program that recognizes and deals with these issues. The chapter is written from the point-of-view of a practicing consultant who has mounted such a program, and who is convinced that this is a useful activity for developing a responsive environment whereby the entire community is served.

In addition to the rationale for training, in this chapter are discussed the personality characteristics of three occupational groups of service employees that contribute to the need for consultation. Unlike some occupations, the emergency care providers described herein—police officers, school principals, and hospital based nurses—need two separate and seemingly unrelated sets of skills: a quick judgment set for decisive action and a slow reflective set for helping activities. With regard to this latter set of skills this consultant is prepared, by education and personality, to provide the needed training. The training objectives, to be identified later, focus on the "helping," or interpersonal relationship, dimension of the Service Providers' job.

Training Service Providers to be effective helpers results in a sense of satisfaction for the consultant. It helps make the Human and Health Service Providers more approachable. With public good will, the Service Provider becomes more effective in the helping process. Instead of being seen as a threat generally, as police officers sometimes are, or as a source of help only when people are in trouble, the approachable service providers are seen as helpful community based resources. A facilitative intervention from a Service Provider in a crisis situation can be a powerful force in influencing behavior.

In this chapter is discussed the use of three techniques (self-analysis, problem solving, and the empathetic and respect modes of good communication) to help service providers who are skilled in crisis intervention, become more approachable. As a consultant, this writer taught and demonstrated these techniques with three different service agencies: Capital City Police Officers, Secondary Principals of the Better County School System, and the staff of the Hopewell General Hospital. Each of the three mentioned groups (using fictional names, of course) varied greatly in their composition, but they shared a common attitude toward their roles. That is, they each saw a need to act decisively in a crisis and yet appear helpful and caring. As agencies and as individuals they recognized a need to learn ways to show caring and respond in a facilitative manner.

AGENCY A: CAPITAL CITY POLICE OFFICERS

The police group, numbering 60, were trained in two groups of 30 each. These groups met three hours weekly for eight weeks. Each group consisted of males and females, rookies and seasoned veterans.

The need for a consultant arose when complaints were made to the administration about numerous situations involving attitudes and behaviors toward the public, poor relationships with subordinates, and the recurring non-productive relationships among staff.

These problems generated the request for a consultant to set up a program to improve communications and to introduce a problem solving technique that could be useful to the agency. The consultative process was designed to deal with both internal and external problems. The approach was to use techniques that would lead to an understanding of the personal characteristics and professional competencies needed and used by the professional in the discharge of his/her duty, and to help the consultee differentiate between two seemingly opposing sets of responses needed for *crisis reaction* and *interpersonal interactions.*

Because of the diversity of the police force and the varied tenure of the members, the consultant had difficulty with maintaining control of the consultative process and keeping focused on the task. The norm for the group was to resist training that might result in change. Senior officers seemed to enjoy their "all knowing" roles. They perceived the consultant as an outsider who was not familiar with police procedures and organizations. As a result of these perceptions, they resisted the concept of humanistic training, especially being brought in from an "outsider" whom they considered naive about what the life of a police officer was really like.

These officers' resistance to change seemed to be anchored in their belief that an effective officer had to maintain a stance of being hard, decisive, cold, and insensitive. This role, in their view, did not allow the officer to be "humanistic." Humanism was equated with softness or indecisiveness and was contrary to their basic personality and beliefs. The "hardcore" type of personality encountered on the police force demanded that his/her consultant use every skill at his/her disposal. Interestingly, this consultant was tested and tried in terms of being facilitative; yet, those were the very skills that helped diffuse the negative attitudes. Some critical survival techniques available to this consultant were the ability to facilitate skeptics, as was the case with the police officers themselves; to absorb any put down remarks that were made; and to be sensitive to emotions and behavior without appearing "soft." The importance of these skills were not anticipated prior to the first meeting. Obviously, the atmosphere at the first meeting demanded the consultant's total attention to the business at hand. An uncertain novice in the business of working with such a group probably could not have managed this first session. This first session is critical in establishing the working relationship between consultant and consultee; therefore, preparation and anticipation can hardly be overemphasized.

Establishing a working relationship requires that the consultant understands the role of the police officer. It is helpful if the police officers believe the consultant understands their role, but they can be convinced as the session progresses if the consultant knows and appreciates the fact that an officer is placed in the position of having to secure his/her survival, both physical and psychological, through the legal aspects of being a "rule enforcer." In other words, an officer forces a set of rules on others, as opposed to being concerned about one's own behavior. For example, in issuing a speeding ticket the officers must use legal power, and at times, force. The action itself may be seen as a confrontation by the citizen. Confrontation may produce a variety of unpleasant situations. Two dimensions of behavior are needed for the police officer to be effective. These are responsive understanding (empathy) and quick decisions (action). If the officer operates only in the action mode as "rule enforcer," he/she creates a public image that causes the individual to appear cocky, and this in turn causes others to be aggressive toward the officer. An officer skilled in communicating caring and empathy, to complement the decisive-action mode, is aware that one's own behavior may escalate confrontation, and in some cases even provoke a conflict situation. Law enforcement officers spend a great percentage of their time during crisis as well as noncrisis situations giving comfort and aid to the community, which is all the more reason they need to be skilled in communicating caring and understanding.

Training Objectives

The consultant formulated two major objectives for the participating officers.

OBJECTIVE 1: To teach a model for effective communication which would give officers a skill: (a) to diffuse highly explosive situations, and (b) to respond appropriately when having contact with the general public; thereby, avoiding unnecessary confrontations.

OBJECTIVE 2: To provide an opportunity through group interaction and personal relationships, to develop an understanding of self and others.

Based upon these objectives, an appropriate instrument was devised to measure the impact of the training on the participants. Certain other instruments were used, primarily as a part of the training package, that would provide systematic information to the participants. Both types of data are discussed and summarized.

The 16 P F Inventory was administered to 18 of the police trainees so they could obtain information about their personality traits as compared to other officers and also with people in general. In Figure 3.1 are displayed means for Capital City Police Officers. The profile for these officers was rather similar to the profile established through studies of the Illinois Police Officers (Cattell, Eber & Tatsuoka, 1970), but they were noticeably different from people in general on several factors. The trainee group, as well as the comparison group of Illinois police, appeared slightly more tough minded (factor I), more self-assured (factor 0), more self-disciplined (factor Q3), and more relaxed (factor Q4) than people in general.

Individual test results were shared with those police officers who took the test as a means for greater self understanding. Group means for officers were discussed with the entire group as part of the awareness activities. Group interpretations helped officers examine their own personality characteristics and to compare their personality traits with other individuals choosing this profession.

A plausible conclusion about police officers is that the effective police officer does behave in a cool, tough-minded, self-assured, and relaxed way in crisis situations, as the personality profile indicates, but these traits can be interpreted by the public as negative, insensitive, and unresponsive in the day to day performance of duties and tasks. Thus, training in communications to help officers transmit an attitude of *competence with concern* seems to be especially important.

Communication Training

"Why are we here?" one police officer asked at the outset of the first meeting.

"The reason you are here is to learn one technique on how to communicate with people."

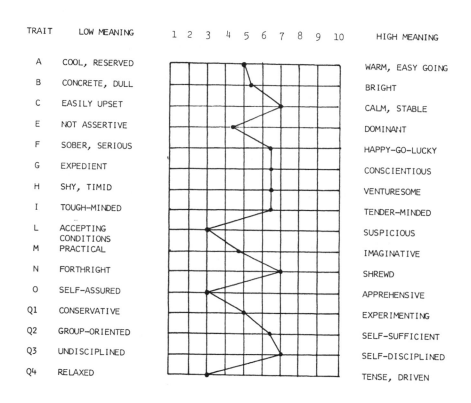

SELF RATING

PERSONALITY PROFILE

TRAIT	LOW MEANING	1 2 3 4 5 6 7 8 9 10	HIGH MEANING
A	COOL, RESERVED		WARM, EASY GOING
B	CONCRETE, DULL		BRIGHT
C	EASILY UPSET		CALM, STABLE
E	NOT ASSERTIVE		DOMINANT
F	SOBER, SERIOUS		HAPPY-GO-LUCKY
G	EXPEDIENT		CONSCIENTIOUS
H	SHY, TIMID		VENTURESOME
I	TOUGH-MINDED		TENDER-MINDED
L	ACCEPTING CONDITIONS		SUSPICIOUS
M	PRACTICAL		IMAGINATIVE
N	FORTHRIGHT		SHREWD
O	SELF-ASSURED		APPREHENSIVE
Q1	CONSERVATIVE		EXPERIMENTING
Q2	GROUP-ORIENTED		SELF-SUFFICIENT
Q3	UNDISCIPLINED		SELF-DISCIPLINED
Q4	RELAXED		TENSE, DRIVEN

Figure 3.1. Capital City Police Profile using 16 PF Inventory.

The most difficult task in getting started was making clear what communication is all about. Terms such as "receiver" and "sender" were discussed and "helper" and "helpee" were defined.

ACTIVITY 3.1: Warm up

A warm-up exercise was used. The consultant asked members of the group to think of an adjective to describe a person that has helped them in some way. A composite list of these descriptive words were written on a chalkboard. As intended, this activity helped the members of the group identify characteristics of persons seen as helpers and relate those characteristics to human relations skills.

The trainer/consultant, using Carkhuff's (1969) model of communication, explained the use of empathy (feeling words) and respect (content) to open communication in a helpful fashion.

A global scale for rating responses, using the concept of Levels 1, 2, 3, and 4, (Figure 3.2) was explained to these police officers, indicating that the focus of the training would be Level 3, the point where communication is open and understanding takes place (Gazda, Asbury, Blazer, Childers, & Walters, 1977).

ACTIVITY 3.2: Practice and Rating

The next phase in learning to understand the Level 3 response was to ask the officers to write a statement that had been made to them and that had generated an unpleasant feeling. These statements were not to be identified as to whom the sender or receiver might be. The next step in this process was to read one statement and ask the group to write a spontaneous response. The responses were picked up and read anonymously and rated by the group according to the global scale. As each response was read and rated (See Fig. 3.2), a discussion followed as to how the response could be improved for each response that was written for each stimulus that was used.

At the next group meeting the consultant reviewed the global scale. The consultant then used one of the previously written stimulus statements as an introductory role-playing statement. Each consultee participated in this exercise on a one-to-one basis. This gave each trainee a change to respond and to evaluate his/her feelings about the response.

Also, this procedure allowed the consultant an opportunity to work with any individual who was having problems with this model.

The officers then were asked if they had had an encounter since the last meeting that they could share with the group. Many examples were given. Using their examples, again the role-playing technique was employed to develop skills of responding. During the exercise the officers assumed both roles, i.e., the police officer and the civilian. This was done to help the police officer identify with the feelings of the citizen involved in the situation with the officer, and to help the officer find a helpful response that would minimize violence or bad feelings, and yet allow the officer to do one's duty.

A Stimuli-Response Assessment Form was administered to the participants prior to and following the training program. This instrument was made up of five stimulus statements that an officer would probably hear while on the job. The mean rating using the Global Rating scale (shown in Figure 3.2) by the police officers on the pre-test, i.e., prior to the training, was 1.2; the post-test mean rating was 2.5. This is an increase of 1.3 points. These ratings are shown in Figure 3.3.

STIMULUS—RESPONSE SCALE

The GLOBAL SCALE FOR RATING HELPER RESONSES were scored according to the following:

LEVEL 1—Not helpful; hurtful. A response by which a helper damages communication.

LEVEL 2—Not helpful; ineffective. A response by which a helper impedes lines of communication.

LEVEL 3—Helpful; facilitative. *A response by which the helper communicates acceptance of the helpee as a person of worth.*

LEVEL 4—Helpful; additive. A response by which the helper demonstrates his willingness and ability to be a helper.

Figure 3.2. The global scale used by police officers to rate communication effectiveness.

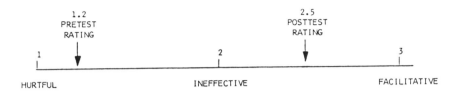

Figure 3.3. Change in mean score on pre-post measure of communication effectiveness.

Problem Solving

At the height of the communication training as officers experienced the impact of their actions on behaviors and feelings of others, several group members became critical and verbal about the poor communications among the rank and file within the department. The trainees were complaining about many problems in the department. In order to channel these gripes into a productive session the trainer introduced the VISUAL approach to problem solving (Kirby, 1979) and secured their agreement to apply it to the problems they were experiencing. (For a discussion of the VISUAL Model see Chapter 2.) The group hesitated because they expressed concern that nothing could be done. However, they were willing to try. A list of problems was solicited from the group in a brainstorming session and listed on the board. The problem-solving model was expanded to include barriers that prevented solution and finally what alternative could be used as a solution. As a result of this exercise, several solutions were put into effect by the department.

In Figure 3.4 are representative problems presented by trainees and is an example of the application of the "barriers and realistic alternatives" aspect of the problem-solving procedure. This is not intended to be inclusive of all problems presented, but illustrates the kinds of concerns and issues the technique generated.

CONCERNS	BARRIERS	REALISTIC ALTERNATIVES
A. Reducing Number of Breaking and Enterings	1. Misplaced priorities (towing, traffic, drunks) consume time.	a. Let wagon man take tows, drunks, etc., or let sergeants do it. b. Increase size of roving patrol. c. Have shift commander inform officers as to which crime has priority for a specific time period. d. Put two persons on patrol wagon to take care of tows, traffic, and drunks.
	2. Inadequate Rookie Training	a. Assign a rookie with a veteran for one year. Be selective in assignments. b. When practical, make assignment of pairing upon request. c. Group rookies periodically for rap sessions with a veteran. d. Have rookie work a month and go to school a month in that order. No academy training. e. Plan more inservice, utilizing talent of staff.
	3. Lack of Inservice Training	a. Change veteran who works with rookie every four months. b. Have continuous inservice by persons who have received specialized training (i.e., a detective who has gone to a crime prevention seminar). Utilize staff persons or retired officer. c. Print interdepartmental newsletter regularly. d. Hire locally. e. Dismiss rookie at eleventh month if he/she cannot make it.
	4. Court System from process to incarceration too time consuming.	a. Eliminate J.P. system. b. Have city clerk sign all warrants. c. Keep county court out of process. Separate county and city jails. Too much time is consumed in processing which keeps officers off the beat. d. Call warrants in on "call for help" phone to one person. e. Deputize secretaries to sign warrants. f. Use proper warrant form in each category as a sample. This should be written by an expert. g. Create a department for evaluating and analyzing information thereby relieving officers.
B. Lack of Communication	1. Fear of repercussion from immediate superior	The acceptance of constructive criticism from within rank.
	2. Veterans in upper rank show no respect for new ideas	Freedom and opportunity to exchange opinions and ideas in rap sessions.
	3. Lack of respect for officers	Interdepartmental exchange of ideas.

Figure 3.4. Concerns, barriers, and alternatives generated during problem-solving exercises with police officers.

Self-Appraisal Rating Scale

A self-appraisal rating scale (Figure 3.5) was administered twice, pre- and posttraining, to the 18 police officers taking the 16 P F questionnaire. This scale allowed officers to rate nine items (presented as 1 to 9 in Figure 3.5) on a six point scale from high to low.

In Figure 3.5 are shown the difference between the pre- and postrating on each of the nine items for the same individuals. The trainer believes that the difference in the self-rating of the officers from before to after the training was due to achievement of greater self-awareness through the process of group dynamics. This assumption seems to be substantiated by the following comments made by officers:

> "The training helped me to know I did not understand myself as I thought I did."

> "Open discussion in the group has helped."

> "In the group I became aware I've been trying to impose my beliefs on others."

> "I always thought I was Mr. Average, now I'm not sure I'm as good as I thought I was."

> "I'm now aware others see me as a threat; I can see how I can work through them."

> "I used this in my personal life, it works. But I'd rather not comment about that now."

Data derived from this checklist was of little value beyond the discussion and self-analysis it generated. Nevertheless, the use of assessment instruments are recommended as an interaction technique to speed up self-awareness and encourage a discussion.

Officer's Evaluation Questionnaire (OEQ)

A questionnaire was constructed to gain an impression of police officers' evaluation of the training experience. From their responses the following conclusions were drawn:

Participants	Genuineness Do I Like Me	Do Others Understand Me	Care, Respect. Do I Like People	See and Understand Needs and Feelings of Others	Allow Others Their Beliefs	Allow Others Belief Without Judging	Talk Without Threatening	Open Mind to Others	Willing to Change— Develop as a Person
	1	2	3	4	5	6	7	8	9
A	− 1	0	0	0	− 2	0	0	0	0
B	− 1	+ 1	− 1	0	1	− 2	0	+ 1	+ 2
C	0	0	0	0	0	0	0	0	0
D	+ 1	+ 1	0	1	0	0	0	0	0
E	0	0	− 1	0	0	0	0	0	− 1
F	+ 1	+ 1	+ 1	+ 1	+ 1	+ 1	+ 2	0	0
G	0	+ 1	+ 1	+ 2	+ 1	+ 1	+ 1	+ 1	+ 1
H	+ 1	− 1	0	0	− 1	+ 1	0	0	+ 2
I	0	0	− 1	0	0	0	− 1	− 1	0
J	+ 1	+ 1	+ 1	0	0	+ 1	0	− 1	+ 1
K	0	0	− 2	0	0	− 1	− 1	0	− 1
L	0	0	0	0	0	0	− 1	0	0
M	− 1	+ 1	− 1	+ 1	0	− 1	0	− 1	0
N	0	0	+ 1	+ 1	− 1	0	0	− 1	0
O	− 1	− 2	− 1	0	0	+ 1	0	− 2	− 1
P	− 1	0	0	0	0	+ 1	0	− 1	0
Q	− 1	− 1	0	− 1	0	− 1	0	0	0
R	0	0	+ 1	+ 1	+ 1	0	+ 1	0	0

Figure 3.5. Differences in rating between pre- and posttraining as obtained on a Self-Appraisal Rating Scale for 18 officers.

1. Ninety-six percent of the trainees indicated the training accomplished all or part of its objectives.

2. Essentially, officers felt that the most valuable part of the training was the group interaction, listening to comments of fellow officers, recognizing needs and feelings of self and others, and learning how to respond to others.

3. Eighty-five percent indicated all parts of the training were of some value.

4. Eighty-seven percent of the trainees indicated they would attend another such type of training.

5. Ninety percent indicated they would recommend this training for fellow police officers.

6. Eighty-seven percent indicated they were able to use the training on the job.

7. An effectiveness scale (Figure 3.6) was utilized to provide an estimation of overall effectiveness of the training on a quantitative scale. Officers were asked to rate the training on a scale from 1 (ineffective) to 9 (most beneficial). The mean rating by the police officers was 7 as shown on Figure 3.6 below.

```
  1    2    3    4    5    6    7    8    9
_____
INEFFECTIVE                   MEAN   MOST
                              GROUP  BENEFICIAL
                              RATING
```

Figure 3.6. Overall effectiveness rating of training with police officers.

As can be noted from rating on the Effectiveness Scale, officers perceive the training to be effective, i.e., rated on upper third of the scale.

Conclusions and Recommendations

The following conclusions seem valid based upon data obtained from several instruments and the observations of the trainer.

1. Officers became more honest and gained self awareness through training.

2. Communication training, provided by a humanistic consultant, can be threatening to police officers who rely on toughness as a model of control.

3. When a facilitative approach (i.e., effective communication) was used on the jobs (as reported back verbally), officers felt this approach was a more positive approach than the more commonly used "authority" model.

4. This training model is more appropriate for certain types of situations, such as communicating with individuals and small groups, than with large demonstration groups.

The following recommendations grew out of this consultant's experiences with police officers:

1. Police officers should be given an opportunity for problem-solving sessions once a month with representatives from different departments.

2. An objective consultant/facilitator (nonpolice personnel) should be provided, on retainer, to lead the group through problem-solving situations, and provide aid to groups and individuals who have job and personal concerns.

3. Upper level administrators and superiors need to give genuine consideration to concerns of officers, such as those expressed in Figure 3.4.

4. All ranks of personnel within the police department should be involved in problem solving and policy making.

5. Officers need to be oriented to goals and objectives of group sessions with the consultant prior to training.

AGENCY B: BETTER COUNTY
SECONDARY SCHOOL PRINCIPALS

The second consultative group to be discussed consisted of secondary school principals from 11 high schools in the Better County School System. These schools served a cross section of students from intercity to rural areas. These schools send from 15 to 50 percent of their graduates to college.

The need for a consultant was generated by numerous complaints and problems brought to the attention of the deputy superintendent who, at that time, felt a need for a workshop with administrators. This writer was requested to present a training program using a problem solving technique whereby the myriad problems could be addressed.

This workshop was set up on school time, beginning at 8:00 a.m. and dismissing at 3:00 p.m., for two consecutive days. The group consisted of secondary school principals and the central office staff which totaled about 40 participants. Attendance was mandatory. Functionally, administrators constituted an interdependent system. Principals, for example, were in an administrative position that needed central office support to resolve and to implement any recommendations arising from this workshop. In this group the consultant had to deal with several levels of administrators and with as many educational philosophies as participants.

A consultant as an *insider* has power based on his/her reputation as a facilitator and helper, and this recognized expertise can be employed to encourage communication and openness. Additionally, in order to have credibility and thereby function effectively, the insider serving as the consultant needs to be recognized as a person who uses good problem-solving techniques and facilitative skills in conducting his/her own school. In dealing with one's own peers, imperatively the consultant must be objective and must concentrate on the work related issues. A colleague working with fellow administrators must develop a sense of trust so that individuals in the workshop do not deal with personnel agenda rather than the work of the group. Under such circumstances a consultant's level of trust and feelings of comfort in the group is an index of the atmosphere within the group.

At the outset the group developed their ground rules. The operating rules were:

• be honest (i.e., say what you mean and mean what you say);

- no comments are to be argumentative; everyone has a right to say what they wish; and,

- only one person can speak at a time.

These rules provided a vehicle for good group interaction. The role as the facilitator, as different from that of a colleague, was explained.

The objective of this workshop was stated as follows: "To demonstrate a problem-solving model that administrators can use in solving individual and group problems." The VISUAL Model (Kirby, 1979, also see Chapter 2) was used. This model was chosen because it makes clear to participants that members of a group can collectively arrive at a possible solution to their common problems. Even problems that do not apply to everyone can be resolved if the group is willing to attend to the issue or concerns of select individuals owning those problems.

Following the establishment of ground rules, participants were divided into smaller groups of five members each. These groups were instructed to brainstorm concerns, their problems, and compile a list that was common to the group. (For a discussion of Brainstorming Technique, see Chapter 2.) About one and one-half hours were allocated to this activity. This allowed enough time to identify a variety of problems to be used throughout the two days the group worked together.

After the small groups finished brainstorming, the recorder for each group read the concerns aloud. A list was compiled on the board so that all could see. One feature of this procedure of writing on the board is that when they see the list it makes a greater impact on them. Once all groups had reported, overlapping concerns were eliminated and remaining ones reworded into measurable objectives. An example follows:

> **Problem Statement:** How can we improve staffing patterns as it related to special education classes, declining enrollment, and continuity between junior and senior high school programs?

> **Measurable Objective:** To adopt a staffing plan that will fit the needs of the county pertaining to present and future projections in regard to special education, enrollment, and articulation between middle and high school programs.

Next, individual administrators were given a list of concerns and asked to prioritize them. The following list is an abbreviated statement of concerns as they were prioritized by participants.

CONCERNS	RANKING (%)
1. Staffing Patterns	96
2. Nonnutritional foods	95
3. Attendance Policy	94
4. Last day for seniors	88
5. Data Processing	88
6. Early graduation or requirements	71
7. English teachers for Vocational Centers	70
8. Eleven months, employment for Vocational Home Economics teachers	69
9. Summer School	67
10. Vocational money	57
11. Area assistants	54
12. Rental Policy	33

The consultant chose a rather simple issue, No. 4, above, as the first problem to be resolved. This activity—"Last day for seniors," gave the group leader an opportunity to teach the consultees the VISUAL Model (Kirby, 1979), let them experience its effectiveness as a group decision-making approach, and deal with group process issues before the group was immersed in a more complex and emotional issue. This lower level problem also was an effective procedure for developing trust in the leader, openness about one's philosophy, and cohesiveness within the group.

The first concern on the prioritized list, i.e., staffing pattern, was so complex that it was subdivided into many areas alluding to staffing patterns. Appropriate measurable objectives were written for each of the subissues addressed by the workshop. The complexity of the issue is seen by the following list of concerns relating to staffing patterns as identified by administrators:

1. Lack of staff for Special Education classes

2. Added student load because of extra math credit

3. Decline in enrollment reduces offerings; lack of staff specialization

4. Lack of continuity between junior and senior high school programs

5. Driver Education increased load and demands

6. Ratio of students to assistant principal and counselors not consistent

This consultant noted to the participants that one concern may lead to several others as indicated by the preceding articulation. In the example offered previously, each of the related concerns were treated as separate issues during the problem-solving workshop.

The VISUAL Method (Kirby, 1979) provided a structure for decision making that appealed to practicing administrators, and at the same time the structure allowed the consultant freedom to manage and to direct the dynamics of the process to encourage creative and innovative considerations of all problems. The workshop sessions were productive. Examples are given in Figures 3.7 and 3.8 of ideas that were generated by the group as they dealt with their common concerns of staffing patterns and data processing.

The last hour of the workshop was devoted to summarizing the work of the group and bringing closure to their involvement. Recommendations, as drafted by administrators to be presented to the central office staff for consideration,were read by the recorder. The consultant recapitulated objectives and commented on the model applied, and to insure that all emotions were left behind, each participant made a statement about their feelings.

Example 1: VISUAL PROCEDURE

V   Problem:

How do we increase teaching staff to effectively handle all Special Education (Sp. Ed.) students that qualify for the resource centers.

I   Alternatives:

       1. Seek increase in finances.
       2. Study staffing at neighboring states to see how they improve utilization.
       3. Regular staff may teach students eligible for the resource center.

S   Survey:

       (Notes: Advantages and disadvantages for each option were identified and

U   Underline:

       underlined to indicate values of group.)

A   Accept one alternative:

       A staff utilization study be implemented.

L   List Next Step:

       The Administrators as a group recommended (in writing) that the board officers implement a county wide study of staff utilization, and that other states be contacted to learn how they managed this problem. (The central office was asked to report back to the school level administrators at a given date.)

Figure 3.7. Summary of problem-solving activity with administrators using the VISUAL Approach to problem solving, Example 1.

EXAMPLE 2: VISUAL PROCEDURE

V   Problem:

How can the data process procedure used in reporting grades be improved.

I   Alternatives:

1. Make due dates more realistic.
2. Change "W" to another code. This drops student from the records.
3. Change code that "add" students will appear.
4. School needs should be anticipated earlier.
5. Improve coordination of other departments.
6. Improve scheduling of printing report cards.

S   Survey:

(Note: Advantages and disadvantages for each option were identified.)

U   Underline:

(Items were underlined to indicate values of group.)

A   Accept One Alternative:

Set up realistic due dates for Data Process Sheets.

L   List Next Step:

The Administrators as a group recommended (in writing) priorities to be set for use of computer. Also realistic due dates for reports be commensurate with last day of school closing.

Figure 3.8. Summary of problem-solving activity with administrators using the VISUAL Approach to problem-solving, Example 2.

Conclusion

The effectiveness of the workshop was evaluated as highly successful by the fact that the following recommendations presented to the Board of Education were implemented.

• A driving range was built at a vocational center to accommodate more students.

• A new attendance policy was implemented clarifying excused and unexcused absences and how attendance was to be implemented.

• Data processing procedure for reporting of grades was improved and effectively implemented.

• Early graduation requirements were effectively implemented.

Some sample statements that were made at closure by administrators were as follows:

"I had a chance to be heard."

"Only relevant dialogue was carried on."

"Discussion was to the point and effective."

"I had my say."

"I felt good that our recommendations will be considered."

AGENCY C: HOPEWELL GENERAL HOSPITAL STAFF

Hopewell General Hospital is a small community hospital. The staff is primarily comprised of local persons. The hospital has approximately 150 beds and it serves a rural county area. For its size it is considered a good hospital staffed with very caring people.

The Director of Nursing approached this writer to set up a program that might help her staff in learning good communication skills. The Director of Nursing was enrolled in a human relations class at the local graduate college and as a result of her experience in the class felt that her staff would benefit from a similar program at the hospital. As the consultant, this writer suggested a workshop to initiate the program, then if the staff was receptive, future workshops could be set up. The goal for the consultant in the initial contact with this group was to help them gain some self-awareness and ascertain if they would be interested in this type of program. While the initial workshop was to be an orientation to a more intense program, procedures used were designed to provide an opportunity for participants:

1. to achieve self-awareness;

2. to learn good communication skills;

3. to learn openness as well as become assertive in their dialogue with each other and their patients; and

4. to learn a problem solving technique.

From the outset the consultant had suggested a one day workshop. This workshop, because of time, was structured so that participants would get an introduction to different techniques.

Procedure

ACTIVITY 3.3: Warm up

The participants were asked to pair off with someone they would like to know better. After about 10 minutes, each participant introduced each other to the group.

This technique seemed to set the atmosphere for the day. The group was involved and excited about the experience.

ACTIVITY 3.4: Nonverbal Awareness

The next activity asked each group member to mill around the room, not speaking, but feeling. They were told to observe nonverbal signs and signals. *Again, after about 10 minutes, each participant was asked to express what they saw and how they felt.*

This technique was another type of warm-up that was designed to help participants get in touch with their feelings.

The consultant's role in these warm-up activities was to facilitate each response as each group member reacted and, also, to explain how messages are sent even though there is no dialogue. Nonverbal signs and body language were discussed at this time.

The group was given a Self-appraisal Rating Form similar to the one used with police officers (see Figure 3.5). When completed, each member was asked if her self-perception was surprising in any way. While these scales were rated by the individual, the instrument caused them to think about themselves in the context of a workshop where awareness was the focus. This activity generated an amazing number of revealing reactions. It seemed this group activity gave individuals "permission" to analyze their own feelings, actions, and beliefs, and seemingly for the first time! This proved to be a useful, nonthreatening approach for this group.

Following these interaction activities, participants were asked to respond in writing to the self-analysis questions indicated in Activity C.

ACTIVITY 3.5: Self Awareness Questionnaire

Part I. Write a short paragraph on each of the following five points:

> *1. What I want to be.*
>
> *2. What kind of person I am.*
>
> *3. What kind of a person do other people think I am?*
>
> *4. How I would like to change the world.*
>
> *5. What I would like to change about the world.*

Part II. If you could be granted three wishes, what would they be?

1.

2.

3.

When each had completed writing, those that volunteered to do so, shared some or all of the information they had written. Some of their responses indicated that they were surprised at the results. This was another exercise in understanding self.

Communication Model

The objective relevant to good communication was excerpted from the model explained earlier in the discussion of the police officers. The trainer/consultant explained the use of empathy (feeling words) and respect (content) to open communication in a helpful fashion. The next phase in learning to understand the Level 3 (see Figure 3.2 for the rating scale) response was to ask each participant to write a statement which had been made to them and which had generated an unpleasant feeling. When each participant had finished, one by one they were asked to read a statement aloud and the group was asked to write a response. Then, each participant was asked to read their response while the consultant discussed the level of response according to the global scale. If their responses were not a Level 3 then it was changed to meet that level. All participants were given a chance to participate until they experienced a Level 3 response.

Problem Solving

The group was divided into subgroups of approximately five each. Their instructions were to list some problems they face. These problems were to be job related. This brainstorming activity gives each group member an opportunity to participate without having to reveal too much about oneself too early.

After approximately 20 minutes, the large group convened and the recorders read their problems and listed them on the chalkboard. Overlapping problems were eliminated and the list of concerns were prioritized.

The VISUAL Model (Kirby, 1979) was explained. The time remaining allowed the consultant to work through one problem with the group.

The evaluation instruments (Figure 3.9) used at the end of the workshop indicated a strong interest for future workshops. All participants indicated that they did learn something about self.

The consultant recapitulated objectives for the workshop and a closure activity was used for the group, thus ending the program.

Reflection

The trainer/consultant's role in this situation was essentially the same as in preceding situations. The director of nursing had set the stage for this consultant and expectations were consistent with the "training" style of the consultant. Even though this group was apprised of this consultant's role, initially a great deal of apprehension and ambivalence was present. The application of low risk awareness activities and the use of issues common to the group allowed participants the option of deciding their individual levels of participation. As trust in the leader and comfort in sharing personal information with colleagues represented by different levels of employment and training were achieved, the group became more and more task oriented. The impression of this consultant was that *pacing* was the critical factor in working successfully with this group specifically, and perhaps in the hospital setting with groups generally. Additionally, an orientation workshop, like this one, that gives room for a "tentative" commitment to consultation/training seems to be a good approach for developing rapport and gaining commitment to more intensive work together.

EVALUATION FORM

Express your opinion by checking the appropriate column after each category.

1. Evaluation of Content Session	Excellent	Good	Adequate	Less than Adequate
(1) Program Format	————	———	————	————
(2) Opportunities for exchange of ideas	————	———	————	————
(3) Strengthened or renewed my interest in the topic	————	———	————	————
(4) Content was related to program title	————	———	————	————
(5) Possibilities for application/ Practicality	————	———	————	————
(6) Provided new ideas	————	———	————	————
(7) Program was related to hospital concerns	————	———	————	————

2. Rating of Program	Yes	No	Undecided
(1) This session expanded my *awareness* of the topic	—	—	————
(2) This session increased my *interest in the topic*	—	—	————
(3) This session may change my *personal behavior*	—	—	————
(4) This session expanded my *knowledge* on the topic	—	—	————
(5) This session may have impact on my *job behavior*	—	—	————

3. Why did you attend this session? (Please check one or more).

    (1) Inservice credit   ————————
    (2) Improve hospital program   ————————
    (3) Interaction with staff members ————————
    (4) Personal   ————————
    (5) Other (please list)   ————————

4. Would you recommend more sessions on this topic?

Yes———— No————

COMMENTS:

Figure 3.9. Workshop evaluation instrument used with hospital based service providers.

REFERENCES

Carkhuff, R. (1969). *Helping and human relations. A primer for lay and professional helpers* (Vol. 1). New York: Holt, Rinehart, Winston.

Cattell, R. B., Eber, H. W., & Tatsuoka, M. M. (1970). *Handbook for the Sixteen Personality Factor Questionnaire.* Champaign, IL: Institute for Personality and Ability Testing.

Gazda, G. M., Asbury, F. R., Blazer, F. J., Childers, W. C., & Walters, R. P. (1977). *Human relations development* (2nd ed.). Boston: Allyn & Bacon.

Kirby, J. (1979). *Second marriage.* Muncie, IN: Accelerated Development.

CHAPTER 4

STRATEGIC SYSTEMIC CONSULTATION

Donald L. Bubenzer, Ph.D.

Donald L. Bubenzer, Ph.D.

Donald L. Bubenzer, Ph.D. is Associate Professor of Marriage and Family Therapy within the College of Education, Kent State University. He is a Clinical Member and Approved Supervisor of the American Association for Marriage and Family Therapy. His consulting activities have included serving as the marriage and family specialist with a multi-disciplinary team of an adult service network, and as a consultant for group homes, mental health centers, and schools. His research and writing have included the study of personality variables related to stress and life adjustment and the training of marriage and family counselors.

STRATEGIC SYSTEMIC CONSULTATION

Donald L. Bubenzer, Ph.D.

During the past couple of decades concern for the mental health of individuals within the community has shifted from almost exclusive attention to interpersonal factors to community based issues that might appropriately be labeled systemic factors. Only recently has the role of environmental forces become a focus of professional consultation and activity. The Mental Health Study Act of 1955 resulted in the establishment of a federal commission, the Joint Commission on Mental Illness and Health (1961), to study the mental health needs of the nation so that the federal government might address those needs. One outcome of the Commission was the establishment of community mental health centers.

The development of professional organizations and training programs to prepare personnel to work in community mental health settings is still in a state of infancy. In 1965 a definition of community psychology was developed for and by psychologists who met to discuss the training of community psychologists (Hersch, 1969) and in 1978 the American Mental Health Counselors Association first developed a definition of the professional counselor (Seiler & Messina, 1979).

Meanwhile, the number of agencies and organizations responding to specific mental health needs within communities has multiplied. These agencies, both privately and publicly supported are tremendously diverse in terms of populations they serve and/or problems they address. Nevertheless, they all are concerned with issues of *coping, growth,* and *behavior.* Some agencies address the particular needs of adolescents and their families such as group homes, foster care, and runaway houses. Some other agencies exist that deal with substance abuse, eating disorders, weight control, and compulsions. Other mental health centers address a full range of mental health problems. Still other centers specialize in specific areas such as the family, child abuse, domestic violence, special concerns of women and unique concerns of men. Certain community organizations address needs of the elderly, of young singles, of new parents, of parents with adolescents, and of persons facing retirement. The list could continue but one can see that the number of agencies or organizations that address the psychological needs of citizens would total in the hundreds and perhaps even the thousands.

The combination of the youthfulness of the field of community mental health, the absence of sufficient numbers of adequately trained professionals and paraprofessionals and the multitude of agencies, organizations, and programs attempting to meet the mental health needs of communities and their residents all point to the need for effective consultants.

Individuals serving as consultants to community agencies function as problem solvers and planners. They intervene with fellow professionals to identify and break inappropriate cyclical patterns of behavior (Blake & Mouton, 1976) and they help professionals and organizations anticipate futures (Lippitt, 1959) so that strategic decisions can be made that will impact long range goals. To accomplish the consultative task, the practitioner needs a working knowledge of a problem solving/planning process that has applicability to community agencies, facilitative skills that help people change attitudes and behavior, and the ability to fulfill differing consulting roles when given the situation, needs of the consultee, and their own professional style. In this chapter, a process of consultation that this writer applies in consultation with community agencies, and some roles and techniques appropriate to various stages of the consultation process will be discussed. Application will be made to what Caplan (1970) terms a *consultee-centered case setting* and a *consultee-centered administrative setting.* In the former, the focus is on helping a professional solve problems in the management of a case and in the latter the focus is on helping solve problems of programming and organization.

ROLES

To apply a consultation model to an actual work situation presupposes possession of basic facilitative skills and knowledge of basic responses appropriately used by consultants. Lippitt and Lippitt (1978) have described eight roles that consultants assume. Consultative roles range from least directive to most directive, and include (1) observer reflector, (2) process facilitator, (3) fact finder, (4) alternative identifier, (5) joint problem solver, (6) trainer, (7) informational expert, and (8) advocate.

The *observer reflector* role allows the consultant to pose questions for others to think over while the *process facilitator* observes problem solving processes used by the agency and raises issues about the effect of those processes. The consultant as a *fact finder* seeks out data relevant to problems the organization is seeking to solve. As an *alternative identifier* the consultant is helping the client to identify resources that may be helpful in problem solving. The *joint problem solver* role is played when decisions are chosen from alternatives. Much work of consultants consists of *training,* i.e., providing assistance in learning specific skills germane to problem solving. At times, consultants operate as *informational experts.* They provide expert information relative to the specific problem presented. Finally, consultants, although they have no power other than persuasion, may *advocate* for a particular course of action or process to be utilized.

All of these roles find expression in the particular model that the author uses in viewing problems. Various phases of the consultative process require different roles to be used by the consultant. Roles as they interplay with phases of the consultation process are presented throughout the remainder of the chapter.

OVERVIEW—STRATEGIC SYSTEMIC CONSULTATIVE PROCESS (SSCP)

Problems and their solutions are multifaceted with each component related to every other component in a systemic manner. An analysis of the system provides the consultant with information about roles, techniques, and processes. Steps of the SSCP and their relationship to the process are depicted in Figure 4.1.

For any intervention to be successful the consultant has to have information about each of seven factors defined: problem, objectives, climate, resources, strategies, implementation plan, and evaluation. The following example shows how the seven steps of the process are interrelated. Suppose the program director of a local community agency, in this instance a group home for adolescents, calls a potential consultant requesting a staff training workshop on group work with teenagers. The request implies the prospective consultant is to play a *training role* in the implementation phase (Step 6) of the SSCP model. However, an experienced consultant will seek additional information to determine whether the request is appropriate to the need.

Immediately the individual contacted assumes consultative roles of "fact finder" and "observer reflector" to make a decision about the appropriateness of accepting the consulting contract. Relative to the *problem* (Step 1, SSCP), the prospective consultant wants to know:

• What needs of the consultee the group work would address?

• What characteristics of residents might best be addressed through the utilization of group work?

• What specific outcomes, objectives (Step 2), of the training are desired?

• Are staff members in need of learning about group dynamics and leadership skills related to particular types of groups, and so forth?

• What is the climate for change (Step 3) from the perspective of how receptive the staff is to assuming group leadership responsibility?

• How receptive are the residents to the idea of meeting in groups?

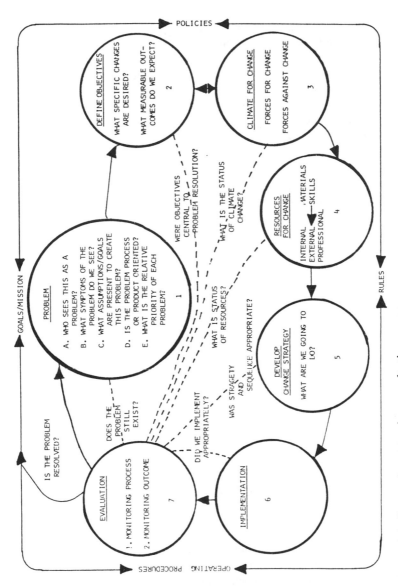

Figure 4.1. Strategic-systemic consultative process.

• What are the personnel and physical resources (Step 4) of the group home relative to conducting groups.

• Questions to be answered revolve around finding out the appropriateness of facilities, the staff members, and the type of continuing support that would be provided through supervision.

If information from the previous questions leads the consultant to believe that training in groups is appropriate and if he/she is willing to provide the training, the groundwork is in place for making strategic sequential decisions (Step 5) about the training. For example, to provide change strategy interventions may be important to increase the receptivity of staff and residents to group work before performing group training functions. In helping to develop a change strategy, the consultant is employing roles of "joint problem solver," "alternative identifier" and perhaps "advocate" if he/she believes a particular strategy is highly favored. Once plans have been finalized the consultative process is ready for implementation (Step 6). Yet to be answered are the evaluative questions (Step 7) of "Did we do what we intended and was it effective?" Information relevant to Steps 1 through 5 may have been obtained in a 15 minute phone call. But at other times the work may be spread over several months with large scale involvement in the planning activity. This brief sketch gives the reader a flavor for the Strategic Systemic Consultation Process used by the writer.

SSCP COMPONENTS

As illustrated in the previous section, various parts of the SSCP are related. To provide a clearer understanding each part will be discussed separately, links to other components will be shown, examples of the application of components to consultation with community agencies will be provided and techniques individuals might use in the consulting process will be presented.

Problems

Consultants are approached by community agency personnel, usually administrators, because the agency is experiencing a problem. A community agency problem, in the broad context might be defined as *a disparity between what the agency is doing and what someone, internal or external, to the agency believes it should be doing.* For some reason the agency is not capable of effectively accomplishing its mission. Usually the agency or specific workers within the agency are experiencing a crisis, i.e., the old way of doing things no longer works. The following are typical requests from community agencies for consultative services:

> EMPLOYMENT SECURITY—"We need some help in working with hostile claimants. With unemployment benefits running out many people we serve are feeling desperate and our workers feel helpless in working with them."

> PROTECTIVE CUSTODY—"Our employees need some help dealing with stress. They feel burned out and we are having a high employee turnover."

> ADOLESCENT GROUP HOME—"We need some help thinking through what we do. So many kids we get today are 'predelinquent' and we still operate and are seen as if we were an orphanage . . ."

Requests for consultative assistance are usually seeking what Schein (1978) defined as *expert services,* the purchase of specific information or expertise, or *process services,* someone who helps define a process by which the organization can surface problems or ideas and assist in seeking solutions or plans. In instances where the consultee's diagnosis appears to the consultant to be appropriate and where the request for services appears consonant with the diagnosis, the consultant simply decides whether or not to become involved. However, in instances where either the problem diagnosis or the service diagnosis seem to the consultant to be insufficient, the potential consultant has to decide on whether to be involved and also develop a strategy for redefinition of the problem and/or redefinition of services to be rendered. An example of the latter might be a request for a stress management workshop when it appears the source of stress within the organization needs modification. Clarity of the problem or need is crucial so that interventions when implemented will be effective.

Answers to the following questions provide helpful information in DEFINING PROBLEMS or needs for an individual human service client or for an organization.

• What is the problem from the perspectives of a variety of people—client(s), service providers, administrators, and so forth?

• Who sees this particular issue as a problem?

• What symptoms of the problem are present?

• What assumptions are present, in order for this issue to be a problem?

• Is the problem due to a lack of skill, resources, knowledge, self-confidence, or what?

• How important is the problem compared to other problems the organization or individual is facing?

Often, various personnel will see the same issue quite differently. What one believes is a problem, others will believe is a symptom. Seeking widespread input about symptoms and common problem definition is helpful (1) in terms of striving for a common solution; (2) to obtain commitment to the solution; or (3) to establish an agreed upon process of finding a solution. If only a few people believe a problem exists or if many people believe a problem exists but believe that it is an insignificant one, then commitment to solving the problem will be low. Articulating symptoms of a problem will help the consultant and consultees sort out symptoms from problems and also will provide guidance in establishing objectives. For example, a mental health center may state "staff morale" as a problem and cite worker absenteeism, use of sick days, staff turnover, and a low number of client appointments as symptoms. Time spent on listing symptoms is well spent because as the consultant progresses to Step 2 the symptoms can be reformulated as objectives for change. The organization mission or goals in combination with budget and daily operating procedures may offer information relevant to problem definition. For example, the institution mission might include service to some of the most difficult populations, yet budget might allow for only entry level pay. Consequently, morale, turnover, burn-out, and low numbers of clients may be symptomatic but the defined strategic solution might center around redefining the type of patient served, or providing staff training. Obtaining broad-based input into problem definition and describing symptoms are valuable in the development of appropriate objectives and the development of strategies for problem resolution.

Techniques for Obtaining
Information About Problems

If problems are presented in a vague manner, the task of the consultant is to help develop a process that will identify problems in solvable ways and establish the relative and sequential importance of problems. The following techniques have proven useful to the writer. Multiple methods of obtaining information should be used to eliminate inherent weaknesses of any single method.

Interviews—Face to face contact with individuals presents to them an attitude that the consultant cares about them, that they are important, and that their perceptions are valued. Consequently, interviews are effective in surfacing organizational concerns. However, a consultant must be clear about one's purpose in conducting interviews. Some personnel will be skeptical that the consultant is working for the "boss" and for them to talk is not in their best interest. Thus, the consultant needs to be focused in presenting reasons for the consulting and interviewing activity and in explaining how information will be used. If the "boss" will explain to personnel the goals of the consultation process and the type of information needed, potential interviewees will feel more willing to reveal their perceptions. These early consultant contacts are designed to increase the trust of consultees.

Group Meetings—If interpersonal trust is very high or very low in the organization, group meetings are effective. In the former case, group thinking will be stimulated and enthusiasm for the process will help generate useful information. *Brainstorming* and *problem ranking* are useful methods of organizing the group meetings to capture the energies and focus attention on task. When trust is low, group meetings can be used to develop trust. Group meetings may be used to help to diffuse rumors, to dispel the notion that some people are secretly favored, and to shatter the belief that regardless of what is said decisions are made by a few who discount the many. Group meetings create a shared body of information and when that information is acted upon trust rises and problems begin to be solved. During consultation transitions and decisions are made in the problem solving process, and thus the group meeting allows appropriate individuals an opportunity to communicate with persons involved, and all who will be affected by changes within the system. Trust and commitment is increased through the group meeting process. Verbal communication is generally more effective than written communication, especially between consultants and participants because it allows individuals to clarify vague points and to obtain additional ideas.

Questionnaires—Two types of questionnaires are appropriate in the identification and definition of problems. The first type of questionnaire simply seeks problem identification and strength from the respondent. An example is shown in Figure 4.2. Of course several questions may be included on the questionnaire and the degree of specificity may vary. This method makes tabulation easy, yet it allows each respondent to identify problems from a personal perspective.

Respond to the following:

"I believe the following five problems are the major problems of X Mental Health Center." Please rank in order of importance with 1 being most important.

1.

2.

3.

4.

5.

Figure 4.2. Sample Questionnaire used for problem and/or strength identification.

A second type of questionnaire focuses on establishing the difference between the present state of affairs and the desired state of affairs. Needs are stated on the questionnaire and the respondent is asked to estimate the intensity of the need in terms of present and future functioning. An excerpt from such a questionnaire is shown as Figure 4.3.

DIRECTIONS

THE QUESTIONNAIRE CONSISTS OF STATEMENTS OF POSSIBLE ORGANIZATIONAL NEEDS/GOALS. USING THE ANSWER KEY SHOWN BELOW, YOU ARE ASKED TO RESPOND TO EACH STATEMENT IN TWO WAYS.

FIRST - HOW IMPORTANT IS THE NEED/GOAL WITHIN THE ORGANIZATION

AT THIS TIME?

THEN - IN YOUR JUDGEMENT, HOW IMPORTANT SHOULD THIS NEED/GOAL BE

IN THE FUTURE?

PLEASE BLACKEN OUT NUMBER AFTER IS AND ONE AFTER SHOULD BE		OF NO IMPORTANCE	OF LOW IMPORTANCE	OF MEDIUM IMPORTANCE	OF HIGH IMPORTANCE	OF EXTREMELY HIGH IMPORTANCE
1. TO INCREASE SECRETARIAL	IS	O	●	O	O	O
SUPPORT IN PREPARING CASE NOTES	SHOULD BE	O	O	O	O	●
2. TO INCREASE THE TYPES OF SERVICES OF	IS	O	O	●	O	O
THE MENTAL HEALTH CENTER	SHOULD BE	O	O	●	O	O
3. TO PROVIDE MORE TIME FOR PLANNING	IS	●	O	O	O	O
PREVENTIVE MENTAL HEALTH PROGRAMS	SHOULD BE	O	O	O	●	O

Figure 4.3. Sample questionnaire used for identifying difference between the present state of affairs and the desired.

The questionnaire provides information concerning the extent to which a problem exists, i.e., discrepancy between "is" and "should be," and also information about the relative importance of various problems by comparing the mean difference between items. Two problems arise. Invariably respondents complain that they are limited to the set of items presented and the "really important" items are omitted. This can be reduced by constructing items from ideas gathered in interviews, group meetings, and open-ended questionnaires and by leaving space at the end of the questionnaire where respondents can write their own items. Also, holding discussions of questionnaire results will allow respondents to verbalize their concerns. Secondly, respondents tend to rate most items as being problems and needing attention. Thus, one is left with many problems that are considered of high importance and decisions still have to be made regarding problem prioritization.

Problem definition is critical for planning intervention strategies. Ideas and techniques discussed previously are those that the author has used in helping community mental health agencies define their problems. Consistent with the SSCP model used by this consultant, problem definitions are chosen that allow results to point to objectives for change and allow the consultant to assess the climate or commitment to change.

Objectives for Change

After an organizational or case problem has been defined, the consultant's task is to assist in the construction of program or case objectives—quantifiable statements of measurable outcomes relative to the problem to be solved. Lewis and Lewis (1983) indicated that process evaluation depends upon assessing the difference between objectives and accomplishments. Thus, constructing appropriate objectives is essential to both success in program and case delivery and the evaluation of that success.

Two types of objectives are usually needed. *Outcome* objectives stipulate results desired relative to agency or case goals while *process* objectives stipulate activities needed to accomplish desired outcomes. The following example statements reflect the three levels of specificity: goals, outcome objectives, and process objectives.

Agency Goal: To provide appropriate educational and therapeutic services to families in the agency's catchment area.

Outcome Objective 1: To provide parent study groups to all families in the agency's catchment area within the next three years.

Process Objective 1: Within two weeks to divide the catchment area into three sub-areas and to target an area for parent education groups for each of the next three years.

Process Objective 2: Within three weeks define a curriculum to be used in the parent education effort.

Process Objective 3: Within four weeks to adequately identify publicity methods in sub area 1 to reach all families.

Additional outcome and process objectives would need to be developed to insure full realization of the goal. The accomplishment of goals and objectives depends on having shared definitions of key terms. The example cited suggests the need for clear definitions for terms: "educational," "therapeutic," "families," and "catchment area." Once definitions have been derived, objectives can be developed.

Techniques of Objective Development. Viable statements of objectives consist of two components: (1) *content terms* i.e., what is to be done; and (2) *performance terms,* i.e., a measurable context for the content. Outcome and process objectives noted within the previous section might be analyzed along the dimensions listed in Figure 4.4.

Several decisions must be made when formulating objectives. Care must be taken to establish objectives that address resolution of the defined problem or goal statement. Inadequacy of either the number of objectives written or the quality of objectives will result in a failure of problem resolution. Redundancy of objectives or too minute or too specific objectives will result in wasted resources or staff frustration. Record keeping and "paper work" will become oppressive and meaningless.

The systemic nature of the consultative process is further evidenced in the working objectives. Just as the problems refinement phase pointed toward the establishment of objectives, the writing of objectives begins to define needed resources and suggest a strategy for change. Once objectives have been established, two related processes can be started. The climate for change can be assessed and an inventory or resources for change can be conducted.

Objectives & Content Terms for Family Services

Objectives	Content Term	Performance
Outcome 1	provide parent educa- tion study program	a. for all families
		b. in three years
Process 1	Divide geographical area and target program delivery	a. three sub areas
		b. 1 area per year for 3 years
Process 2	Identify curriculum	a. within 3 weeks
Process 3	Identify publicity methods in sub area	a. adequate to reach all families
		b. within 4 weeks

Figure 4.4. Sample analysis procedure for outcome and process objectives.

Climate for Change

The existence of a problem, whether programmatic or case specific, usually implies a condition of homeostasis. From an organizational perspective, Lewin (1951) addressed the idea of homeostasis. His concept of force-field analysis suggests that systems solidify around forces that resist change and pressure forces that seek to promote change. The result is a balance between these forces. Lewin also proposed when change is desired by some members of the organization and they attempt to increase the forces for change, other members will rally to maintain the status quo; thus tension and resistance increase. If one is able to reduce the forces that resist change, change is likely to occur with minimal stress and to be more stable. In mental health clinical practice, therapy has been defined (Haley, 1976) as a change in the repeating sets of a self regulating (homeostatic) system. Thus human problems may be viewed as a kind of "stuckness" where a rigid sequence and narrow range of behaviors are employed.

Techniques of Assessment of Climate of Change. Climate of change refers to attitudinal and value laden forces as well as more objective data that support values and attitudes. In assessing the climate for change one is attempting to decipher forces that focus on change and forces that resist change in a problem specific manner. Identification of forces affecting both process and outcome objectives is important.

In identifying forces "favoring" and "resisting" change, information may be obtained from those persons who desire change and from those who are resistive. They are "experts" concerning relevant forces. However, as a consultant the exercise of caution is important in filtering these forces. People usually have both personal and objective reasons for supporting their perspective and both reasons should be identified. Figure 4.5 displays the forces that favor/resist accomplishment of the first objective specified under "Objective & Content Terms or Family Services" discussed earlier.

In consulting about a specific case, the consultant may use varied approaches to assess the climate for change. The consultant may interview only the consultee or the consultant may interview and/or test the consultee, the client, and significant others. The purpose of this climatic assessment is to decipher attitudes, beliefs, norms, and rules that are affecting the ability of the client to change.

In the case specific setting, the consultant usually explores four broad areas:

1. What is the attitude and level of professional objectivity of the consultee toward one's own client?

2. What is the consultee's level of self-confidence with regard to being an effective agent of change with one's clients?

3. What is the client's belief about his/her own ability to change?

4. What is the attitude of significant others in the life of the client regarding their ability and the ability of the client to change.

Climate for Change

Outcome Objective 1: To provide parent study groups to all families in the agency's catchment area within the next three years.

Forces Favoring Objective Accomplishment	Forces Resisting Objective Accomplishment
I. Social Climate	
A. Many parents have expressed concern about parenting skills.	A. Agency is viewed as an outsider and as "expert" and both are to be distrusted.
B. The incidence of substance abuse, teenage pregnancy, and misdemeanors among children has been rising.	B. Belief that how one "parent" is the province of the home and not community mental health agencies.
C. Community has many dual career and single parent families with little communication interparentally about "how we as a community want to raise our kids."	C. Sense of embarrassment that parents feel over needing help to be effective parents.
II. Interagency Climate and Mission	
A. No other agency is fulfilling need	A. Awareness of other agencies that this is an area of need and a service opportunity for them.
B. Support of some churches for parenting education activity	B. A mood of interagency competition.
	C. An economic climate in which agencies are having accountability and find something new is looked on skeptically.
III. Agency Climate	
A. The agency is having difficulty justifying current staffing levels.	A. Most staff prefer to work in one-on-one rather than group settings.
B. Some staff desire to work in preventive-educational models rather than remedial-therapeutic models.	B. Few staff have knowledge or skills relative to parent education.
	C. Staff prefer to work in agency office space rather than in community.
	D. Most staff prefer therapeutic rather than preventive work.
	E. Agency budget is severely limited.

Figure 4.5. Climate for change—forces favoring and forces resisting accomplishing a specific objective.

Resources for Change

Concomitant with the assessment of the climate of change associated with objectives is the process of assessing resources for change. Resources both internal and external to the agency need to be assessed. With regard to resources for change the concept of a *discrepancy model* is helpful. The discrepancy specifies the distance between resources needed to accomplish objectives and resources available to accomplish objectives. The discrepancy model uses an inventory approach to assessment. An inventory of internal resources available relative to accomplishment of each objective is generated. Establishing inventory categories for each objective simplifies the process. If the agency is seeking outside assistance, the inventory also should include external resources. Again, resources germane to both outcome and process objectives must be identified. Figure 4.6 provides a display of inventory data for one objective from the family study center example discussed earlier.

Seldom will the consultant do the actual work involved in conducting a climate for change inventory or a resource inventory. However, the consultant is expected to provide the expertise necessary to structure the task and organize the information. The information format should provide the consultee a quick reference for determining actions needed to accomplish each objective. The format used in the example (see Fig. 4.6) makes the discrepancy between available resources and needed resources quite clear. In this example, the agency knows that 150 parenting books are needed for the family study centers and that the cost will be covered by parents. Six group leaders are needed but money has been found to pay their costs. A one-quarter time secretary is needed and internal monies are not available. Thus, either external money will need to be sought or an alternative plan, such as a volunteer, will be needed.

Development of Change Strategy

At this point in the strategic systemic consultation process the strategy shifts from data collection to data analysis and integration. The sought for outcome is a detailed outline of a plan of action that will be utilized in meeting the community agency's need for solving a specific problem. The consultant's role is that of "process facilitator."

Data gathered from the Climate of Change Survey and the Resources Inventory need to be integrated to develop a strategy for addressing outcome and process objectives established in relation to the original problem.

Resources Inventory

Outcome Objective 1: To provide parent study groups to all families in the agency's catchment area

Category of Need	Need	Internal Resources	External Resources	Discrepancy
I. Facilities & Equipment				
A. Adequate rooms scattered in catchment area	7	1 room in agency	4 rooms in centers	0
B. Film projector	2	2	2 rooms in schools	0
C. Parenting books	150	—	—	150
II. Personnel				
A. Group leaders	14	4 staff lead 2 groups	0	6 group leaders
B. Secretary to coordinate groups	¼ time	0	0	¼ time secretary
C. Contact person in each parent group	14	—	—	14
III. Budget				
A. Rental for 3 rooms	$150	From facility's budget	—	0
B. 150 bks @ $10	$1500	—	Charge parents for materials	0
C. 6 group leaders @ $1200	$7200	—	Special grant United Way	0
D. ¼ time secretary	$2500	—	¼ time donation from . . .	0

Figure 4.6. Resources inventory with inventory data for one specific objective.

The consultant at this point assumes the role of "observer-reflector" and "process facilitator." Although the consultant is usually skilled at integrating climatic and resource variables, to perform this task for the consultee will result in resistance characterized by apathy. For the change strategy plan to be successfully owned, developing the plan must be in the hands of those who will deliver and receive services. The participation of these "deliverers and receivers" has been emphasized earlier in the formulation of objectives and again in the gathering of climatic and resource information, and that participation must be continued in the development of the strategy for change.

Overcoming resistance is the major issue in analyzing climate of change information. As mentioned previously, Lewin (1951) stated that change will be less stressful and more stable if attention is focused on reducing resistance to change rather than accelerating forces for change. Watson (1969) provided a number of principles that are helpful to keep in mind when attempting to reduce resistance to change. The following ideas of Watson have special application to the consultation process.

1. Resistance will be less if community leaders and the receivers of services believe the project is their own and not one devised and operated by outsiders.

2. Resistance will be less if the project is fully supported by the agency's top administrator.

3. Resistance will be less if participants believe the change will lessen their burdens.

4. Resistance will be less if the program reinforces already held values and ideals.

5. Resistance will be less if participants believe their autonomy and security will be maintained.

6. Resistance will be less if participants are involved in all phases of the planning process.

7. Resistance will be less if it is anticipated that misunderstandings will likely occur, thus ample feedback opportunity is planned.

8. Resistance will be less if participants experience acceptance, support, trust, and confidence in their relations with each other.

9. Resistance will be less if the plan is open to reconsideration and revision is expected.

In an earlier example (Figure 4.5) forces resisting change have been enumerated. These resistive forces included skepticism of the agency as an outsider, the belief that parenting is in the province of the home and not community agencies, and the preference of the staff for working one-on-one rather than with groups. Thus, applying Watson principles a strategic plan can be formulated that will reduce the forces of resistance to change. An example follows.

1. To reduce skepticism of the agency as an outsider:

> Community leaders and residents will be included in the planning process. The agency will play a facilitative role, not trying to sell a product, but rather surfacing and crystalizing a concern that exists in the community. This strategy would be employed throughout SSCP.

2. To maintain the view that parenting is in the province of the home:

   a. people from "the homes" are involved in planning,

   b. the consultant stresses the value of parenting and reinforces the belief that parents should be in charge of the families, and

   c. shows through the actual parenting meetings that a goal is to help parents do a better job and reduce the burden and increase the joy of parenting.

3. To reduce resistance to group work use the efficiency of the group approach:

   a. provide employees a reduced client load, and

   b. provide participating staff with additional planning and professional development time.

These ideas are far from exhaustive in reducing the resistive climate for change in the example cited. However, they do illustrate the applications of suggestions by Watson for reducing resistance.

Techniques of Strategy Integration. Planning flows most smoothly when one task force is used to develop the strategic plans for producing a better climate with regard to objectives and another task force is formed to develop plans for finding resources to accomplish objectives. After these two plans have been developed, the two task forces can be merged to formulate a Master Plan that includes both climatic and resource components. Care must be taken to assure that the merged task force functions as a single unit concerned with a common objective. The possibility always exists that groups will polarize around their original membership and thus shift into a competitive mode.

The strategic plan should be shaped to fit the particular problem. The following questions address important content areas to include in the plan.

What are we going to do?

How are we going to do it?

When are we going to do it?

Who is going to do it?

How will we know we have done it?

Thus, the following categories may comprise the form for the action plan: objectives, activities/methods, resources needed, person(s) responsible, time lines for accomplishment, and evaluative procedures. Figure 4.7 is an example of an abbreviated action plan—a method of providing information.

Implementation

Consultants usually serve as "informational experts" or "trainers" during the implementation phase of the SSCP. In the informational expert role, the consultant is available to provide information in the event an unforseen problem arises. As a trainer, the consultant may provide direct service to those responsible for implementing the agreed upon problem-solving procedures, or they may provide direct training or therapeutic services to consultees or their clients.

Abbreviated Action Plan

Outcome Objective 1.0: To provide parent study groups to all families in the agency's catchment area within three years.

Process Objective 1.1: To reduce resistance to group work on part of staff through reduction of client load, provision of preparation time, and provision of professional development activities.

Process Outcome	Activity	Resources	Person Respon.	Time Line	Evaluation
1.11 One to one client load reduced by 25% for involved staff	a. referral of parenting related concerns to parent-ing groups b. refer clients to other agen-cies at a rate producing desired result	Solicit coopera-tion of other agencies	Clinical Director	Within 3 months of project start	Check # of clients in load compared to pre-vious load
1.12 That planning time of 1½ hrs. per week be pro-vided.		Time will be gained through reduced counsel-ing load	Clinical Director	At time of project start and continue	Check of work schedules

Figure 4.7. Example of abbreviated action plan.

Process Outcome	Activity	Resources	Person Respon.	Time Line	Evaluation
1.13 Professional Development occurs weekly in agency and every 6 months external to agency	a. weekly staff meeting of participants will occur to discuss common problems and ideas for future parent meetings. b. staff will attend external workshop on either topic of parenting or effective group leadership	leader for weekly meetings, funds for attenders at external workshop	Clinical Director	Begin at project initiation	Check with participating staff

Process Objectives 1.2 Recruitment of Group Leaders

Process Outcome	Activity	Resources	Person Respon.	Time Line	Evaluation
1.21 To fill 8 leadership units internal to agency	appropriate staff contacted		Clinical Director	Select by 10/6/83	8 leadership units filled by date indicated
1.22 To fill 6 leadership units external to program	a. graduate programs in area contacted b. other community agencies contacted	Funds for salaries	Clinical Director	10/6/83	6 units filled by date indicated

Figure 4.7. Continued.

In the example cited, a consultant might be utilized to train group leaders to conduct a parent education program or a consultant may be used to help leaders develop group leadership skills. Consultants also may serve as facilitators to help group leaders process issues related to the effectiveness of their parent groups. The over-riding goal of the consultant is to insure that efforts put into assessment and planning by the consultee come to fruition.

A caution may be extended at this time. A consultant may become overly invested in the implementation stage. A consultant may view the implementation phase as a kind of trial exam where one's value as a consultant is judged. Such a feeling in indicative that the consultant is no longer maintaining a consulting role but has assumed an identity with the consultee that confuses areas of responsibility. When this role shift occurs the consultant should back away and allow the organization to address their own problems.

Evaluation

Evaluation focuses on three separate but related activities. These include (1) evaluating processes, (2) evaluating outcomes, and (3) evaluating the effect of treatment. The consultant focuses on helping the consultee define methods of monitoring progress and of measuring success. Consultants may render appropriate service by performing evaluations or by helping the consultee define a process for evaluation. Knowledge of evaluative procedures is important for consultants to possess.

In a strategic systemic consultation model, evaluation is a continual process. Evaluative information should be gathered at each stage so that progress toward meeting objectives can be ascertained far in advance of the production of outcome data.

Periodic checks need to be scheduled relative to each part of the process. The following questions are germane to respective components and the task of the consultant is to raise the questions and assist the organization or individual in finding answers.

1. Problems/Needs

    a. Does the problem still exist or has a change occurred, perhaps external to problem solving efforts, so that the problem no longer exists?

    b. At the end of problem solving efforts, one asks the question, "Is the problem solved?"

2. Do the objectives still appear to be central to problem resolution?

3. What is the status of the climate for change?

4. Are additional resources to be identified or have resources been lost?

5. Change strategy

    a. Were strategic activities appropriate to objectives?

    b. Were resources adequate for activities?

    c. Has the person assigned responsibility assumed responsibility?

    d. Are completion dates appropriate?

    e. Were the evaluative indicators appropriate?

6. Has the program been implemented, i.e., activities conducted, time lines honored, evaluative information gathered?

7. Has evaluation been continual and have data been compared to objectives?

Process evaluation requires the participation of all who are involved in each phase of the problem-solving endeavor. Attention is focused on monitoring activities, targeted completion dates, the appropriateness of objectives, and so forth. Charts specific to objectives and activities are helpful in compiling and integrating information relative to the completion processes. Figure 4.8 is a sample form for objective completion and objective-process monitoring. Figure 4.9 is a comparable form for activities.

Objectives—Process Monitoring Form

ITEM	CHECK POINT DATES
1. Is outcome objective still viable/feasible? What new data supports/reflects the objective?	
2. Is outcome objective still viable/feasible? What new data supports/reflects the objective?	
3. Repeat for each objective	

Figure 4.8. Sample form for objective completion and objective-process monitoring.

Activities—Process Monitoring Form

Objective:_____

Activities	Start Date	Final Date	Date Completed
1.			
2.			
3.			
4.			
5.			

Figure 4.9. Sample form for activities completion and activities-process monitoring.

As important as monitoring whether activities are completed is monitoring whether activities are conducted appropriately and/or had the desired impact. Methods and materials available for such evaluation include direct observation by the evaluator, planning materials used by service providers, and information that might be gathered from program participants either through interviews or the use of questionnaires.

Once data are gathered a report is usually prepared by the consultant to provide an accurate picture of activities that were implemented and the impact of the services on the targeted population. Of particular importance in evaluation is the development of a time unit versus cost versus usage analysis so that the most effective application of resources can be made.

Outcome evaluation focuses on the results of activities. Attention may be given to the result of the consultant's interventions, the result of program interventions or the result of therapist intervention. *Outcome measures attempt to discern the degree to which objectives are met.* With both individual clients and organizations, measures are often idiosyncratic to the specific client or program. For example, a consultee and client may agree on certain objectives such as weight loss, sobriety, display of cooperative behaviors, etc., and the outcome is the degree to which the client achieved the stated goal.

At times direct behavior observation is impossible and then indirect measures, such as standardized instruments, may be used. Often a pre-treatment/post-treatment measure is taken and the difference between these two measures is judged as an indicator of growth or decline.

Finally, client perception is often used as an outcome measure. Agency users can be asked to rate their satisfaction with agency services or their sense of well-being in instances of therapeutic treatment.

Most outcome measures do not provide information about the effect of the consultation on the consultee's clients. To find out about the effect of consultation on treatment one needs to employ a research design. Such designs often necessitate the use of pre-post testing, explicit descriptions of services, control groups, and time series analysis. The reader is referred to Selltiz, Wrightsman, and Cook (1976) for further information about measuring treatment effects in human service settings.

SUMMARY

Consultants are employed by community human service agencies to assist in planning and problem solving relative to case specific or organizational program issues. In either instance the consultant needs to have a model for planning and problem solving and the skills to involve the consultee(s) in the problem solving/planning process. In this chapter was presented a model of problem solving/planning to assist consultants in thinking about how to intervene in community human service agencies. Methods and tools relative to the model were described to assist the potential consultant in making model application. The focus for the remainder of the chapter is on case studies in which the SSCP model was utilized.

CASE CENTERED CONSULTATION USING THE SSCP

Case Example: Adult Services Network

The Adult Services Network (ASN) of the Forest Clear Valley is composed of about 70 social service agencies in a 4 county area that provide human services to adults within the area. At the request of the network, a multidisciplinary consulting team (MDT) was formed to staff complex adult cases. The team performed diagnostic functions and assisted in the evaluation and management of cases. The MDT served in a consultative function in that presenters were free to accept or reject recommendations.

The team consisted of a social worker who served as team coordinator, a psychiatrist, an information/referral specialist, a psychiatric nurse, a family therapist, and an attorney. Meetings were held for one and one-half hours on a twice monthly basis and one case was presented at each meeting. Any agency could refer cases to the team but the primary case worker of the agency had the responsibility to present the case. The presenting agency could request the presence of other agencies who had been or perhaps should be involved with the client.

The MDT focused deliberations on four areas: (1) the danger of the client to self or others; (2) the optional treatment recommendations; (3) the identification of a responsible party for each treatment strategy; and (4) the identification of data based indicators relative to "success" in handling the case.

Meetings largely followed the SSCP model. The presenter first defined a presenting problem relative to the client and provided information about the client on a number of variables that were germane to the professional expertise of MDT members. This particular team was supplied with information relative to (1) emotional well being, (2) physical well being, (3) interpersonal skills, (4) behavior control, (5) personal management, (6) ability to cope with environment, (7) cognitive skills, and (8) ability to perform relevant roles. After a general discussion of the case was conducted a problem or problems were identified and refined and tentative treatment objectives were stated. The climate of change was assessed from the perspective of evaluating previous interventions. Resources were examined relative to each of the eight dimensions listed previously. A strategy was then developed at the meeting for addressing agreed upon objectives. Appropriate agency personnel agreed to assume responsibility for implementing the strategy and a follow-up meeting was scheduled to evaluate progress.

Each MDT member contributed to the consultation process by providing expert information, by seeking significant facts, by observing and reflecting on problems and strengths of case management, by identifying alternative methods of handling the case, and, in some instances, advocating for a course of action.

Case of Betty. The case of Betty was presented to the MDT at the request of several agencies. Several feared that she might be dangerous to agency personnel and community members. Betty tended to "use" an agency until her welcome was exhausted and then tap into another agency. Interested professionals from eight agencies in addition to the presenter agency attended the meeting when Betty's case was presented. Figure 4.10 displays the complexity of the systemic interaction with Betty. Information contained in the Climate and Resource Columns of Figure 4.10 was presented to the MDT and the attending agencies at the beginning of the consultation process. Information in the other columns was filled in at the meeting as the result of consultative discussion.

I. Identifying Information

Age ____37____ Sex ____Female____

Marital Status ____Separated Common-Law____

Living/Residential Situation ____Unknown____

Presentor ____Marge Pell*____

Children and Others in home

____1 perhaps____ age ____unknown____

_____ age _____

_____ age _____

II. Presenting Problem: Client has shown up at 8 agencies in the past 3 weeks demanding services, i.e., shelter, money, or clothing; sometimes doesn't seek service but simply creates a ruckus, is very loud, has threatened to beat up agency workers and has threatened two families. She indicated she would start a riot at a public gathering and gave specific data about doing so. Evidently started two fights at a shelter. Warrants have been sought on two occasions but not served.

III.

Problem Area	Objectives	Climate-Past Intervention & Effect
A. Emotional (self) (e.g., depression, anxiety, affect)	a. Outcome: seek professional evaluation at next encounter with agency through 1) voluntary submission; 2) hearing before Mental Hygiene Commission	Volatile--explodes--has "exploded" at all agencies involved; threatened lives of workers and their families in four agencies.
B. Physical (self) (e.g., disease, general problems, medication)		Apparently no physical problems
C. Interpersonal (e.g., isolation, sexual problems, interpersonal effectiveness, family discord)	a. Process: Client contacts with all agencies will be referred to one agency	Demanding is only mode of contact with agencies. Apparent prejudice against whites. Apparently dreads being alone but intimidates others. Common law husband absent.
D. Behavior Control (dangerous, anti-social, illegal acts, substance abuse)	a. Process: To get all persons who have been threatened to submit to record consolidation point statements of threat within 2 days b. Plan for how to handle week-end contacts	Verbally abusive, threatens physical violence (to beat up workers), has set fires in public accomodations.
E. Personal Management (e.g., nutrition, medication management, finances, leisure, hygiene, community and inter-agency interactions	a. To consolidate all agency records at central location.	Never has money. Fails to keep appointments.
F. Environmental (e.g., income, employment, situational crises, residential)		Homeless. Barred from shelters and most hotels because of disruptive behavior. Demands and receives services but behaves to cancel.
G. Cognitive (e.g., orientation, psychosis)		Thought patterns reflect violence. Psychotic thought processes were present while hospitalized.
H. Role Performance (e.g., wage earner, parent, marital instrumental)		Mother--but child is not present Wife--husband absent
I. Other		

IV. Resource Persons Requested

Name ____Ralph Paul____ Agency ____Legal Aid____ Name ____John Neer____

Name ____Mary John____ Agency ____Voc Rehab____ Name ____Sheila Cory____

Name ____Paul Low____ Agency ____Human Service____ Name ____Bill Page____

Figure 4.10. Profile sheet for case of Betty.

Employment	None
Income Source	SSI
Income	$324.00/month

Known Agency Involvement		
	Legal Aid	Employment Security
	Voc. Rehab	Information & Referral
	State Hospital	Community Mental Health
	Human Services	Salvation Army

Resources	Strategy	Responsible Person/Agency
Never seems to try, stubborn, single minded	a. At point of client-agency contact, client will be urged to seek assistance at community mental health center b. If violence occurs or threatened warrant will be sought to take to Mental Hygiene Commission	Paul Low, central contact at Human Services
Apparent health		
Survivor, great manipulative ability.	a. all agencies at meeting agreed that upon contact of client, they will refer to Human Services	Agency representative
Has at times been in control. Achieves her ends although means are unacceptable.	a. by tomorrow morning people who have been threatened agreed at meeting to submit reports to Human Services. b. Meeting took place between personnel to discuss week-end arrangements.	Persons threatened and Paul Low CMH, Human Services, Legal Aid
Street-wise	c. Client had previously signed relase of information form. Representative of each agency to submit relevant material to Human Services.	Agency Representative
Receives SSI, always been able to find food, shelter, clothing		
Some workers have had contact with husband/appears supportive		

*All names are fictitious

Agency	Information & Referral	Name		Agency	
Agency	CMH	Name		Agency	
Agency	State Hospital	Name		Agency	

Figure 4.10. Continued.

At the problem phase consultants sought from agency personnel information relative to the client's condition and to the commotion she was causing for the community and agencies. Typical of this phase in general was the need for involved personnel to provide "their story of the encounter with Betty." Although the consultant may desire to short-circuit this emotional material, the process usually can not proceed until this emotional catharsis has occurred. Blake and Mouton (1976) indicate catharsis takes place at the beginning of most consultation processes. Consultants use this problem definition phase to gather information about the climate of agencies relative to the client and the response of the client to past intervention. In addition personal resources of the client are explored. A question-answer discussion format is used. The discussion centers first about what is going on currently with the client and moves then to historical information.

The following information relevant to Betty was significant in establishing outcome and process objectives. Evidence was substantial that in the past two weeks she had set two fires in public living areas. She had threatened lives of four persons present and their families. According to record she had had psychotic thought processes while hospitalized at a state mental institution only two months previously. The belief of those present was that she was not now on medication. Agency personnel documented that Betty usually had no money and demanded from the personnel that they find shelter, food, and clothing. Places of lodging refused to serve Betty and in fact had confiscated her possessions as security against past bills. The number and seriousness of symptoms and the fear agency personnel had of Betty led the team to recommend the outcome objective that a psychological evaluation be sought to determine the appropriate short-term treatment approach. Believing that Betty would not volunteer for evaluation, process objectives focused on establishing a sequence of steps that might be taken to insure the evaluative process.

Process objectives in sequenced order of implementation included:

1. To name one agency to act as the central referral agency to which Betty would be directed for assistance.

2. To gain commitment from all attending agencies to send relevant records to the central agency by noon of the day following the meeting.

3. To gain commitment from all persons who had been threatened by the claimant to send statements of each threat to the agency by noon of the day following the meeting.

4. To gain commitment of agency representatives to go before the Mental Hygiene Commission if necessary to obtain an order for evaluation.

5. To gather key agency personnel for a discussion of how weekend emergencies relative to the client might be handled.

Commitment to these objectives was obtained. In addition a meeting to plan how to handle weekend emergencies took place. Evaluative criterion (i.e., did people complete their assignment) that were contained in the objective statements became the responsibility of the contact agency for monitoring.

In this case consultants served as "process facilitators" helping explore approaches to the case, as "fact finders" to seek more information about the case, as "informational experts" to supply information relative to the client's case, and as "joint problem solvers" to establish a strategy to be implemented.

ADMINISTRATIVE CONSULTATION

Administrative consultation using the SSCP focuses on clarifying and defining processes and procedures relative to specified variables that will help the organization accomplish its mission more effectively. The target of the consultation may be a specific unit of the organization or the target may be the total organization including the interplay between supportive publics, staff, facilities, and clients. The following case began with a specific request for training in group work, and expanded to the larger organizational functioning. Because of the complexity of the consulting process and the length of the time involvement, three years, only critical turning points are reviewed in the light of the SSCP model.

Case Example: Beacon Youth Home

The Beacon Youth Home is a private facility providing residential care for pre-delinquent adolescents. Capacity of the facility is 20 males and 10 females. The primary staff consists of an executive director, three social workers with at least a bachelor's degree and twelve houseparents.

The author received a phone call from the executive director of the Beacon Youth Home seeking assistance in providing group leadership training for staff members. The caller indicated residents were in need of socialization skills training and small groups were the method of choice for providing training. Aspects of the conversation left the consultant in doubt that training in small groups was sufficient or appropriate at the moment to address organizational needs. Doubts were raised because personnel who were to serve as group leaders had not requested the training and seemed resistant. A number of the resident's behavior problems were enumerated, some of which seemed highly unlikely to be affected through group activities. The expertise of the staff seemed to necessitate the learning of skills more elementary than those needed by group leaders. Also, the youth home seemed to be undergoing a transition. The nature of the resident population was changing and the rate of turnover of staff was high.

Given numerous indicators of problem areas, an initial information gathering visit to the campus seemed appropriate to help clarify the situation. As a potential consultant, this writer asked permission to visit the home, meet with staff and residents, and see facilities. Also, to respond to the original request, a meeting with houseparents and social workers was arranged with the understanding that small group methods would be used in working with them. The purpose of this meeting was threefold: (1) to increase trust between staff and consultant, (2) to gain information about the levels of staff skills and organizational need, and (3) to use and illustrate group methods.

As a way of seeking maximal participation during the campus visit, a paper-pencil technique was employed along with discussion. While the consultant wanted to hear from everyone, the paper-pencil activity gave everyone a chance to respond anonymously and engage in some level of participation. The following incomplete sentences were used to stimulate ideas:

    1. I believe that as a cottage staff our major strengths are. . .

2. I believe the major strengths of the Beacon Youth Home are. . .

3. I would like to see our cottage staff. . .

4. I would like to see our Center staff. . .

5. I believe that as a cottage staff, our major weaknesses are. . .

6. I believe the major weaknesses of the Beacon Youth Home are. . .

A discussion of the responses followed. Small group leadership skills were brought into play and the individuals involved experienced the dynamics of the group's interactions. In addition to learning something about small groups, a listing of problems as seen by the staff was generated. The following major problems were identified.

1. The lack of a programmatic approach to treatment, i.e., treatment goals for individuals were lacking, programs which addressed resident problems were not identified, indicators of success were not stipulated.

2. Staff had a lack of knowledge, held biased opinions, had limited trust in each other, and felt that team work was at a minimum, if any.

3. Staff perceived the lack of a shared vision about the mission of the Center.

4. Staff did not believe residents were capable and thought residents were irresponsible.

5. Residents were not involved in the life of the Center. Residents lacked chores, meaningful activities, and opportunities to get together in encouraging ways.

Identified problems were listed and possible solutions appeared numerous. Given the apparent ease with which some problems could be stated as objectives and addressed, this writer felt it was important to identify why they had not been solved. The assumption on the part of the consultant was that reasons would be found in the climate for change and in the resources for change.

To obtain information about climate for change, the consultant reviewed minutes of staff meetings, and interviewed staff, selected residents, and board members. In general, units at the Home, i.e., cottages, houseparents, social workers, operated in a very isolated fashion. Thus the climate was one of distance, fragmented communication, and hesitation. Morale factors, trust, and knowledge seemed to be highly related to the following structural problems.

1. Cottages functioned as separate entities. Staff from cottages did not get together on an informal basis and supervision or programming did not necessitate intercottage staff functioning.

2. Social workers were assigned to cottages and consequently did not jointly staff residents or work with each other.

3. Staff shift changes did not overlap and, therefore, information was not passed from one shift of workers to the next.

4. No staff meetings had occurred in which all staff attended and no method was in operation for passing information to those not in attendance.

5. Program was defined as a cottage function rather than a campus wide function and possibly seen as an "extra" because staff saw household tasks as consuming all their time.

Several houseparents especially prided themselves on food preparation and were, therefore, reluctant to involve residents in the kitchen. As an outcome of this attitude residents were seen as irresponsible and staff as overworked. Part of the lack of involvement of residents stemmed from the belief that involvement would mean more work for staff. Job descriptions and expectations had never been made explicit because, "we are family and, therefore, people should/will contribute what is needed."

Although resources for change were lacking, these deficits were not nearly as impactful as the norms and unwritten rules that had evolved over the years. The Center lacked a program specialist and many staff members lacked the training and knowledge to be able to work with residents in a helpful manner. Facilities tended to encourage physical separation of staff and residents. Through the consulting process many resource deficits were revealed and some of these situations were remediated. An activity building used by all residents was constructed, staff training was provided, and a campus wide program director appointed. Problems still persisted. Staff did not want to go over to the building to supervise their residents and certainly they did not want to take responsibility for residents of other cottages.

Over the next year, progress was made by assigning residents to social workers rather than cottages to social workers. These social workers had responsibility to residents in multiple cottages. This provided the impetus for interstaff communication. Plans were made for a new assignment of overlapping shifts and a program based upon resident need was developed. Because the potential for positive change was so great, the consultant had to guard against leading and becoming over-involved. Although the plans seemed adequate, the rate of implementation was slow. The organization was not "hurting" enough to raise forces for change and the excitement and benefits of the change did not seem great enough to reduce resistance.

At this point it seemed a catalytic event would be necessary to provide impetus to the change process. The crisis event that stimulated plan implementation was threefold: (1) accrediting bodies of the Center raised questions about the adequacy of resident treatment plans, (2) funding sources asked questions concerning accountability, and (3) the number of referrals to the Center dropped.

Because the SSCP had stressed problem oriented planning with clear statements of objectives and evaluative criteria, the Center had at hand those tools needed to respond to the crisis. The crisis had increased forces for change and hastened the implementation process.

As stated earlier, only highlights of the consulting process have been presented in this case study. Other elements that had an impact that were not involved in the description included such activities as the development of newsletters, mailings, and other communication devices. A family counseling program was initiated to work with families of residents and a coeducational independent living cottage was developed for older residents.

Process evaluations and outcome evaluations offered conclusive evidence that the SSCP approach involving administrative structures and operations was highly successful, albeit long term.

REFERENCES

Blake, R. R., & Mouton, J. S. (1976). *Consultation*. Reading, MA: Addison-Wesley.

Caplan, G. (1970). *The theory and practice of mental health consultation*. New York: Basic Books.

Haley, J. (1976). *Problem-solving therapy: New strategies for effective family therapy*. San Francisco: Jossey-Bass.

Hersch, C. (1969). From mental health to social action, clinical psychology in historical perspective. *American Psychologist, 24,* 909-916.

Joint Commission on Mental Illness and Health. (1961). *Action for mental health*. New York: Basic Books.

Lewin, K. (1951). *Field theory in social science*. New York: Harper & Row.

Lewis, J. A., & Lewis, M. D. (1983). *Management of human service programs*. Monterey, CA: Brooks/Cole.

Lippitt, G. L., & Lippitt, R. (1978). *The consulting process in action*. San Diego, CA: University Associates.

Lippitt, R. (1959). Dimensions of the consultant's job. *Journal of Social Issues, 15* (2), 5-12.

Schein, E. H. (1978). The role of the consultant: Content expert or process facilitator. *The Personnel and Guidance Journal, 56,* No. 6, 340-343.

Seiler, G. S., & Messina, J. J. (1979). Toward professional identity: The dimensions of mental health counseling in perspective. *American Mental Health Counselors Association Journal, 1,* 3-22.

Selltiz, C., Wrightsman, L. S., & Cook, S. W. (1976). *Research methods in social relations* (3rd Ed.). New York: Holt, Rinehart and Winston.

Watson, G. (1969). Resistance to change. In W. G. Bennes, K. P. Benne, & R. Chin (Eds.). *The planning of change*. New York: Holt, Rinehart & Winston.

CHAPTER 5

CONSULTATION IN HOSPITALS: DEVELOPMENT OF A TRAIN-THE-TRAINER PROGRAM

William C. Childers, Ph.D.

William C. Childers, Ph.D.

Dr. William C. Childers is a faculty member at the University of Georgia, in the office of Adult Counseling at the Georgia Center for Continuing Education. In this position he provides occupational competency programs for helping professionals and supports staff with a special emphasis on health care programs. His professional interests center around skill development in interpersonal communication, an area in which he has co-authored four textbooks and conducted hundreds of workshops.

The hospital-based patient relations program he directs, A Step Ahead in Caring, is gaining wide acceptance as an economical method of hospital-wide training in interpersonal skills. In conjunction with A Step Ahead in Caring, Dr. Childers is completing development of an audio-visual package that will enhance the ability of in-house staff to serve as instructors.

CONSULTATION IN HOSPITALS: DEVELOPMENT OF A TRAIN-THE-TRAINER PROGRAM

William C. Childers, Ph.D.

Hospitals, like other large organizations, have employees from one end of a continuum to another on virtually every variable one could mention. Hospitals, though, have personnel who have heightened sensitivity to the quality of the interactions with health care providers. Many reasons exist for this heightened sensitivity, but perhaps the most obvious reason is that patients and their families enter the hospital with apprehensions that result from not knowing for sure the outcome of the hospitalization. Something routine could become something very serious: symptoms could result in a diagnosis that has little impact on the patient and his/her family, or the diagnosis could be devastating to those involved. Patients and their families pay close attention to both the verbal and nonverbal behaviors of health care providers. Consequently, the quality of the patient/guest-staff interactions affect how patients and guests feel about the hospital in general. This fact exerts a great deal of pressure on hospital staff as they go about their routine at work. The problem that exists in many hospitals is that the staff has had no training in dealing effectively with others on a one to one basis. There are many possibilities for consultation around the theme of patient relations. In this chapter is described the development of one such program, including the qualifications necessary for the consultant and barriers to overcome.

Historically, hospitals received patients who delivered themselves to the building and, in essence, placed their full faith in the health care team to take care of them. This blind faith in the expertise of health care workers reinforced the mystique of health care and placed virtually all these workers into a "more knowing/less knowing" dichotomy with patients and their families. Needless to say, the evolution of thinking in this area has necessitated many changes for health care workers, and presently a general expectation exists that explanations will be given, questions answered and procedures explained as a matter of course during the hospitalization process.

Many hospitals have programs presented to staff that deal with interpersonal relationships, but upon examination most fall short of true training and involve mostly motivational/inspirational talks or lectures about what employees *should* do. While the motivational talks probably increase sensitivity to the need for attention to interpersonal interactions, skill development requires instructing, modeling, and practice. The program presented in this chapter involves twelve hours of training; thus, an appreciable commitment of time and involvement is required for this program to be effective. Commitment to a program of "training" as the consultative model becomes the first critical factor in implementing a skills building workshop designed specifically to help make a hospital environment supportive for workers and comfortable for patients and guests.

A Human Service Provider offering consultant services to an agency that has as its major concern the delivery of health care may be seen as not quite understanding the situation, or not having the necessary medical background to speak with authority, or perhaps even as injecting a disruptive element into an otherwise cohesive group. Gaining acceptance to enter the consultative relationship necessitates a bit of "selling."

The source of persuasive power is the clear articulation of goals of the training, procedures that will be employed, and the length of time the participants will be involved in the skill building workshops.

The experience of this writer has been that hospital personnel look for assurance of the consultant's credibility and expertise. We are able to sell our consultative services to hospitals because we do the following things:

1. Use the name of the University of Georgia prominently.

2. Establish credibility by discussing our health care background, research base for the training, publications, and previous users.

3. Offer economical consultation.

4. Offer options for training site and dates.

5. Offer to train members of hospital staff to teach in-house course.

6. Help hospital personnel select trainers.

7. Listen closely to their perception of the problem before offering help.

8. Let hospital personnel know that unless they are fully satisfied no charge will be made for the training.

9. Offer to develop refresher courses as needed.

10. Offer to make a presentation on the program to the administrator, medical board, board of trustees, department heads, or others who must approve the expenditure of funds.

11. Get a corp of employees interested—try to get representatives from as many units of the hospital as possible.

12. Offer telephone consultation upon request, and visit for consultation on a regular basis after the program is initiated.

RATIONALE FOR THE PROGRAM

This section describes the rationale for and development of a major staff development program that allows hospital officials to train members of their own staffs to serve as instructors. The program, the Patient/Guest/Co-Worker Awareness Training Program, is designed to train all hospital staff members in interpersonal skills that will have a positive impact on patients and guests in the hospital and that will increase and improve communication among staff members.

Many comments and criticisms, both justifiable and not justifiable, are being directed toward health care delivery systems in the United States because of what patients believe to be a lack of concern by health care staff members, both professional and support, for their needs and the impersonal way services are being offered. Criticism ranges from the "quick, impersonal inspection" by a physician to the way in which a food service worker delivers the hospital meal. It also extends to the way in which the hospital switchboard operator handles calls from the public to how the patient accounts staff respond to questions about bills and other charges. In essence the reaction can be formed as a result of interaction with any employee, no matter what the level of training of that employee might be. In many ways the hospital is a victim of rapid scientific and medical breakthroughs that encourage, through mechanization, the impersonalization of health care. However, at the same time a growing awareness is occurring on the part of patients and their families of their rights in terms of information about the treatment being delivered. Add to this the fact that lawsuits are at an all-time high from disgruntled patients and their families and one easily can see that a need to find solutions to the problem are present. The solution involves maintaining the dignity and rights of the patient as a person in spite of the impersonalization of advanced technology.

If hospital patients are asked to describe the characteristics of their favorite staff members, chances are those characteristics will be included in the following list: kind, caring, smiles a lot, listens, spends time with me, sweet, friendly, good sense of humor, warm, honest, understanding, gentle, or helpful. One thing that is obvious from this list is that for the most part these characteristics are *interpersonal skills* as opposed to technical knowledge or training that one generally associates with health care personnel. If this finding holds up across many health care institutions, and so far it has in our work with hospitals, then those problems hospitals have had in the last several years with disgruntled patients and their families can be explained in part by a deficit in interpersonal skills training on the part of the staff. Generally, a hospital staff can be broken down into two main categories, professional and support. For the most part, the professional staff has been trained in technical skills with little emphasis in the interpersonal area. After all, not too many years ago patients allowed health care professionals to do just about anything they wanted to with them and no questions were asked. Support staff such as aides, orderlies, dietary workers, housekeeping personnel, and so forth, spend more minutes during the course of a day with patients than professional staff and yet persons at this level have had virtually no training in dealing effectively with people.

These findings point to an area that is wide open for consultation by human service providers who have training skills in interpersonal relationships and the prerequisite work background or understanding of health care as mentioned above. The program to train individuals to serve as "in-house" trainers for hospital personnel that was developed by the author (and is copyrighted by the University of Georgia) is described in the following section.

DEVELOPMENT OF THE PROGRAM

The task of the University of Georgia sponsored hospital based training project was to develop and deliver a true skill-development program to all levels of health care staff, and do it in such a way as to mesh the knowledge of how adults learn with the skill components of human relations model all within the reality constraints of a hospital. The result of this effort is the Patient/Guest/Co-worker Awareness Training Program. Commonly referred to as the Patient Awareness Program, it is a program that allows hospitals to have members of their own staffs trained as trainers to deliver the workshop hospital-wide. For the cost of sending two or three employees to a seminar, a hospital can have a program that impacts all employees.

In order for the Patient Awareness Program to be a true cooperative effort, a hospital in Georgia was identified that was willing to serve in a pilot capacity during the development of the program. A small committee was formed that represented the major divisions of the staff. This writer, as the Adult Counseling Specialist at the University of Georgia Center for Continuing Education, worked with the committee in a consultative role, and was responsible for pulling the committee's ideas together to formulate a program that could be delivered to all levels of health care staff. After several months of deliberation, the following decisions were made that allowed the consultant to start work on materials:

• The program would be delivered by existing hospital staff who would be trained by the consultant as *Trainers.*

• An attempt would be made to select Trainers from all areas of the hospital so that rapport and empathy would be enhanced.

• The number of hours of training would be 12, and the delivery of the 12 hours would be variable to accommodate the schedules of hospital staff.

• Group size would be under 15 to encourage participation by all members.

• A training manual would be provided to each employee.

• An evaluation would be performed to determine if the training was making a difference with patients, visitors, and co-workers.

• A trainer's manual would be developed so that all Trainers would be using a similar format for delivering the workshop.

Armed with the framework mentioned in the preceeding decisions the consultant developed the program. Ten years of experience as a trainer in human relations skills and six years of work experience in hospitals qualified the consultant for this task. After a literature review and interviews with a cross section of hospital staff to find out what the major interpersonal problems were as perceived by the staff, the following objectives were developed for the program:

Health care workers will learn:

    1. To understand the impact of each employee's verbal and nonverbal responses on the perception of patients, visitors,

and the community about the hospital and the health care it provides.

2. To become more perceptive of the type of request the patient or the visitor is making and learn to respond to the request in an effective way.

3. To appreciate the hurtful effects of rumor, gossip, and chronic complaining and to respond in an effective way to inappropriate communication.

4. To apply a model for listening, responding, and problem solving.

5. To develop skill in dealing effectively with anger (within and from others).

One important requirement for the Patient Awareness Program was that the training materials had to be flexible enough to be used with all levels of staff. Since hospital staffs are generally composed of persons with a range of ability from highly skilled professionals to those who are non-readers, the materials had to have multiple options for use by the trainers to accommodate the diversity of training and sophistication. The materials needed to offer the flexibility that would allow trainers, when appropriate, to go into detail about the theoretical rationale behind the training program, and at the same time be equally useful for the groups with little or no reading ability. This type of flexibility did not create any difficulties for the consultant as trainer, nor later for the hospital based trainer in using the materials.

In selecting trainers for the program, certain prerequisites were established. Since these persons would become instructors, the feeling was that some kind of teaching experience was important. Some candidates had had informal teaching experience in church activities, boy scouts, or civic clubs, and others had been teachers in traditional classrooms or in in-service departments of hospitals. Another prerequisite was that they be willing to give at least two hours a week to the program. This requirement ruled out some whose jobs would not allow this kind of commitment. A third prerequisite, and one harder to measure, was that the candidate have both an awareness of the interpersonal deficits in the hospital and a willingness to be part of a team that was designed to do something about the problem. This attitude was determined through interviews with all applicants. Since no restriction existed as to what level of employee could apply, applicants came from all areas of the hospital. One strength of the program was that persons were trained as Trainers from support areas, administrative areas, and professional health care delivery areas. One discovery made during the implementation of the program was that employees responded positively when an instructor was a person who worked in the same general area of the hospital as the trainee. Consequently, every effort was made to pair the trainer with a group that was similar to the trainer in job description and/or education.

Once the materials were developed and trainers were selected, the actual Train-the-Trainer sessions were scheduled. Since the plan was to use essentially the same program at more than one hospital, materials were copyrighted by the University of Georgia Center for Continuing Education and the training materials became the transportable product; thus, participants who became Trainers were granted permission to use the materials in their hospitals. The Train-the-Trainers program was conducted by the consultant in six days. This six day program constituted the majority of the cost to the participating hospitals of the program. Following the training sessions, the cadre of trainers was ready to continue the program in their respective hospitals. Of course the consultant-as-trainer observed the new Trainers in their first training session and critiqued their performance. After this, through the Office of Adult Counseling Services, the University of Georgia Center for Continuing Education continued to offer its services on a consulting capacity as needed.

After the pilot was completed, the program was repeated in several hospitals and the materials have continued to be refined. Presently, the Office of Adult Counseling has taken on the largest training program in its history. Grady Memorial Hospital in Atlanta, a 1,000 bed teaching hospital, has contracted with the University of Georgia Center for Continuing Education to train enough Trainers to put their entire staff of 4,300 employees through the 12 hour program. A total of 26 trainers have completed the six day training session and are currently teaching the Patient Awareness Program to employees on a rotating basis.

To this point, with five hospitals having trained over 4,000 staff members, evaluations have been very positive from both Trainers and their trainees. Also, hospital administrators in the state are talking to one another about the program and many inquiries are coming in from all over Georgia. Evidence is growing that this grass roots attempt to change a community's perception of its hospital from negative to positive is working. The greatest need at this point in the development of the program is devising a follow-up schedule that will keep Trainers up to date with current training techniques and program content. Development of follow-up materials have been hampered by the demand from hospitals for the program that has already been established. This constant updating need will keep consultants in close contact with hospitals that are using the program on a regular basis.

OVERVIEW OF THE TRAINING PROGRAM

The training program has two major phases: *Training-the-Trainers* and supervising the process of the *Trainers training their employees in their hospitals.* During the six day Train-the-Trainer portion of the program, approximately three days are spent putting the trainers through the program as participants. At this point, pressure is on the consultant to model appropriate behavior and to "sell" the Trainers on the effectiveness of the program. (Since modeling is so important, yet difficult for a novice consultant, experience suggests that new consultants should apprentice with experienced consultants before attempting to train a group solo.) Following the initial phase of instruction, the consultant then works with Trainers on their teaching skills. Each candidate is repeatedly evaluated by the consultant/trainer and the apprentice/trainers. Videotape is used extensively in our program, and is a highly recommended procedure, to provide feedback to trainers about both verbal and nonverbal strengths and deficits.

At the conclusion of the six day program, the consultant evaluates the skill level of each trainer and either certifies the person to teach the class or recommends additional training. Then the Certified Trainers are paired and the consultant helps with the development of a strategy for implementing the program within the hospital. We recommend that the consultant stay with the program at least through the first 12 hour program that is taught by the novice trainer. There is a difference between the *practice* training that occurs in the Train-the-Trainer program and actually training a group of regular hospital employees. The consultant can provide feedback to Trainers at this point as well as support and encouragement.

The consultant's role after the program appears to be running smoothly falls into two categories: maintenance and development. The first thing the consultant needs to do is maintain periodic contact with the hospital administration and Trainers so that any problems can be addressed as soon as possible. Telephone consultation is effective at this stage if a trip to the hospital is inconvenient. This communicates interest and provides continuing visibility for the consultant, and maintains a continuing association with the Train-the-Trainer program.

Periodically, needs will arise for development of supplemental materials and also to conduct workshops for the purpose of updating Trainers. This development phase can be on-going with the hospital and the hospital will look to the trainer/consultant for help based upon the perceived success of the original program.

BARRIERS TO CONSULTATION IN HOSPITALS

Many issues and reality constraints must be taken into account when contemplating consultation in hospitals or other health care institutions. In this section some of the barriers confronting the consultant are discussed. Responses to these barriers are based on our own experience of consultation in hospitals for the last ten years and observing how the hospital works. Major barriers to hospital consultation are as follows:

1. The desire on the part of many hospital personnel is to bring in someone who is "one of them." This can be accomplished easily, of course, if the potential consultant has had some work experience in hospitals. Even a short period of time in a non-patient-care capacity (candy striper, and so forth) is acceptable. If the consultant does not have a health care background, he/she should be well versed in the inner workings, jargon, stereotypical power struggles, hierarchy, and humor of health care institutions. This "homework" by the consultant will help to establish his/her credibility. Failure to prepare in this area can create a crisis in the training session if the consultant's background or credentials are questioned.

2. Work schedules and work loads pose a problem in working with hospital personnel. With three shifts, either the consultant-as-trainer or consultees-as-trainees are inconvenienced when session times are established. A consultant in hospitals can go far toward establishing a good relationship with the administrative staff by being very flexible in terms of when training is offered. This may necessitate classes on the 11 to 7 shifts (2 a.m. seems to be a good class time for night personnel) or classes may need to be more frequent and shorter in duration than one might suggest for other organizations.

3. A potential obstacle for hospital-wide programs is the wide range of abilities represented on the staff. This may range from the non-reader to the highly skilled medical specialist. If one program is suggested for all staff, this diversity of ability levels necessitates a number of training approaches. Allied with this problem is the fact that in many cases when hospital-wide programs are implemented, some staff members will refuse to participate, or will simply not show for a scheduled session. Consistent with the philosophy of building on the strength of interest and motivation of volunteers, this writer has always been inclined to go with those who show up without attempting to "force" participation, since forced participation tends to create additional problems which may be more serious than some staff members not attending. In some instances, administrators view this issue as an institution's decision to make; thus, a conflict of values has the potential of becoming another barrier.

4. When proposing programs or consultations to hospitals, several people typically must be "sold" in order for money to be appropriated. Obviously this obstacle can be overcome, but the smart procedure is to take it slow and maintain an air of professionalism throughout the negotiations. One negative reaction can kill the project. Skills that seem to be important for success are tact, perseverance, and a high level of frustration tolerance.

5. One problem that can be partially or completely overcome with planning is interruptions of training by persons being

called out of sessions to attend to patients or paperwork. This can happen even if training is conducted outside the main hospital building. It can be prevented by discussing with administrative personnel, prior to the session, the importance of everyone participating at all sessions. This way personnel usually can have someone else cover their duty stations as if they were not on the premises.

6. Of course other problems arise when consulting in hospitals. Good interpersonal relations on the consultant's part can go a long way toward breaking through red tape and helping people work together in planning. A good rule to increase one's probability of success in hospital consulting is to sell the program to the top person—usually the administrator or the medical director. With support from the top, doors are opened for the consultant up and down the hall.

COMPONENTS OF THE TRAINING

The actual training program discussed in this chapter is designed to be delivered in twelve hours. Many hospitals, because of scheduling constraints, elect to send personnel to six two-hour sessions. This plan works well because it allows ample time between sessions for course content to be processed and practiced. The material is divided into 12 one-hour units which allows as much flexibility as desired by the person doing the scheduling.

The following material presented by hours of training represents an abbreviated "notebook" for the Train-the-Trainer program. The sample exercises that are included may be sufficiently detailed and comprehensive enough for the experienced consultant to use in developing a similar program of training. The total program, described herein, may be obtained from the author.

HOUR 1
PRETEST AND INTRODUCTORY INFORMATION

Pretest

Use a pretest to establish baseline data so that participants can evaluate their own progress (see Section entitled "Hours 10 and 11") and the trainer can assess the overall impact of the program. The pretest, also to be used as the posttest, can be constructed by the trainer to elicit the usual of "typical" response the trainee makes to patients and others when understanding is being solicited. The test might be comprised of 5 to 10 statements (similar to those included in practice exercises 5.7 and 5.8) that reflect real life situations and work experiences of trainees.

Open the first session with an explanation of the purpose of the pretest. Then distribute the pretest to trainees. (Before the beginning of the group discretely determine if any persons in the group are not able to write. Administer the pretest orally to those persons individually and prior to the first session.) Begin the group pretest by asking if any persons have already completed it. No explanation for these persons is necessary. Allow approximately 10 minutes for all persons to complete the pretest. Collect the forms and put them away until the end of the training. The forms should contain the namc of the group member, the consultant's name, and the date.

Introduction of Leader

A short introduction of the consultant as trainer is appropriate. Since the consultant will be introduced in more detail in the following exercise, this should be kept short. If everyone already knows the leader or if the leader has already been introduced by someone else, skip the introduction.

Getting Acquainted

This phase of the training sets the stage of everything else that happens. Even though participants may know each other's names, the group should still go through a get-acquainted exercise such as the one suggested in Activity 5.1.

ACTIVITY 5.1: Get Acquainted

The most efficient way to do the get acquainted activity, although there are dozens of possibilities, is as follows:

1. *Divide into pairs—attempt to pair individuals with someone they do not know well.*

2. *Each person questions the other for 3 to 4 minutes. Focus on:*

   Name
   Hometown
   Job
   Family
   Hobbies and interests
   Other information that makes the person unique

3. *Bring group back together and have each person introduce his/her* **partner** *to the group.*

This method works better than asking persons to introduce themselves because it generates more unique information without giving the appearance of boasting.

Purpose of the Training

A concise explanation should be provided at this point. This must be done in a way that does not insult the group member but at the same time communicates that the program has something to offer that will help him/her deal more effectively with others. A suggested outline is as follows:

1. Health care workers are being "forced" nationally into a more patient oriented position. Patients are no longer passive recipients, but are more and more becoming knowledgeable consumers. Also, litigation is on the increase, partially as a result of impersonalization in health care delivery.

2. Most nursing schools, medical schools, and allied medical training programs do not focus on human relations training in a major way. Even for those who may have had some experience in human relations training, a current review of

theory and revalidation of skill are important. Those group members who come into the group as excellent human relations practitioners can be used as models and even as co-facilitators. Certainly recognition and utilization of the entire range of skills of participants in the training are important aspects for the program to succeed.

3. Patients and guests remember the interpersonal skill variables after leaving the hospital—even more than the professional expertise of the health care workers.

4. A comfortable feeling comes from the knowledge that one can handle all—even tough—interpersonal situations.

5. The skill learned and practiced in the training program generalizes from the work setting to friends, family, and other interpersonal situations, which improves the *general* quality of one's interactions with others.

Characteristics of a Helping Person

To assist the consultees in better understanding the characteristics of a helping person have them do Activity 5.2. Then discuss the characteristics they identified and have them relate those characteristics to themselves.

ACTIVITY 5.2: Helper Characteristics

In this exercise give the following instructions: "Think about a person you like to be around and with whom you could talk if you had something important to discuss. Think of one-word characteristics that would describe this person. Tell us the word that describes the person to whom you would talk and I will write the word on the board."

Encourage the group to brainstorm and don't stop until you have at least 15 words. After all are listed, make the following points about the list:

• *This would be the perfect friend, counselor, co-worker, spouse, and so forth.*

• *Virtually all are skills, and as skills they can be learned.*

- *Virtually all are interpersonal characteristics as opposed to technical knowledge or innate behaviors.*

- *If these are characteristics you would like in others, it makes sense that these are also characteristics others look for in you.*

- *The remainder of the training will involve looking at the extent to which you communicate these qualities as you interact with others.*

HOUR 2
REQUESTS AND PHASES OF HELPING

Types of Communication Requests

The consultant as trainer moves into the skills training aspect of the program by providing information about the work instruction and the model to be taught. The consultant might offer the following explanation:

"Many times in the course of a day we are called upon to respond to a patient's request or the request of a member of the patient's family. A common tendency is to *respond spontaneously.* We might be busy or running late for something else or just want to get away from the patient. Sometimes we want to help but simply do not know what to say or what to do. We typically make a response and go on about our business. Sometimes this way of being with people is not satisfying because we are left with the feeling that we have done less than we could have done—and this may well be the case. We are left with a feeling of incompleteness and the patient, by his/her verbal and nonverbal responses, lets us know that an issue is still unresolved or that he/she is not satisfied with the response."

"The first step in the helping process is the skill of identifying the type of communication request that the patient/guest/co-worker is making. Unless you know the type of communication request, you will have difficulty in knowing how to respond. In the following section each type of communication request is briefly described and an example is given."

Request for Information. This is a very common type of request in a health care setting. Patients ask for information, and guests ask for information. The care giver sometimes asks *them* for information. The skill component here is to distinguish between the information request that is only an information request and the one that has other motives. If a request is strictly a request for information, then providing the information is the appropriate response—unless, of course, the request involves confidential information or is inappropriate for other reasons. A section will follow on responding to the inappropriate request.

Determining the type of request has to be a personal decision that is made using one's own personal experiences together with understanding the verbal and nonverbal behavior of the other person. The following is an example of a request for information:

"What time does Dr. Johnson usually make rounds?"

The appropriate response would be to provide the answer. If one doesn't know, the appropriate action would be to respond "I'll find out and get back with you." To merely respond "I don't know" without a follow-up will be perceived negatively by the patient. If the doctor in question does not follow any regular schedule in making rounds, an explanation of that fact is usually sufficient.

The following request sounds at first like a request for information, but the way it is presented and the patient's nonverbal behavior, together with the health care worker's (HCW) knowledge of the patient, will determine whether there are "underlying" reasons or feelings involved in the request.

"Does the pain usually take this long to go away?"

The underlying element here could be fear on the part of the patient that something additional is wrong or that he/she is not progressing satisfactorily. However, if the care giver can rule this out from one of the factors previously mentioned, then responding to the request as a legitimate desire for information is appropriate. When persons are discouraged, an encouraging response can help them feel better about themselves. Maybe the results are not obvious after one response, but a series of encouraging responses tends to have a cumulative effect on the other person. The following responses would be encouraging:

"You are doing very well. The pain will gradually disappear."

"Some people do get over the pain a little faster, but you are making a great deal of progress. In fact, I can tell a difference between yesterday and today."

The following response would be for the person who, in fact, is not progressing well. Again, it would be encouraging.

"I know it has been hard for you. Once the pain starts going away, it should go quickly."

If the patient's request is clearly more than a request for information, your response can come from a different area. The other types of requests follow.

Request for Action. The request for action differs from the request for information in that action implies that one does something for the other person as opposed to providing information. So any request by another person for one to do something for him/her is likely to be a request for action. In the health care setting this request is a very frequent one as a result of the nature of the clientele. Patients are thrust into a relatively helpless situation, at least when compared to their normal environments. In addition to not having their clothes on and being in bed, they are many times too ill to do for themselves. Several factors to consider before responding to a request for action include the following:

1. Is this something the other person should do for oneself rather than having the care giver do it for the patient?

2. Does the request involve confidential information?

3. Is the request contrary to the doctor's orders?

4. Are there obvious underlying reasons for the request?

5. Are there reasons why providing the action would be ill-advised?

If the care giver can answer no to the preceeding questions, then the appropriate response would be to provide the action requested.

Read the following requests for action, and discuss the possible reasons why providing the action would be inappropriate.

"Would you please get me a match?"

"I need some help to the bathroom."

"I would like for you to call my doctor and tell him that I need to see him tonight."

"Would you put a 'no visitors' sign on my door?"

"They took my pitcher. Would you get me a glass of water?"

The preceeding requests may be genuine and, if so, some action is appropriate. Of course, if one is not sure, it is essential to *check it out*. A good rule in the hospital is *don't assume anything*. Making mistakes as a result of making assumptions is a crucial error that can result in severe consequences in a health care setting.

REQUEST FOR INAPPROPRIATE INTERACTION

In this category, the patient/guest/co-worker makes some kind of request that, for one reason or another, a care giver is not willing to fulfill. Several main categories of this type request follow:

1. Rumor/gossip

2. Unethical/unprofessional/illegal practices

3. Chronic complaining

4. Practices counter to the good of the organization

5. Requests that are contrary to the value system for the HCW

6. Requests the HCW, for whatever reason, considers to be in-appropriate

The appropriate response to items 1 through 4 is politely to have no part of it. The skill is in the word *politely*. Many ways exist to decline participation, but to do it politely will increase one's probability of maintaining a relationship with the other person. When a person is encouraging one to participate in something that is considered to be inappropriate, refusal to participate frequently will generate negative feelings in the other person. So all one can do is stand up for what one considers to be appropriate and do it in a polite, yet firm, way. In the long run a person will be respected for taking a position and for knowing where one stands, even though the initial response from others might be negative.

Types of Inappropriate Requests

A section of this training will be devoted to responding appropriately to request for inappropriate interaction. In this section the care giver should learn how to recognize this request for what it is—an attempt by others, either consciously or unconsciously, to pull the care giver to their level by involving him/her in something that is considered to be inappropriate.

The following examples illustrate some types of inappropriate requests.

Rumor/Gossip. Rumor usually has to do with a situation. Gossip usually refers to a person. Either type is inappropriate in that the source of the rumor or the victim of the gossip is not present to defend him/herself. When individuals repeat second-hand information, and when they make negative statements about an individual in that individual's absence, they take the risk of distorting the accuracy of the situation and also depriving the individual of his/her right to explain circumstances as they really exist. The consultant might suggest to the trainers that they think about times in their past when gossip has circulated about them. Most will probably agree that it is a helpless feeling to be victimized in this way. And the longer the gossip persists, the more distorted it becomes.

Help trainees understand that one way to avoid being part of the problem is to develop a personal philosophy to decline participation. Even though this may be an unpopular position, inasmuch as the person is ready to share the information with the care giver, the long range reaction is usually respect.

Examples of rumor are the following:

"Did you know that we are not going to get a cost of living raise this year?"

"I heard that they were bringing in *more* consultants. Why don't they use that money for salaries!"

Examples of gossip are the following:

"You'll never guess where I saw Mary last night!"

"Have you noticed how Dr. Brown's personality has changed lately? I heard he was having problems in his marriage."

Unethical/Unprofessional/Illegal Practices. Sometimes in a large organization, practices become established that are unhealthy yet occur with regularity. Many times these situations occur over a long period of time, and an informal network is in operation within the organization. Even though one is told that something is common practice, if that behavior is unethical, unprofessional, or illegal, it is always appropriate, though not always popular, to refuse participation.

Examples of these three situations are as follows:

Unethical: "Dr. Roberts will chew you out if he finds out Mrs. Brown didn't get her treatment. Go ahead and chart it; nobody will ever know."

Unprofessional: "I can't wait to get home and tell my aunt that her boss was in for treatment of alcoholism."

Unprofessional: Respiratory Therapist to patient: "You probably don't need this IPPB treatment. These doctors order everything in the book for their patients."

Illegal: "We always take left-over medications home. My medicine cabinet is fully stocked from the hospital. Besides, it is already charged out to the patients. Go ahead and help yourself."

Chronic Complaining. Some individuals continually complain about the same situations, day in and day out, without getting around to doing anything about those situations. True many persons have unfortunate family situations, and some persons have problems that have no easy solution; but it is inappropriate to complain about them continually, particularly when the complainer is taking valuable time from other employees.

Many times the appropriate behavior is to listen to others. But there comes a time when continuing to listen simply reinforces the inappropriate behavior of others. That is, for many persons it is easier to complain than to take action, and complaining makes those persons feel better—temporarily. The problem, though, is that the relief is so short-lived that later in the day, that night, or early the next day, the person/complainer needs another dose of listening because the same tensions have reappeared. There is no mystery to this phenomenon. There are persons around who have listened to a friend, co-worker, or patient discuss the same unfortunate situation for ten or more years. The listener at some point finds him/herself avoiding this person whenever possible because the topic of conversation is so predictable.

One can be more helpful by declining to participate in the discussion, because by doing so a care giver begins to encourage the other person either to take appropriate action with the problem or, in the case of a problem without a solution (death of a spouse, for example), to turn his/her thoughts and energy to more productive avenues of expression. Difficult to do? Yes, but very rewarding for those who make the effort.

Examples of chronic complaining:

"Mrs. Martin on the 11 to 7 shift must not do anything but sit around all night. She leaves us with most of what she should have done."

"I wish they would do something about these old worn-out hospital gowns. Half of them don't even have ties in the back. I guess they're just too cheap to buy new ones."

Counter to the Good of the Organization. This category is primarily for things that are done that are against policy, thus harmful to the organization. Avenues other than rebelling against regulations are available to get changes made. When persons begin behaving as if they are "beyond rules and regulations," then the organization itself cannot operate effectively.

Examples of this category are as follows:

> "Just take clean sheets and towels home with you and bring the dirty ones in every week. The laundry will never know the difference. Lots of people do that—especially single people like yourself."

> "We always take a long break while the head nurse is gone for meals. Nobody cares."

Request For Understanding/Involvement

Many statements made during the day by patients/guests/co-workers are other than requests for information or action but rather are requests for understanding/involvement. Another way to think of understanding/involvement is that the other person is asking someone to *listen*. The skill of listening is one that seems very simplistic. One probably thinks that everyone knows how to do that, listening is easy. The fact is that many of us think that we are listening but if the patient is asked, he/she perceives it differently. It is not enough simply to think we are listening. The real test is whether or not the other person feels listened to.

As hospitals become more and more automated and technical in the health care area, the skill of listening becomes increasingly important. The technological advances, which mean better patient care, are frequently interpreted as impersonalization by the patient. As machines do more and more of what the care giver used to do, the human element of listening becomes more essential for good patient care.

Much of the training that is remaining will focus on the skill level necessary to guarantee that the other person *feels* listened to. This component will allow trainers to have an opportunity to try out new ways of responding to others, and also have the experience of really being listened to as they talk with others about their own interests.

Examples of the category of request for understanding/involvement are the following:

"I've been here seven days now and no one has been by to see me."

"I try to be cheerful, but it gets harder every day."

"I was planning to go home today, but the doctor just told me that she wanted to do some more tests."

ACTIVITY 5.3: Communication Requests

In the following exercise, mark each statement according to the type of request being made.

Unless otherwise noted, all are patients speaking:

1. *"What is my temperature?"*

2. *"Can I go home today?"*

3. *"The longer I stay here, the more discouraged I become."*

4. *"Can you slip me something to drink?"*

5. *(Co-worker) "Just write in an earlier time when you get here late. Don't punch the clock late."*

6. *"That lady on duty from seven to three is bad. She calls herself a nurse but all she does is visit all day."*

7. *"My brother-in-law gets on my nerves. Would you tell him I can't have any visitors tonight?"*

8. *"My doctor says I'm getting along fine, but I don't know. It seems like I'm going downhill fast."*

Theoretical Overview

A number of factors on the helping continuum determine from which position to make the most appropriate response. Those factors are discussed in this section and examples are given for each position on the continuum. Understanding the type of request, as discussed earlier, together with the knowledge of the helping continuum, and how to respond at each position, will increase the trainee's probability of being effective in interpersonal relationships with patients, guests, and coworkers.

Present the continuum as shown in Figure 5.1. The detailed description of each of the three phases (positions) identified on the continuum need to be shared with the trainees.

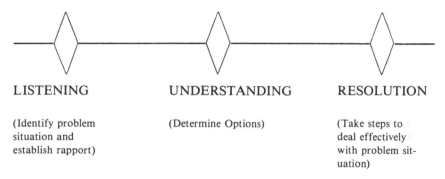

LISTENING   UNDERSTANDING   RESOLUTION

(Identify problem   (Determine Options)   (Take steps to
situation and   deal effectively
establish rapport)   with problem sit-
                                                       uation)

Figure 5.1. Helping skills continuum.

Listening Phase of Helping

The starting point for the majority of helping relationships is the *listening phase.* As described earlier, at times the HCW is not called upon by the patient to answer questions, nor to do anything for the patient, and the patient is not making an inappropriate request; instead, the request is simply for understanding involvement—for a listening ear. By understanding these categories of requests, the HCW can know very accurately the type of response that will be appropriate for any given situation. Responding to requests for information, action, or inappropriate interaction is relatively easy; these responses usually come from the content expertise of the job. The difficult request many times, is the request for listening.

One of the most serious mistakes most persons make in responding to the request for listening is to make an action-oriented response too early. That is to say, *the HCW provides options prior to understanding the problem*. This mistake is easy to make, and it usually grows out of a genuine desire to help. The problem, of course, is that the solution comes from the HCW's own frame of reference and value system, which might well be inappropriate for the patient/guest/co-worker. In addition, by making a suggestion, the HCW may well be suggesting an option that either has already been tried unsuccessfully or has been ruled out for one reason or another.

Effective and ineffective protocols are presented in this section. In the first, the HCW responds from an action position. In the second, the care giver tunes into the other person and listens carefully. Both conversations take approximately the same amount of the HCW's time, however, these two approaches differ greatly.

Ineffective

Patient: *"I really wish my son would visit me. I told him about the operation."*

HCW: *"Maybe he will come. It's early yet."*

Patient: *"I doubt it. His wife won't let him come."*

HCW: *"Oh, don't talk like that. I bet they will **both** come."*

Patient: *"No. My daughter-in-law and I don't get along well at all."*

HCW: *"I don't get along well with my husband's family either, but they would still come if I really needed them."*

Patient: *"I can tell our situations are different, but ..."*

HCW: *"I would just as soon my relatives stay at home when I'm sick. When you're sick you need peace and quiet, and there's no such thing as peace and quiet with my relatives."*

Patient: *"Well, thanks for stopping by."*

Effective

Patient: *"I really wish my son would visit me. I told him about the operation."*

HCW: *"You seem a little bit down over the fact that your son has not been by to see you."*

Patient: *"Yes. His wife and I had some trouble a few years ago, and he seems to side with her."*

HCW: *"That must be uncomfortable for all of you."*

Patient: *"I think about it all the time. The solution is so simple, but I haven't made the phone call yet."*

HCW: *"Sounds like you know what you need to do, but for some reason you've never done it."*

Patient: *"I suppose the situation of being in the hospital would give me a good excuse to call. It couldn't hurt."*

HCW: *"I'll stop by a little later and find out how it came out. It seems like you are doing something you really want to do."*

Patient: *"Thanks a lot for stopping by."*

Understanding Phase of Helping

The second point of the continuum, *understanding phase,* is reached automatically if the first phase, listening, is done properly. The more the HCW listens, the better the patient/guest/co-worker will understand his/her situation. In addition, effective listening allows the HCW to gather valuable information about the patient/guest/co-worker. A third thing that happens is that rapport is developed between the HCW and the patient/guest/co-worker. *Rapport development is valuable in patient/guest/co-worker management as well as in encouraging understanding.* Patients/guests feel better about the care giver, about the hospital, and about the treatment when they have experienced a satisfactory level of interpersonal interaction with the staff.

In ordinary HCW-patient/guest/co-worker interactions, the HCW may never accomplish the "understanding" phase of the helping relationship. A couple of factors contribute to that. One is, most HCW's are not psychotherapists. At some point in HCW-patient/guest/co-worker relationships, a referral of the other person to someone who has the time and is trained to deal with emotional problems may be appropriate. The rapport between the HCW and the care receiver is the key to making the referral. The HCW can use the strength of his/her relationship to encourage the patient/guest/co-worker to seek help elsewhere. Another factor is the willingness of the patient to self-disclosure. It often happens that the HCW-patient/guest/co-worker interactions remain at a relative superficial level. This is as it should be for brief admissions, and for many co-worker situations. A good gauge is the willingness of the other person to self-disclose.

The majority of HCW interactions will be in the listening area of the continuum. The natural progression is to understanding, but in many cases this phase will not be reached. In special cases, however, the understanding will be necessitated. For examples, the patient who stays a long time, or the patient who by the nature of the illness requires more attention. Also, of course, some patients or guests expect a great deal of attention, and others are the ones with whom the HCW simply enjoys spending time. Another example is the co-worker who the HCW gets to know well through spending time with him/her on or off the job. Because of special cases, some of the training time will focus on the understanding dimension of helping; however, the primary focus will be on the listening phase.

Resolution Phase of Helping

The final stage of helping, *resolution phase,* is where problem solving actually takes place. It is an action phase in the sense that some action generally is taken on a situation as a result of the listening and understanding phases that have preceded it. By the time the patient/guest/co-worker reaches this point, making a decision is easier because the exploration has taken place in the listening phase and options have evolved during the understanding phase.

Again, because health care workers are not psychotherapists or mental health counselors, the care giver will not always be required to work through the entire process with the other person. However, knowledge of the process is important and special skill development training is appropriate at the listening phase of helping.

HOUR 3
LISTENING SKILLS

As discussed earlier in the training, when the request from the other person is for understanding/involvement, listening constitutes the appropriate response. This section of the training will focus on the verbal components required for effective listening. The next section will deal with nonverbal components.

An important point to keep in mind is that, while the intentions of the listener may be very genuine, the speaker may nevertheless not feel listened to. The real test of the listener's success is whether the other person feels listened to. The listener's task becomes one of *demonstrating* that he/she *is* listening through both verbal and nonverbal means. The approach used in this training has been demonstrated through years of research and practice to be an effective method of interpersonal communication. The model allows a tremendous amount of flexibility so that each HCW can personalize the approach to fit his/her style. Nevertheless, unless one is already skilled in this method, the initial reaction may be negative. Thus, recognize that an important aspect for learning the listening skill is to stick with the process through the phase even if at times it seems rigid, mechanical, or simply "not me."

Usually a helpful action at this point in the training program is to remind trainees that any changes they have made or any change they will make in the future involves going through a period during which the newness feels unusual—the feeling that "this is just not me." Pushing oneself through this awkward stage is the key to movement in a positive direction, to growth. Suggest that they try to recall feelings of being the first to wear a new style of clothing. They will no doubt remember feeling a bit self-conscious, and wondering what the reaction of others, particularly their friends and co-workers would be. They may also recall that their feelings of comfort in this situation occurred with the passage of time and as they noticed others similarly dressed. Likewise with interpersonal skill development, one will likely feel uncomfortable at first and more comfortable with passage of time. An added feeling of confidence will occur as one observes others responding positively to one's new style.

Two major components to any response are the *content* of the message and the *feeling level* of the message. In any given response to another person, we can communicate that we heard one component, both components, or either component. If we miss both, that response would be considered ineffective. Our intentions might be good, but we would not be listening effectively. If we respond to one but not both, we would be partially listening. If we communicate that we accurately heard both content and feeling level, we would be listening. True listening requires the accurate communication of both elements. Evaluating the effectiveness of the response may be done by applying criteria presented in Figure 5.2.

LISTENING

Level A: Communication of accurate *content* and accurate *feeling level*

PARTIAL LISTENING

Level B: Communication of *either* accurate content *or* accurate feeling level

INEFFECTIVE LISTENING

Level C: Communication of *neither* accurate content *nor* accurate feeling level

---

Figure 5.2. Communication effectiveness.

Therefore two main tasks are necessary for responding effectively to another person who is asking for understanding/involvement. The task of communicating accurate content will be considered first, followed by a discussion of the accurate feeling level. These two elements will be pulled together in a third section on effective listening.

Communicating Accurate Content

The key word in communicating accurate content is *essence*. The task of the listener is to capture the essence of the message. As one can imagine, this increases in difficulty with the length of the other person's statement. We will begin with Activity 5.4 which contains three examples and a request to practice identifying key content words and phrases.

ACTIVITY 5.4: Communication Exercise—Content

Statement	*Key Content Words and Phrases*
"I really feel funny being here in the hospital. Every time somebody walks in the door I'm afraid it's going to be bad news."	*Being hospitalized. Feels that bad news is imminent.*
"I hope my job is waiting for me when I get out of here. They didn't make any promises when I left."	*Job security. No commitment from employer.*
"I've been paying the man for my policy every week for a long time. I hope it covers everything because I don't have any money."	*Question adequacy of insurance policy. Has no money.*

Write three other statements. Then identify the key content words and phrases.

Unless one responds to the content part of a message, the other person may not be sure the receiver really heard. Merely to tell the person one is hearing really is not enough; the listener has to demonstrate that fact. Parroting back the exact words of the other person is not appropriate either. It is monotonous and tends to put the other person on the defensive. **The solution is to capture the essence of the message.** *In the three examples provided the "essence" is shown in the right hand column. By responding with the key words or phrases one communicates the essence of the other person's message.*

Communicating Accurate Feeling Level

In communicating the feeling level accurately, a basic distinction has to be made: whether the feeling word is *surface or underlying.* A surface feeling word is one that seems accurate based on the statement(s) the other person makes together with the nonverbal behavior and any additional, accurate information one might have about the speaker. An underlying feeling word is one that might possibly be accurate, but one can not be sure based on the information one has. Dozens of feeling words can be used for any given situation, and many can be used accurately in the first response to another person. A safe rule, if the person with whom one is talking is not a close friend, is to use a surface word early in the interaction.

Examples in Activity 5.5 are to illustrate the difference between underlying and surface feelings.

ACTIVITY 5.5: Communication Exercise—Empathy

Statement	Feeling Level	
	Surface	*Underlying*
"I feel really funny here in the hospital. Every time somebody walks in the door I'm afraid it's going to be bad news."	Uncomfortable	Insecure
	Powerless	Overwhelmed
	Afraid	Lonely
"I hope my job is waiting for me when I get out of here. They didn't make any promises when I left."	Uncertain	Defeated
	Confused	Depressed
	Frustrated	Incompetent
"I've been paying the man for my policy every week for a long time. I hope it covers everything because I don't have any money."	Concerned	Helpless
	Worried	Angry
	Upset	Anxious

Give some statements typical to your situation and then identify surface feelings and underlying feelings in each statement.

The surface feeling words are understandable from the situation itself. The underlying feeling words are possibilities, but one cannot be sure based on the information provided.

In making an initial response to another person, unless one knows that person quite well, respond with a surface word. *By using a surface feeling word, one is tuning into the emotional world of the other person without attempting to go any deeper than he/she feels like going. This is a comfortable response style that communicates that one is listening,* **really** *listening, without creating anxiety or defensiveness on the part of the other person.*

We can see by looking at the list of underlying feeling words that they are all **possibilities,** *but without additional data we cannot be sure they are accurate. If a care giver uses one of these words in an initial response, one of three things will happen:*

1. *It will be inaccurate, and the other person will feel that the care giver is* **probing** *and not really listening.*

2. *It will be accurate, but because it has come so early, before rapport has been established with the other person, it will be denied.*

3. *The response will be on target, the other person will agree with the statement, and the response will have actually gone beyond the surface level.*

Clearly being able, accurately, to go directly to underlying feelings would be advantageous. The main problem with attempting to communicate what one perceives as underlying feelings early in the interaction is, for reasons mentioned above, the other person is likely to disagree with that feeling level. Since the goal is the establishment of rapport between the care giver and the other person, **the highest probability for success is to stay with the surface feeling level until one earns the right, through the relationship with the other person, to go beyond.**

HOUR 4
FACILITATIVE RESPONDING

Remember that we said earlier that a listening response was composed of two primary elements: content and feeling. When the request of the other person is for understanding/involvement and one responds with words that include accurate content and an accurate surface feeling word, the following things will happen.

1. A process will be set in motion for a dialogue, if desired.

2. The other person will feel listened to.

3. The other person will begin feeling good about the care giver as a helping person.

4. Rapport will begin to develop between the two individuals.

5. The other person can feel comfortable self-exploring.

6. A positive perception of the hospital begins to develop.

7. The tone becomes encouraging and healthy rather than discouraging and sick.

We can easily demonstrate the process of making a listening (facilitative) response by using our three example items. By definition the response must include accurate content and an accurate surface feeling, therefore, the task for the caregiver becomes one of combining these two in a way that feels comfortable.

Study examples provided in Activity 5.6 to understand how the content and feelings are combined. Then practice writing listening responses to statements provided in Activity 5.7.

ACTIVITY 5.6: Communication Exercise—Facilitation

Statement   *Listening Response*

"I feel really funny being here in the hospital. Every time somebody walks in the door I'm afraid it's bad news."

"You seemed concerned both about being in the hospital and about what you might hear."

or

"I guess it's uncomfortable for you right now, always wondering what will happen next."

or

"Being here and worrying about what they might tell you can be a pretty powerless feeling."

"I hope my job is waiting for me when I get out of here. They didn't make any promises when I left."

"You seem pretty uncertain about your job, especially since no promises were made when you left."

or

"I guess it is pretty confusing, since you didn't get a clear understanding about your job when you left."

or

"Not knowing whether or not your job will be waiting for you when you get back can really be a frustrating situation."

"I've been paying the man for my policy every week for a long time. I hope it covers everything because I don't have any money."

"Even though you have been paying on the policy a long time, it is hard not to be concerned until you are sure the coverage is adequate."

or

"You seem a little worried about whether the policy will pay off."

or

"It's upsetting to think that your insurance might not be adequate, especially since you don't have the money to pay a hospital bill."

ACTIVITY 5.7: Practice Exercises—Listening

Write listening responses to the following three statements.

1. *Elderly patient to HCW: "Those people downstairs upset me so while we were checking in. They got mad because I couldn't answer all the questions."*

2. *HCW to HCW: "With three children at home I feel like I have already done a day's work when I get here at three."*

3. *Patient to HCW: "My family needs me at home. I don't know how they'll manage while I'm here."*

HOUR 5
RATING RESPONSES

Pass out a blank 3 x 5 card to each person in the group. Tell them that they will be asked to write responses but they will not be asked to read their responses. Also tell them that they are about to hear a situation that they should assume is coming from a person they do not know well. After hearing the situation they are to write a response exactly as they would say it. After a short period of time offer the option of writing a second response, i.e., "what the trainer wants me to say and what I would really say." Indicate that both responses will be evaluated. Use one of the situations in Activity 5.8, or a more appropriate one and say it in a realistic way.

ACTIVITY 5.8: Practice Exercises—Responding

    Situation: (One health care worker to another) "I think the real reason I feel dissatisfied with the job is that we have so many patients assigned to us that we are not able to spend enough time with each one of them."

    Situation: (One health care worker to another) "If I had it all to do over again, I don't believe I would have gotten into hospital work."

    Situation: (One health care worker to another) "When I get home after work, I like to get outside and do things. My family seems so dull. It seems like all my family wants to do is stay glued to the TV set.

Allow five minutes and collect the cards. Read the cards anonymously and let the group decide upon a rating based on the scale suggested earlier in Figure 5.2. Write the scale on the board for reference.

HOUR 6
NONVERBAL COMMUNICATION

One cannot avoid communicating with others. Every action or nonaction is a communication of something. We can *define nonverbal communication as everything observable by others except the words we use.* Using this definition it is easy to understand how pervasive the nonverbal domain is. It is extremely important to become aware of signals that *we send* to others and also to be able to accurately observe and respond to the nonverbal behavior *of others.* This section focuses on both of the above and utilizes a roleplay format for practice.

Every aspect of our interaction, or non-interaction, has a nonverbal component. When a patient is asleep, for example, an HCW can make a number of observations without any words being spoken. Even in a telephone conversation, though we cannot see the other individual, emotions such as anxiety, fear, excitement, or anger can be readily detected and responded to. More subtle emotions also can be detected as we become more skilled at listening for them.

In order to help the care giver better understand the broad range of nonverbal communication, present the following outline. Help the group think of examples around them as they go over the list.

Categories of Nonverbal Communication Behaviors

1. Nonverbal Communication Behaviors Using Time:

   Quickness of response
   Amount of time spent

2. Nonverbal Communication Behaviors Using the Body:

   Eye contact
   Eyes
   Skin
   Posture
   Facial expression
   Hand and arm gestures
   Self-inflicting behaviors
   Repetitious behaviors
   Signals or commands
   Touching

3. Nonverbal Communication Behaviors Using Voice but Not Words:

   Tone of voice
   Rate of Speech
   Loudness of voice
   Diction

4. Nonverbal Communication Behaviors Using the Environment:

   Distance
   Arrangement of the physical setting
   Clothing
   Position in the room

As one can see from the preceeding categories, the nonverbal domain covers more areas than most persons realize. The trainer can suggest to the trainees that one way to practice the skills of becoming more
aware of nonverbal behavior is to think of these broad categories when
observing others and to find examples of each type. A practice exercise
follows.

ACTIVITY 5.9: Nonverbal Communication

The trainer gives the following instructions:

*"In the following exercise, you will be given an index card that con-
tains one of several feelings. Your task is to communicate this feeling
nonverbally to the remainder of the group. Group members will guess
until they hit the correct feeling. Some of the emotional states are easier
to communicate than others, and it may take longer for the group to
guess certain ones. The goal is not to see how fast the group can guess,
but rather to give you practice in thinking about and verbalizing certain
affective states that can be communicated nonverbally. Remember, you
can use anything other than words to get the feelings across."* The list of
words to use are provided in Figure 5.3.*

Feeling Words			
caring	humorous	intense	left-out
courteous	proud	strong	tearful
friendly	assured	blue	awkward
patient	authoritative	defeated	confused
elated	brave	discouraged	agitated
excited	energetic	humiliated	nervous
nauseated	shaky	timid	angry
bullying	rude		

Figure 5.3 List of words to use in Activity 5.9.

Many times in interpersonal situations a discrepancy occurs between words that a person uses and the nonverbal behavior of that person. In cases like this, **a person will almost always believe the nonverbal.** Discuss the following incident:

> "Suppose you are talking with another HCW in the coffee shop and that person tells you that he/she has plenty of time to talk. As you talk, you notice the person frequently checks his/her watch. What would your assumption be?"

Most people agree that they would believe the nonverbal behavior over the verbal. We find that the nonverbal tells the truth, even when words are not accurate.

As we discussed in the section on listening skills, the most effective response when the other person is asking for understanding is one that combines the affective or feeling domain within the accurate content of the message. Because the feeling domain is often expressed nonverbally, one easily can see the importance of understanding nonverbal communication. A care giver can often help the patient, a member of the patient's family, or a fellow HCW to better understand his/her situation by accurately responding to what one sees nonverbally. Many times the emotion will not be in conscious awareness but will be obvious from the language of the body. By responding to this, one can push the other person closer to a self-understanding of a situation.

The previously mentioned area is tricky and was not meant to imply that nonverbal behavior is simple to interpret and respond to. When presented without other evidence, any interpretation of nonverbal behavior should be extremely tentative. Examples of this are as follows:

> "You seem a little angry."

> "This may or may not be right, but I get the feeling that you are skeptical of the diagnosis."

> "When I mentioned your family, you seemed to cheer up immediately."

One should always remember that many, many potential reasons may exist for a given nonverbal response. In addition to being tentative, any interpretation should be accompanied by other evidence that makes *the assumption likely. For example, while one reason for a person's crossing his/her arms tightly is to defend against verbal attack, other reasons might also exist; and the available other data, as well as the context in which the nonverbal behavior appears, helps to determine the interpretation. Arms might be crossed because the person is physically cold, not defensive!*

In summary, nonverbal behavior is a very complicated domain that only **appears** *simplistic. The skill of using it as adjunct evidence in understanding others facilitates the helping process. Exercises in Activity 5.10 are for the purpose of enabling the group to practice with each other to refine this skill.*

ACTIVITY 5.10: Nonverbal/Verbal Communication

Vocal emphasis will frequently change the meaning of words. Using the same words, in the same order, it is possible to communicate a variety of meanings. Form groups of four and assign one of the following sentences to each group. Ask that they think of as many different ways to emphasize meanings as they can, and keep track of ways in which the sentence is delivered and the message that is communicated. After five minutes have a representative from each group read the list that each group developed. Study the following example to get an idea of the task for this exercise.

Sentence: *I didn't say you took the phone order incorrectly.*

Emphasis: **I** *didn't say you took the phone order incorrectly.*

Message: *Somebody else said it.*

Emphasis: *I* **didn't** *say you took the phone order incorrectly.*

Message: *I deny having said it.*

Emphasis: *I didn't* **say** *you took the phone order incorrectly.*

Message: *But we both know you did.*

Emphasis: *I didn't say you* **took** *the phone order incorrectly.*

Message: *You may have taken it accurately but transmitted it inaccurately.*

The example could be expanded, of course, but one easily can see from the above that vocal emphasis is crucial in understanding and responding to others. Sentences for groups practice are provided in Activity 5.11.

ACTIVITY 5.11: Meaning Communication Practice

    1. "Why do you always question new administrative policy?"

    2. "Every time the phone rings, I panic because I'm afraid it is terrible news from home."

    3. "All of the new staff members work harder than people who have been here awhile."

    4. "Sometimes when I go into the cafeteria, the odor reminds me of a particular patient's room, and I lose my appetite."

    5. "When Mary wears those old-fashioned clothes, she really looks silly."

HOURS 7 AND 8
ROLE PLAY RESPONSES

Various types of role playing situations may be developed by the trainer to practice responding according to the guidelines presented in the program. Feedback is given on both verbal and nonverbal communication. The plan is to move from hypothetical situations that might be supplied by the trainer to personally relevant situations. This evolves at a rate that is related to the rapport in the group. The trainer, when appropriate can model degrees of self-disclosure. The configurations that are used are fishbowl role play, triad role play, and dyad role play.

HOUR 9
DEALING WITH ANGER

Anger is an emotion that frequently is encountered in the health care field. Most commonly, the anger can come from the patient, but it also may come from a member of the patient's family or a co-worker. It is a difficult emotion to handle because the person who is angry is unable to have dialogue with another person; or at least is unable to listen during the period when anger is at its height.

An HCW who encounters anger in another person or persons can respond in a number of ways. Some of these responses may be appropriate, and others may be inappropriate.

Even though we sometimes know that an angry response is misdirected or inappropriate, our bodies may not respond to that knowledge. Consequently, our bodies will "gear up" for a fight. Being able to control a verbal and nonverbal response in such a situation is difficult, probably one of the most difficult tasks in interpersonal relations. A natural tendency when attacked is to defend oneself; a tremendous amount of concentration will be needed to detach oneself from the situation, refuse to personalize the attacks, and respond appropriately. During this session we will examine anger and some of its causes and offer suggestions for responding to it in a helpful, professional manner.

Physical Characteristics
of the Angry Person

Anger sometimes can be detected in a person before an "anger outburst." Physical characteristics stereotype the angry person, and most are related to signs of stress or pressure. Add to the list in Activity 5.12 any additional characteristics that help you detect anger.

ACTIVITY 5.12: Anger—Nonverbal Behavior

> *Voice level changes (becomes louder)*
> *Face becomes flushed*
> *Individual is jittery, with abrupt movements*
> *Individual acts as if he/she is "about to explode"*
> *Eyes become "fiery"*
> *Others*

Of course, one of the preceeding nonverbal signs alone is not usually enough to predict anger; but each additional one that is detected increases the probability of being correct in the diagnosis. Why, one might ask, is it important to know whether or not a person is angry, since one will find out soon enough anyway. The reason is simple. If a person has some prior warning of an impending attack of anger, the mind and body will have time to prepare for it. The physiological response is easier to control with prior warning, and the verbal response is likely to be more effective with time to think before the anger emerges verbally.

Causes of Anger

Being hospitalized, for the patient and for the family, creates conditions that allow anger to flourish. The patient, who is perhaps used to being in control in the family and/or work situation, is thrust into a relatively helpless situation. The patient is in someone else's domain, not his/her own. In addition, being in bed without the normal amount of clothing adds to the feeling of helplessness. The patient is frequently scared, yet afraid or not able to express the fear; this creates frustration. Many times fear is caused by the unknown, for example scary symptoms of disease on which the verdict may not be in yet. This situation can become volatile.

Families of patients likewise experience some of these same pressures during the hospitalization, and anger can easily result. In addition, the family member may well be taking care of the house, the children, the bills, holding down a full-time job, and then visiting the hospital every evening. It is easy to see how anger could result and also how it could be misdirected or displaced. The pressures that have just been mentioned are in addition to many other possibilities that occur with regularity and are exacerbated by hospitalization.

Guidelines for Responding
Effectively to Anger

1. Try to imagine all of the pressures on the patient and the patient's family. Empathize *to yourself:* how would I respond to similar sets of circumstances? By looking beyond the words to the circumstances you can, many times, get a valuable insight into anger. This will help the care giver remain detached from it. (Verbal empathy, such as, "You seem angry," is generally inadequate in the midst of the attack.

The problem is not so much with the words as with the intensity of the response. In order to equal the intensity of the angry person, the caregiver by necessity, would have to respond aggressively, a response that would probably be perceived negative by the angry person.)

2. Become consciously aware of how you normally respond to attack by an angry person. Even though the way you normally respond might not be appropriate in the health care setting, being aware of it would alert you to the point that you consciously could ward off this response to the patient and the patient's family. This guideline requires a lot of practice and self-control, because the response is relatively automatic. If this guideline is followed, the payoff is great (and reinforcing), because it allows one to remain in control and, exhibit objectivity in the face of possible irrationality on the part of the angry person.

3. Realize that everyone has a right to be angry. Arguing the validity of the anger will not change the fact that the person is angry. Acceptance of this fact will help us allow others to be angry when they *are* indeed angry. This puts less pressure on the care giver and, ultimately, less stress on the angry person, since one is not challenging the person's right to be angry.

4. Speak only when the angry person communicates that it is your turn to speak. The longer the anger is being expressed, the quicker it will dissipate. A good analogy would be releasing pressure from a tire. It comes fast and furious, and as long as one holds in the valve stem the air continues to be released. As the pressure gets low, the air loses some of its force, and eventually stops escaping completely when the outside pressure equals the inside pressure. Anger works in a similar fashion. If one tries to talk at the same time the other person is expressing anger, the response extends the anger dissipation time and may even heighten the anger.

5. Remember that listening to anger without responding is in no way admitting guilt and is in no way a complete answer to the problem either. Something sparked the anger, and *the best way to discover what happened is to allow the anger to dissipate and then to talk about it.* Though at first the

caregiver may seem to be doing less than one could do, remember that the first goal is to do whatever one can to dissipate the anger so that communication lines may be established or re-established.

6. Communicate listening without crowding the angry person. To do so remember the things that were discussed during the session on nonverbal communication. An angry person needs more space than a calm person. Touching is usually inappropriate; it is frequently mistaken for aggression. So the key here is to stay back, yet with eye contact and appropriate nods communicate listening.

7. Once the anger begins to dissipate, "test the waters" with an empathic response that implies some action, e.g., "This is *really* important to you. Let's see what can be done." Try to stimulate self-exploration on the part of the angry person in order that you and the person might better understand what sparked the anger. Without this phase, the probability is increased that the anger will recur.

8. Many times the angry patient or family member will have a legitimate complaint. A crucial step is to handle the complaint directly and honestly. If the complaint is legitimately directed at *you,* the care giver, an immediate apology to the angry person is appropriate. Honesty in admitting fault can facilitate development of rapport. If the legitimate complaint concerns other staff members, an appropriate response is to tell the patient or family member that you will check it out and get back with him/her. And, again, recognize the crucial step of handling the complaint directly and honestly by promptly investigating the problem yourself or reporting it to the appropriate person and informing the patient or family member of your actions. This keeps communication open and models appropriate behavior.

In summary, the guidelines for responding to anger are the following:

1. Understand your own reaction to anger.

2. Respect the right of others to be angry.

3. Listen to allow anger to dissipate.

4. Attend nonverbally without invading the space of the other person.

5. Speak only when the angry person expects response.

6. As anger dissipates, respond with empathy and action.

7. Admit fault, if appropriate.

8. Follow-up with action.

ACTIVITY 5.13: Anger—Practice in Responding

Form pairs to role play the following situations. Ask the trainee to follow the guidelines for responding to anger as they role play to gain practice in appropriately responding to anger.

> *1. The patient has been discharged and is waiting for a wheelchair to arrive to take her to her car. Ten minutes pass, and no wheelchair arrives. She grabs your arm as you are walking down the hall and says, "This is the most inefficient place I have ever seen. I've been ready to go for half an hour and still nobody has come with a wheelchair!"*
>
> *2. A patient calls you from the hall. As you walk into the room, he says, "Last night I was up half the night because of the noise across the hall. I'm really tired of this, and if something isn't done about it, I'll call the administrator tomorrow."*

HOURS 10 AND 11
ROLE PLAY SITUATIONS

Continuation of role play situations using a variety of stimulus situations is recommended. The key to the effectiveness of the program is whether or not patients and guests detect a difference between trained and untrained personnel. In order to increase the probability of success, role playing should be used extensively. By this stage of the training program have trainees within the role playing groups working on extremely personally relevant problem situations. When this happens generalization from the group to the work setting is very direct and tends to be effective.

Use pre-posttest comparisons to help the group examine the changes they have made in the way they respond to others. The procedure recommended is as follows:

1. Administer the posttest. (This is the same test used as the pretest and discussed in the Section entitled "Hour 1.)

2. Collect from paticipants their posttests and give them their individual pretests.

3. Ask trainees to evaluate their pretest responses by applying criteria learned during Hour 3 (see Fig. 5.2) of the program.

4. Give trainees their posttests and ask them to evaluate their repsonses on this test in the same manner, i.e., using Fig. 5.2.

5. Have trainees compare their pre- and post-response measures.

6. Have the group discuss changes they have made and what effect, if any, this has had on their work relationships.

7. Collect all data (pre- and posttests) for purposes of group analysis and program evaluation.

HOUR 12
ADDITIONAL HEALTH CARE ISSUES

In addition to the listening amd responding skills presented in this workshop, other related issues impact on the perception of the institution by the public. Any of the following could become mini-workshops in conjunction with the Patient Awareness Program. All, of course, are not appropriate with every group.

- Confidentiality
- Personalizing health care
- Courtesy
- Encouragement techniques
- Professionalism (many sub-units here)
- Touching in health care
- Use of jargon
- Explaining delays and changes
- Psychological reactions to hospitalization
- First impressions
- Telephone procedure

RESULTS

From a small beginning, with an idea being tossed around, this program has caught on in a big way and the future is bright for it. On the individual level, hospital workers learn to be more effective caregivers. The Train-the-Trainer approach is cost-effective in that hospitals are training their own employees to train others and positive spinoffs are a result of persons crossing departmental lines to either conduct the training or participate in it. Also, the problem being addressed in the workshops is probably one of the most nagging with which hospitals have to deal. Training is clearly the most efficient way to combat a negative community perception. The program was developed as a result of blending the expertise of university based personnel with the expertise already at the hospital, through establishment of lines of communication between these two institutions, and incorporation of adult learning principles to the theoretical plan. And it's working!

BIBLIOGRAPHY

Childers, W. C. (1983). Patient relations in hospitals: A train-the-trainer approach. *Innovations in Continuing Education,* Iowa City, IA: The American College Testing Program.

Gazda, G. M., Walters, R. P., & Childers, W. C. (1975). *Human relations development: A manual for health sciences.* Boston: Allyn & Bacon.

Gazda, G. M., Childers, W. C., & Walters, R. P. (1981). *Realtalk: Exercises in friendship and helping skills.* Atlanta: Humanics Ltd.

Gazda, G. M., Childers, W. C., & Walters, R. P. (1982). *Interpersonal communication: A handbook for health professionals.* Rockville, MD: Aspen Systems Corporation.

Gazda, G. M., Asbury, F. R., Balzer, F. J., Childers, W. C., & Walters, R. P. (1984). *Human relations development: A manual for educators* (3rd ed.). Boston: Allyn and Bacon.

CHAPTER 6

CASE CONSULTATION: THE COMMUNITY MENTAL HEALTH CENTER'S ENTREE TO THE SCHOOL SYSTEM

John D. West, Ed.D.

Terry R. Berkeley, Ed.D.

John D. West, Ed.D. is an associate professor of counselor education at Louisiana State University. John has been a consultant for mental health centers and school systems in the northwestern, midwestern, and southern regions of the United States. Recently, he has studied the impact of family counseling with cases where a youngster is presented as the identified patient and in-school behavior is described as a presenting problem. In general, John has found that consultants are often invited into the school system when the faculty, pupil personnel staff, and administration are unable to work successfully with a particular student. As a result, John believes that consultants can benefit from pragmatic models for case consultation.

*Terry R. Berkeley is assistant professor of special education at Louisiana State University in Baton Rouge. He received his training in early childhood special education at the University of North Carolina at Chapel Hill and obtained his doctorate at Harvard University's Graduate School of Education where he focused his attention on the relationship of child development to social policy. He has served in a variety of positions and has held numerous consultantships with local, state, regional, and national organizations working with the handicapped and disadvantaged children. His current research interests include an examination of curiosity in non-handicapped, at-risk, and handicapped children between the ages of six and eighteen months, the study of human behavior in the development and analysis of social policy in education, the discovery of variables impacting family dynamics in those units with handicapped children, and an analysis of humanism in special education. Just prior to this time, he completed work on an extensive examination of systems theory in relation to policies and practices regarding the deinstitutionalization of developmentally disabled individuals (with Angela Novak) that was published in the **International Review of Research In Mental Retardation (Vol 12).***

CASE CONSULTATION: THE COMMUNITY MENTAL HEALTH CENTER'S ENTREE TO THE SCHOOL SYSTEM

John D. West, Ed.D.   Terry R. Berkeley, Ed.D.

In this chapter the focus is on the use of mental health personnel to conduct Case Consultation within the schools. The utilization of a Community Mental Health Center (CMHC), as the external provider of consultative services to the local public schools, is posited as a way of meeting the need for new energy and fresh ideas. In addition, Case Consultation can be utilized to alleviate individual and group problems and to help establish a climate conducive to learning and personal development. In this instance, the Community Planning Council (CPC) is one mechanism for bringing the CMHC and the school system together.

While the CMHC and the local school district have worked together in the past, the consultative skills needed to operationalize an inter-disciplinary team approach to Case Consultation are concerns addressed in this chapter. The approach is based, in part, on the "first hand" experience of several proximal communities in central New England, where the local mental health center staff was used as a consultant in cases involving students with behavior problems or social-emotional disorders. With this limited case-specific clientele, consultative services were effectively provided to communities. Also, we propose that consultative services can be applied to a broader client population, and that successful application of the Case Consultation approach is limited only by the perceived needs of school personnel and by the range of expertise found within the mental health center.

According to Blake and Mouton (1978) "human behavior, whether occurring in an organization or involving a large social system, tends to be cyclical in nature and tends to remain constant or to change only quite slowly" (p. 328). Nevertheless, large social systems (e.g., communities) and organizations (e.g., schools) are being encouraged to change more rapidly than at any other time in our history, thus increasing stress and tension. Reasons for the rapid pace of change include, but are not limited to, an explosion in available information, an increase in diverse populations being extended the right to participate in all phases of life, an escalation in technological innovations, and an extensive re-thinking of values relative to how we should develop as a society.

In special education, the provocation for consultation, through the auspices of an outside or external agency, has been accelerated by increased numbers of students being served due to the enactment of Public Law 94-142, The Education for All Handicapped Children Act of 1975. In regular education, compensatory programs have been developed nationwide, since 1965 on a formal basis, to ensure an expansion of educational opportunities to the poor, the disadvantaged, and other diverse populations representing various ethnic groups. The extension of educational opportunities leading to equality can be viewed as having implications for both the community and the schools (Jencks, 1973; Lightfoot, 1973).

During the current period of accelerated development in educational practices, a plan for change to ensure orderly transitions is essential. Over a decade ago, Tyler (1969) referred to the need for a smooth modification in educational practices by noting problems that emerge from too rapid of a change,

> Accelerating development in education has created a collection of concepts, facts, generalizations, and research instruments, and methods that represent many inconsistencies and contradictions because new problems, new conditions, and new assumptions are introduced without reviewing the changes they create in the relevance and logic of the older structure. (p. 3)

While a challenge to tradition can become an opportunity for innovation, Tyler's warning has relevance for today's educators. Consultation is an emerging method professionals find useful for quenching their thirst for new knowledge and in adapting to new conditions.

CONCEPT OF COMMUNITY
FOR CASE CONSULTATION

Communities are large and complex social systems regardless of their urban, suburban, or rural locations. When establishing a consulting relationship within these social systems, a helpful procedure is to view their complexity in terms of actors, associations, and actions which have a place in the community's daily life. These actors, associations, and actions form the structure of the community (Kaufman & Wilkinson, 1967). While some communities may be "controlled" by a central leader, most communities are interactional. That is to say, according to Kaufman and Wilkinson (1967), "The essence of the interactional community is the organization of locality relevant actor roles and groups through which the needs of the local society are met and the social identity of the locality is maintained within the larger society" (p. 3). Thus, within the community's structure a pathway for community action can be established. Moreover, in the past decade communities have shifted their focus from responding to national and state priorities (Nisbet, 1953) to considering their own identity and meeting needs provoked by the establishment of local priorities (So, Stollman, Beal, & Arnold, 1979). This shift in focus can be used to encourage interagency local cooperation and consultation. The concept of community, then, involves all of the system's needs and priorities, including municipal finances, human services, public education, local government, regional industry, and area recreation.

In human services and education, community planning has been uniquely imperative. Both human and education service providers have attempted to respond to citizenry, regardless of socioeconomic status, whose needs are greater and whose requests for services are more insistent than in the past. Demands and expectations from the members of the community are not always compatible with philosophies of human service institutions nor are they always consistent with traditional roles of professionals from these institutions. Gil and Lucchesi (1979) have discussed the consequences of this phenomenon,

> It should be emphasized that the citizen participation of the 1960's and 1970's developed its frequently strident form of urgency and its attempts at comprehensiveness of control because it arose not from a philosophical belief in democracy, nor a belief in the duty of citizens to participate, but rather from basic unfilled needs—both physical and social. (p. 553)

Furthermore, in order to respond to changes within communities and to meet the real and unfulfilled needs of the people, Community Planning Councils (CPC) have evolved. The councils provide a vehicle from which different local entities can develop cooperative networks (Lewis & Lewis, 1977). Representative agencies found under the CPC umbrella usually include schools, court system, parks and recreation systems, churches, welfare agency, and mental health agency.

The function of the Community Planning Council (CPC) is to provide a mechanism from which needs of the community can be defined, agency resources can be made known, and social services delivered. As agencies develop and implement procedures for keeping records of cases served, data retrieval systems permit the CPC to stay abreast of community needs. Useful information, then, can be obtained from an institution's "termination summary sheet." Agencies and school systems often retain such a sheet in order to have a record of those cases that received services. Termination data found on the summary sheet may include

1. a statement of the client's presenting problem and diagnosis;

2. a summary of the treatment and reasons for termination;

3. a review of problems resolved during treatment and problems that yet remain; and

4. a prognosis and statement of recommendations made to the client.

Obviously the CPC is in a position to encourage cooperative endeavors and interagency linkage. Thus, the CPC is uniquely situated to help identify problems and issues where the Community Mental Health Center (CMHC) can intervene to bring about a desired change.

ENTERING THE SCHOOL SYSTEM THROUGH THE CASE CONSULTATION DOORWAY

Meeting the School System's Administration

As a result of the needs that the school system defines, and contacts established through the CPC, the CMHC representative initiates a meeting with the school system's superintendent and school board or the superintendent and building principals. Parallel administrative levels, such as the school superintendent and CMHC director, should be involved in the first meeting to ensure that adequate authority for negotiations is possible. If for example, the agency's director is not present, an incongruity in the administrative hierarchies exists and, consequently, negotiations relative to contracting for services may flounder, and interest and commitment to the idea may not be regained.

The CMHC director can claim his/her position as the agency's executive by introducing the concept of the interdisciplinary consulting team and explaining the use of the Case Consultation approach. The strength of the Case Consultation approach resides within the divergent views of the interdisciplinary team members. For example, the CMHC team might include (1) a psychologist, who has expertise in procedures related to educational and psychological assessment; (2) a special educator, whose expertise includes remedial work with a variety of learning exceptionalities; and (3) an agency counselor, whose training includes working with teachers relative to classroom management as well as a speciality in individual, group, and family therapy. The consulting team is often from the CMHC's Consultation and Education Unit and our bias is that the consulting team in particular, and the Consultation and Education Unit in general, be made up of professionals with differing areas of expertise as well as divergent styles to problem solving.

The consulting team uses the initial meeting to acquaint school administrators with the business of Case Consultation. Case Consultation is commonly described as a triadic arrangement in which the consultant (representative from the consulting team) and the consultee (faculty or pupil personnel staff from the school system) work to stimulate client (student) growth and development. Moreover, the client is most often not present during consultative sessions between the consultant and the consultee.

As part of this meeting, usually a helpful procedure is for the CMHC's team spokesperson to make a distinction between *client-centered case consultation* and *consultee-centered case consultation* as articulated by Caplan (1970). When the consultee merely desires an evaluation of the client's case and suitable recommendations for client management, the *client-centered case consultation* modality is utilized. The assumption is that the consultee is knowledgeable and skillful in implementing the recommended interventions. However, when the consultee requests an evaluation of the client's case and suitable recommendations for client management, plus guidance in implementing the recommendations for client management, *consultee-centered case consultation* becomes an appropriate modality. For example, if the school's special education staff have not been able to develop effective treatment recommendations for a specific client, the consultant can review the test data and perhaps reassess the client. Next, the consultant develops recommendations for case management and, consequently, utilizes a *client-centered* approach to Case Consultation. In the *consultee-centered* relationship, the consultant is active in providing the consultee with guidance for implementing case management recommendations. This guidance is required since a knowledge or skill deficit exists relative to implementing the recommended intervention. For instance, the consultant could offer the consultee instruction in integrating and implementing educational and developmental activities for the benefit of a particular client. The consultant might instruct the consultee in how to combine motor development tasks with math functions and reading exercises in short, easy-to-direct, challenging, and, yet, success-oriented activities such as adventure games, obstacle courses, or dramatic plays.

Consequently, emphasize the difference—*client centered case consultation* provides the consultee with recommendations for case management, *consultee-oriented consultation* incorporates an additional step of helping the consultee implement the recommendations by increasing the consultee's knowledge base or repertoire of skills. Our experience suggests that the consultative relationship will often be initiated with a request for *client-centered case consultation* and the relationship frequently progresses on to *consultee-centered consultation.* Werner (1978) has commented on this phenomenon and suggests that the progression can lead to consultation that focuses on systemic or organizational concerns. Nevertheless, apparently the *client-centered case consultation* model frequently opens the school system's doors to the CMHC.

During the initial meeting, school administrators may appreciate knowing that the consultant and the consultee will develop a formal written working agreement as part of the consultative process.

The *working agreement* is refined as consultation progresses and can specify

1. the client's identified concern(s);

2. the goal(s) the consultee hopes the client will attain;

3. the list of *possible* interventions developed by the consultee and the consulting team, to aid the consultee in advancing the client toward the desired goal(s);

4. the *jointly* constituted consultant-consultee intervention plan, developed to aid the consultee in moving the client toward the desired goal(s); and

5. the consultant-consultee's evaluation of the consulting process.

Throughout the initial meetings with the school's administrative staff, the consulting team needs to be aware of administrative concerns regarding Case Consultation. Some examples of these concerns are as follows:

1. Will the community become aware of the school's in-house problems?

2. Will personnel conflicts within a school surface and possibly be intensified?

3. Will all building personnel need to become involved in the consultative process or only those who desire to participate?

4. Will members of the consulting team respect individual school building rules and procedures?

5. How will school personnel know if the consultant has done a good job?

When such concerns surface, Caplan (1970) suggested that the CMHC's team provide a further explanation of *Case Consultation* by noting that

1. the consultative relationship is voluntary;

2. the consultee will be involved in designing the educational or therapeutic interventions;

3. the consultee will remain responsible for managing the case and, as a result, is the individual who decides whether an intervention is actually implemented; and

4. the consultant will respect the confidentiality of the relationship and remain problem focused rather than personnel focused.

Throughout the explanation of Case Consultation, the CMHC team wants to make it clear that they are entering the work world of the faculty or staff member for the purpose of a brief collaborative relationship. Here, the intent is to assist the consultee and client beyond a point of impasse.

Once the CMHC team has explained and answered questions pertaining to the consultative process, the CMHC director will want to indicate whether the agency's services are provided as part of their mission to the community or whether remuneration is necessary for services rendered. Philosophically speaking, community mental health is concerned with social and environmental stress factors that can contribute to psychosocial disturbances of various types and, consequently, the mental health agency has a responsibility to work in the various corridors of the community. Mann's (1978) comments suggest the school system to be one such corridor,

Teaching has been described as an extremely lonely profession, and those who are familiar with the situation have remarked often on the special condition of an adult closeted in a classroom with large numbers of children day after day . . .

> Moreover, they may or may not have opportunities for open and clear communication between themselves and curriculum supervisors, principals, or other administrative personnel . (p. 372)

If a contract is required for the Case Consultation, each consultative session can be assessed according to the agency's basic fee schedule. Frequently, the agency will have a sliding fee scale for clients and, as a result, the director will need to have a rate per session in mind that also takes into consideration administrative overhead; for example, travel time to and from the school, materials needed for consultation, as well as costs relative to record and bookkeeping expenses. The school system can be billed once a month or on a quarterly basis. A second method of assigning fees is to charge a set fee for consultative services provided over a specified period of time. Here, the school system may negotiate with the mental health center and an agreed upon fee will be established by both parties. All consultative services are to be paid for through this contract. The first type of contract may be appropriate when intermittent consultation occurs, while the latter type of contract lends itself to situations where consultative services are continuously provided during a specified period of time. To insure that misunderstandings over fees do not interfere with the consultative relationship, the type of contract to be implemented should be agreed to as soon as possible.

While the CMHC director and the team want to remain receptive to questions from the school system's administration, we believe that a structured initial meeting, such as the one presented here, will help familiarize participants in attendance with Case Consultation. In turn, this increases the probability that consultants will be viewed as having an organized and viable set of competencies to offer school personnel. Toward the conclusion of the initial meeting, the CMHC team summarizes what they believe to be the school system's level of interest in establishing a Case Consultation relationship with the mental health center. If the school administrators are desirous of entering a consultative relationship, a time in which individual school building personnel can meet with the CMHC team should be established. In this way, an orientation to the consultative process can be planned.

Meeting the Faculty and Staff

As a result of the preparation provided by the building principal, the CMHC's consulting team can be scheduled to meet with faculty and pupil personnel staff for the purpose of explaining the availability of Case Consultation. At the orientation session, the building principal introduces the CMHC team, and school personnel are made aware of each team member's area of expertise. School personnel may appreciate having *consultation* differentiated from *inservice education* and *supervision.* Bloom (1975) has noted that,

> Consultation can be distinguished from education on the basis of (1) the relative freedom of the consultee to accept or reject the ideas of the consultant, (2) the lack of a planned curriculum on the part of the consultant, and (3) the absence of any evaluation or assessment of the consultee's progress by the consultant. (p. 109)

With regard to differentiating consultation from supervision Bloom (1975) commented,

> Consultation can be distinguished from supervision on the grounds that (1) the consultant may not be of the same professional specialty as the consultee, (2) the consultant has no administrative responsibility for the work of the consultee, (3) consultation may be irregular in character rather than continuous, and (4) the consultant is not in a position of power with respect to the consultee. (p. 109)

Throughout the orientation session the consultation team needs to remain receptive to questions, sensitive to vaguely expressed concerns, and active in providing examples of effective *Case Consultation.* Examples of Client-Centered Case Consultation should highlight how the collaborative effort between the consultant and the consultee can lead to a more in-depth understanding of the client's case and culminate in alternative educational and therapeutic interventions. Again, consultants want to mention that they are entering the world of the faculty member or staff member for a brief period of time with the stated intent of assisting the consultee and client beyond an impasse. While the primary aim of Case Consultation is the relief of a specific presenting problem, a subsidiary goal is to broaden and refine the consultee's knowledge base and skill level in order that similar concerns may be resolved independently in the future. Moreover, CMHC team members can further clarify their role by mentioning that while working toward problem resolution they will respond frequently to the consultee by

1. paraphrasing and summarizing content,

2. employing content confrontations to clarify discrepant information,

3. utilizing open ended questions to probe for additional information,

4. applying theoretical knowledge to arrive at a broader understanding of the case, and

5. offering recommendations in order that alternative educational or therapeutic interventions might be considered.

These consultant behaviors are quite similar to leads outlined by Blake and Mouton (1976). Also, recognize that the role of the consultee includes being actively involved in sharing perceptions of the client's case, establishing goals for the case, developing and implementing alternative interventions, and continually evaluating the consultative process. While the consultant has specific knowledge and skills at her/his disposal for evaluating the client's case and developing interventions, the consultative procedure is process oriented in nature. While Schein (1978) referred to "clients" and we refer to "consultees," his comments relate to process oriented consultation and match our beliefs, "For many kinds of problems the clients face, the only way to locate a workable solution, one that the client will accept and implement, is to involve the client in the diagnosis of the problem and the generating of that solution" (p. 342).

By the end of the orientation session, the first two stages of the Facilitative-Directive Process Model (see Kirby, Chapter 1) have been initiated. That is, answers are provided to the following questions:

1. What is Case Consultation?

2. What is the role of the CMHC team in the consultative process?

Naturally, as the relationship between the consultant and the consultee matures, answers to these questions will undergo additional refinement.

The consulting team begins to close the orientation session by asking school personnel if they believe that Case Consultation would be a valuable service for their school. If an affirmative response is received, consultants can assist school personnel in tentatively identifying issues where consultation may be beneficial. For example, the broad areas that can be suggested include

1. requests on how to "mainstream" exceptional learners,

2. questions relative to identifying the psychological effects of family life on school performance,

3. appeals for procedures to use in side-stepping power struggles with students, or

4. inquiries concerning strategies for counseling with the reluctant client.

Faculty and staff are informed that as individuals, or as members of small groups, they may become concerned with a particular case and can request consultation with one or more members of the CMHC team.

School personnel also are informed that in order to make contact with the consulting team they merely need to provide the principal with a brief description of the case and an indication of which consulting expertise they believe is required. This description may include

1. an indication of the client's age and grade level;

2. a notation relative to the purpose of the consultation;

3. a statement about the family history, if available; and

4. a synopsis of previous client assessment information, including diagnostic information, and any recommendations concerning educational or therapeutic interventions.

Upon receiving this information the principal, or the consultee, will telephone the appropriate team member or members and share the case description. It is critical for the consultant to respond promptly to the consultee's request and establish an appointment at the earliest opportunity. These steps in referral and contact are highly recommended because they affirm the school's administrative hierarchy, acknowledge the consulting team's competency, and suggest that benefits are to be derived from collaborative Case Consultation.

STEPS IN THE CONSULTANT-CONSULTEE RELATIONSHIP

Problem Identification
and Outcome Clarification

Initially, the consultant wants to clarify and articulate concerns which bring the consultee to the consultative relationship. The consultant attempts to attend to the consultee by paraphrasing and summarizing content. Frequently, specificity will need to be added to the consultee's remarks and, consequently, the more accepting type responses can be followed-up with probes (open-ended questions). Probes that can be integrated into the interview are typified by the following:

1. What problematic behavior is the client displaying?

2. When was the problem behavior first observed?

3. What environmental changes were occurring during the onset of the client's problematic behavior?

4. What environmental stimuli seem to intensify the client's problematic behavior?

5. How do others, including children and adults, respond to the client's problematic behavior?

6. What behavioral deficits is the client displaying?

7. How does the client evaluate the problematic behavior?

During the exploration and definition of the consulting problem, the consultant often becomes aware of discrepant information pertaining to the client's case. These discrepancies may be unraveled by utilizing a content confrontation. For example, the consultant may respond in one of the following manners:

1. "You've indicated that Jack has always had difficulty with algebra, yet you've only recently become concerned about his performance. What has occurred recently to increase your concern?"

2. "You've indicated that Susan seems isolated socially and, also, that Katherine has been her best friend. What behaviors does Susan display to suggest she's isolated and what behaviors have allowed her to develop a best friend?"

3. "So Jim is in danger of failing his English class, yet he's making satisfactory progress in his history, science, and mathematics classes. What can you tell me so that I might

better understand these discrepancies in Jim's performance?''

Such confrontations and probes can be of invaluable service in helping the consultant and consultee arrive at an operational definition of the concern that precipitated a request for consultation. Because confrontations focus on content discrepancies and encourage a clearer understanding of the client's behavior, the consultee perceives the interview as a joint effort in bringing clarity to the consultative picture, rather than receiving a sense of being personally challenged by the confrontative inquiries.

When the consultant believes that an operational description of the client's problematic behavior exists, the consultative problem should be summarized in order to discover whether the consultant's perceptions match those of the consultee. Often, more than one consultative problem is defined and the concerns are then prioritized for resolution. Depending on how time consuming the portrayal of the problem has become, the first session may be entirely devoted to problem identification. Consequently, the consultee's "homework" assignment might entail contemplating goals for the identified problem or, in other words, considering the desired outcomes of consultation.

Stum (1982) has suggested that after the client's presenting problem has been defined, the consultant and consultee will want to operationally identify the desired goals or outcomes of consultation. Probes the consultant can use to facilitate the development of a goal may be characterized by the following statements:

1. How does the client's problematic behavior interfere with progress in school?

2. When the consultative problem is resolved, what will the client be doing differently?

3. What behavioral goals has the consultee already established for the client?

4. What behavioral goals has the client established for him/herself?

5. What positive consequences can occur for the client as a result of meeting the consultee's goals?

6. What negative consequences can occur for the client as a result of meeting the consultee's goals?

Probes, such as these, may reveal that client resistance to change has evolved from a lack of clearly defined goals or as a result of the client not valuing the consultee's goals. Naturally, in order to avoid building a consultative atmosphere that is interrogative in character, the consultant will want to follow-up the probes with such active listening responses as paraphrasing and summarizing.

By the end of the first or second consultative session, the consultant and the consultee have begun to develop a *working agreement* (See Figure 6.1). At this point the agreement contains a statement of the client's presenting problem and the goal toward which the consultant and consultee will work. Eventually, when the consultant and the consultee engage in an evaluation of the consultative relationship, the *working agreement* provides a point of reference for opinions and conclusions. Near the end of the second meeting, the *third consultation stage* of the Facilitative-Directive Model (see Chapter 1) will presumably have been addressed. That is, the problems to be resolved during consultation are likely to have been defined and, in addition, the expected outcomes of consultation are likely to have been clarified.

As a management technique, the CMHC team conducts a "weekly review" of all open cases. Whenever a consultative relationship has been initiated or opened, the case is included in the consulting team's weekly review. We believe it is essential that a review be scheduled into the team's calendar at a specific time each week, in order that other appointments are not allowed to replace the meeting. During the weekly meeting each case is reviewed with the following checklist in mind:

1. Have the presenting problems and outcomes of consultation been defined?

2. Are assessment reports comprehensive enough or should additional assessments be considered?

3. Based on assessment findings, what educational and therapeutic interventions have the consultants considered as *possible* recommendations?

Client's Name:_____ Consultee:_____

Consultant:_____

Date:_____ Grade:_____

Identified Concern(s):

Goal(s):

Possible Intervention(s):

Jointly Constructed Intervention(s):

Evaluation of Consultation

    Concern(s) Resolved:

    Remaining concerns with recommendations:

_____

Figure 6.1. Form for developing the Working Agreement.

4. Have the consultant and consultee *jointly* developed educational or therapeutic interventions that can be implemented in the school?

5. Has the consultant conducted a follow-up interview with the consultee in order to ascertain progress in administering the *jointly* developed interventions?

Obtaining answers to the first item in the checklist ensures that consultation has been properly initiated and attempts to guarantee that the presenting problem has been defined in a solvable manner. Utilizing the second item will stimulate consideration of the need for further assessment, perhaps an assessment that is not included in the team's repertoire; for example, a medical or psychiatric evaluation. Consultants may view the third item as an opportunity to "brainstorm" with colleagues prior to writing a *case report* and, thus, this process lends itself to developing a rather extensive list of *possible* interventions for the consultee's consideration. By using the fourth item the consultant is provided an opportunity to present to team members any intervention which was collaboratively developed with the consultee. Team members are impartial observers and may be able to detect potential pitfalls in interventions and recommend minor alterations. The fifth item is a reminder for the consultant to review the effectiveness of the consultative process. More will be said in the remainder of this chapter regarding the development of educational and therapeutic interventions, as well as discussing the review of the consultative relationship.

Client-Centered Case Consultation

Once the desired outcome of consultation is identified, the consultant and the consultee may decide that a more detailed assessment of the client's presenting problem is appropriate or that a confirmation of an earlier assessment should be established; consequently, *client-centered case consultation* is initiated. Obviously, the CMHC team needs to have a number of assessment procedures at their disposal. For example, a simple but useful tool that can be used by the consultant to gather systematic observations of individual behavior is displayed in Figure 6.2. Similarly, a helpful procedure for making home visitation observations is offered in Figure 6.3. Home visits are often conducted by a CMHC team member who has been trained in the area of family therapy.

Student's Name_____Age_____Observer_____

Grade_____Date_____

Setting_____Reason For Observation_____

Time: From_____ To _____   _____

                                          _____

Describe conditions (such as structure, task, close/distance supervision:

_____

_____

AREAS OF BEHAVIOR   OBSERVATIONS MADE

Attending to task
                              _____
                              _____
Interacting with peers
                              _____
                              _____
Interacting with teacher
                              _____
                              _____
Listening to instruction's
                              _____
                              _____
Speaking
                              _____
                              _____
Decision-making
                              _____
                              _____
Others
                              _____
                              _____
Summary:_____

_____

_____

Recommendations:_____

_____

_____

_____

Figure 6.2. The systematic student observation form. Illustration of a systematic procedure for making observations during a home visitation.

Student's Name_____ Age_____ Consultant_____

Date_____ Time_____ Reason For Visit_____

Grade_____ _____

OBSERVATIONAL AREAS & BEHAVIOR WITHIN FAMILIES

Physical Conditions:

      1) Home care
      2) Socio-economic status
      3) Opportunity for family group activities
      4) Accommodations of individual needs
      5) Integration into neighborhood

Atmospheres:

      1) Cultural context
      2) Interpersonal interactions

Adult relationships (describe, e.g., husband-wife):

      1) Structure of family authority
      2) Division of labor
      3) Financial responsibilities
      4) Communications styles/patterns

Parent-Child Interactions:

      1) Care giving behavior of parents
      2) Childs role in family
      3) Attitude of child to parent
      4) Approach to discipline and management

Child-Child Interations:

      1) Competitive roles
      2) Shared values/goals
      3) Controlling behaviors

Figure 6.3. A form for home visitation observations.

Prior to agreeing on an assessment procedure, the purpose or function to be served by the assessment must be clarified. In exploring the purpose of the assessment with the consultee, the consultant again relies on paraphrasing or summarizing content, confronting and eliminating discrepant content, and probing with open-ended questions for additional information. In turn, this dialogue assists the consultant in selecting an appropriate assessment procedure or battery. The consultant recommends a preferred method of assessment and follows-up the prescription by offering a theoretical explanation of the preferred procedure.

In conducting a client assessment, we concur with Caplan's (1970) conclusion that an evaluation should be completed at the school rather than at the mental health center. Naturally, the client benefits from being evaluated in a familiar setting. This procedure also allows the consultant to become familiar with the particular school building and, as a result, facilitates the development of educational or therapeutic interventions that have relevance to that environment. That is, completing the client assessment at the school increases the consultant's understanding of the consultee's level of conceptualization relative to the assessment, and suggests the consultee's potential for implementing various interventions. Obviously, then while the consultant's focus of observation remains primarily centered on the client's case, the degree to which the school environment can accommodate a change also is considered.

After completing the client assessment, a brief *case report* is written. Borrowing from Caplan's (1970) work in the area of *client-centered case consultation,* we believe the case report can address the following issues:

1. a statement of the problem to be resolved and the goal to be attained in consultation,

2. an indication of how the client's efforts to cope have led to a disturbance in behavior,

3. a description of the assessment procedure used during Case Consultation,

4. a synopsis of the assessment findings,

5. a listing of possible alternative educational and therapeutic interventions designed to stimulate more effective behavior from the client, and

6. an indication of the consultant's interest in receiving follow-up information relative to the disposition of the case.

After the consultee has read the case report, but prior to jointly developing an educational or therapeutic intervention, a helpful question for the consultant to pose is, "Do you believe this is a problem or task you would like to work at resolving or do you believe the case is hopeless?" This inquiry, and the ensuing discussion, are designed to clear the air regarding any hesitancy to participate in consultation, to weigh the consultee's investment in establishing and implementing an alternative intervention procedure, and to provide an opportunity for a verbal commitment to the consultative relationship. It can occur, that rather than being invested in developing an alternative intervention, the consultee is motivated through discouragement to show that the client's case is hopeless. The consultant should not try to convince the consultee into a commitment but, rather, rely on those leads and responses which have been previously mentioned in order to help the consultee evaluate her/his interest in pursuing Case Consultation. If the consultee expresses an interest in a *joint* effort at building an educational or therapeutic intervention, the consultant may find the following probes useful:

1. "What interventions have previously been effective for you in working with similar cases?"

2. "What interventions have you already used with the client in order to resolve the presenting problem?"

3. "Based on assessment findings, the list of *possible* alternative interventions, and your previous experience with the client, what intervention do you believe could be developed in order to resolve the presenting problems?"

These probes are designed to discover which educational or therapeutic procedures have previously succeeded and failed. Helping the consultee refine a formerly useful intervention can encourage the implementation of an adapted procedure, and the listing of unsuccessful interventions can facilitate a declaration of "bankruptcy" and result in an increased receptiveness to developing a joint recommendation. The consultant needs to observe whether the consultee seems interested in reworking the list of possible interventions or whether the consultee wishes to build an entirely new intervention. Working together to produce an educational or therapeutic intervention signifies a realistic level of optimism in regard to the consultee's competence and the consultant's desire to be of assistance. Thus, from this collaborative endeavor, a genuine effort is made to construct a joint recommendation for client management. Placing the jointly created intervention into the working agreement (as suggested in Fig. 6.1) concludes an active attempt to ensure that the intervention has relevance for the school environment.

If dialogue with the consultee indicates that the school is unable to implement the recommended interventions and a referral appears appropriate, the consultant can be of assistance by helping the consultee think through the referral process. First, the importance of sharing the *case report* with the appropriate school administrator and with the client's parents needs to be mentioned. Second, the necessity of providing the family with several referral sources should be reviewed. Describing the services provided by each potential referral agency can promote the family's ability to make an informed choice. The family's first efforts at scheduling an initial appointment with the referral agency may be facilitated by the consultee. For example, the consultee may accompany the family to their first session and offer to provide the agency with information relative to the client's case. The consultant also can review with the consultee the importance of keeping channels of communication open between the school and the agency, while at the same time warning the consultee to avoid being caught in a "middle-man" position between the client, the family, and the agency. That is, perhaps the school can facilitate the agency's treatment interventions by putting into effect recommended modifications in the client's educational environment.

By this time, *client-centered case consultation* has reached a point where the *working agreement* contains a definition of the problem to be resolved, a statement of the consultation goal, as well as a list of *possible,* and eventually, *jointly* derived recommendations pertaining to case management. Within the *client-centered case consultation* framework, the consultant is not concerned with helping the consultee develop a list of steps for administering the recommended intervention. Developing procedures for administering the recommended intervention would place the focus of consultation on the consultee's level of knowledge and skill and, as a result, would begin to approximate what Caplan (1970) refers to as consultee-centered case consultation. *Client-centered case consultation* can be viewed as ending after a recommendation for case management has been developed and similarly, terminates Phase I of Facilitative-Directive Process Model proposed by Kirby (see Chapter I).

Consultee-Centered Case Consultation

Caplan (1970) noted that during consultee-centered case consultation the consultant works to correct the consultee's biased judgments, to remedy a lack of consultee knowledge, to resolve a lack of consultee skill, or to support a consultee who lacks self-confidence. He mentioned that *consultee-centered case consultation* frequently must focus on the consultee's lack of professional judgement and indicated that a lack of professional judgement may emanate from any of the following:

—a personal involvement with the client,

—an identification with the client,

—a misinterpretation of the client's case due to characterological distortions, or

—a displacing onto the case of a problematic and unresolved issue or theme in one's own life.

In these situations, the consultant may accept the consultee's prejudicial and problematic perception of the client but call into question the biased and "inevitable" outcome for the case. Caplan, concluded, that as the negative and "inevitable" outcome is effectively challenged the consultee's anxious and ineffectual handling of the case can be reduced. He referred to the process of increasing consultee objectivity as "theme-interference" consultation. However, Bloom (1975) has questioned the effectiveness of this procedure as is illustrated by his statement: "It is possible that consultation of any kind is unusually effective in situations in which consultees have initially low objectivity and thus that the finding linking theme-interference-reduction consultation with increased objectivity is a spurious one" (p. 127). Bloom went on to suggest that differing initial levels of consultee objectivity, as a research variable, are needed in order to study accurately the effects of *consultee-centered* consultation.

We believe that many consultee-centered consultations can be managed using two other approaches described by Caplan (1970): (1) satisfying the consultee's lack of knowledge and (2) correcting for the consultee's lack of skill. As with client-centered case consultation, in the consultee-centered paradigm the suggestion is that the consultant and consultee (1) need to have conducted a joint appraisal of the presenting problem, (2) need to have established the desired outcomes of consultation, and (3) need to have developed procedures for resolving the presenting problem and reaching the desired goal. Then, whether as a result of an initial consultation or whether as a result of following-up a client-centered case consultation, the consultee may recognize the need for additional assistance in implementing an educational or therapeutic intervention.

If the consultant and consultee agree that a deficit in consultee knowledge exists, the consultant may provide the consultee with theoretically based or research specific input. Some examples of deficits in knowledge that could hinder the consultee's work with a client and that could be resolved with appropriate input are, (1) insensitivity to the impact of parental divorce on a child's school performance and little knowledge on how to counteract the impact, (2) a limited understanding of the social and academic effects produced by bussing a client to a new socioeconomic environment and little knowledge of how to make the adjustment easier, and/or (3) a lack of understanding of the anxiety associated with certain learning disabilities and recommended procedures for reducing anxiety and increasing the client's attention span. Based on experiences with consultee-centered consultation a consultee may display a behavioral or performance deficit as well as a knowledge deficit. That is, a consultee may have knowledge relative to a specific educational or therapeutic intervention but lack finesse in implementing a particular technique or skill. For example, a consultee may be aware of the negative impact a parental divorce can have on school performance, but not be familiar with techniques such as the "parts party" (Dobson & Kurpius, 1977) that can be used during group counseling to help the client clarify emotional confusion and regain a sense of mastery with regard to one's own life. Another consultee may know that a client has transferred to their school from a socioeconomic environment where aggressive behavior was the order-of-the-day, but be inexperienced with active listening skills which could help disarm the client's frustration. In a similar situation, the consultee may know that peer tutoring can be utilized to resolve problems of under achievement and may want to use this procedure to encourage the client who has moved into a new socioeconomic environment, but not know how to employ a sociogram to ensure an appropriate tutorial relationship. The consultee may be familiar with dietary interventions which can be used to lower anxiety and assist in increasing a learning disabled client's level of concentration but, perhaps, has not had practice in administering systematic relaxation procedures with clients. The examples can go on endlessly, however, the point is that skill deficits can usually be resolved through a brief instructional period between the consultant and the consultee. In turn, the instructional period may be followed by a demonstration or by role playing. In role playing the consultee may assume the role of the client, while the consultant demonstrates a particular intervention and, then, the consultee can practice the intervention with the consultant playing the client's role. As the consultant and consultee review the practice session, the consultant can provide helpful feedback and reinforcement to the consultee.

As has already been mentioned, consultee consultation differs from teaching and supervision. If lengthy training is required to resolve an extensive knowledge or skill deficit, the consultee should seek help from some other source such as his/her supervisor, a program in continuing education, or extensive study. In such a case, the consultee's client should be referred so that appropriate interventions can be initiated without undue delay. The consultant's responsibility for training must be limited to a brief period of time in order to help the consultee beyond a specific impasse. In case consultation a consultant and consultee determine what interventions will be adequate for resolving the presenting problem, thus, together they can usually distinguish those conditions that require considerable amounts of additional knowledge and skill for the consultee. Naturally, a member of the CMHC team may step out of the role as a consultant and provide continuing education to specific supervisors or members of the faculty and staff, but this training component would not be a part of the Case Consultation.

The Group Modality

Group consultation is a justifiable alternative to the consultant working with a single consultee and it is especially appropriate within the consultee centered model. Group consultation may be initiated by asking the individual, who originally requested the consultation, to explore with colleagues whether they have experienced similar or additional concerns regarding a particular client. If an affirmative response is received and if these colleagues are interested in working together in order to arrive at a more effective procedure for managing a particular case, the consultation group may be quickly established. During group consultation multiple problems and goals are likely to be identified along with various interventions for attaining the desired outcome. Consultees seem to appreciate and enjoy the opportunity to work together toward problem resolution, consequently, the wise consultant facilitates the sharing or responsibility for the consultative process rather than trying to single-handedly direct the eventual outcome. The group's multiplicity of resources are exactly what makes it an effective modality.

The group is often comprised of three to four consultees who have day-to-day contact with the client. Since the consultees are assisted in resolving specific problems, the group becomes quite task-centered and rather open-ended in character. Sessions generally last for 45 minutes, or one class period, and extend for five or six meetings.

In discussing group consultation, Kevin (1963) identified three rather broad phases of the group's development; they are, Phase I which encourages *member involvement,* Phase II which emphasizes *problem solving,* and a Phase III which includes *group termination.* We have witnessed many of the group dynamics reported by Kevin.

In the involvement phase, for example, it is not unusual for members to express anxieties relative to being in a consultation group by presenting vaguely defined complaints about the client and pressing the consultant for an immediate solution. Most often, the consultant will be more successful if he/she avoids quick solutions, utilizes accepting leads, and increases group involvement through a universalization response such as "Has anyone else had a similar experience with the client?" Self disclosures by members and by the consultant, relative to common frustrations when struggling with a difficult case, can help to lower performance anxieties and increase group cohesiveness. As with individual consultation sessions, the consultant can move toward increased confidence in the consultation process by operationally defining presenting problems and establishing goals.

During the problem solving phase it is often quite appropriate to rely on the group's resourcefulness. For example, a brainstorming exercise may be used in order to develop educational or therapeutic interventions. At first, all possible interventions are recorded. Next, those interventions that seem most inappropriate are discarded. Then, the preferred interventions are prioritized and one is selected as the most feasible to implement. Again, the consultant is attempting to ensure the development of an intervention that the school environment can accommodate. Consequently, the consultant encourages group members to create an intervention for their unique situation. If knowledge or skill deficits exist for one or more of the consultees, the consultant, or preferably a group member, can provide a mini-theory input on the use of a specific intervention. Naturally, the consulting group also can be turned into a laboratory as specific members demonstrate the proposed intervention for others and then the remainder of the group role plays in order to gain practice with the intervention. Finally, the group can provide corrective feedback and reinforcement to members as they process the demonstrations that were conducted during the practice sessions. Since a specific intervention can often be developed from the recommendations of consultees, the intervention may be bestowed with additional credibility and, consequently, the commitment to put a specific plan into action is made with positive expectations from all.

The concluding phase of group consultation occurs as the presenting problem is resolved, and since the problem and the desired outcome have been specifically defined, the group's termination point is clearly conceptualized. Again, because we are suggesting a brief period of consultation in order to minimize any semblance of consultee dependence, consultation can be terminated by summarizing the importance of developing specific definitions for problems and desired outcomes and, then conferring credit on the consultees for building and implementing precise interventions.

The following illustration demonstrates how *consultee-centered case consultation* can be carried out in a group format:

> Tom was a fifth grade student whose school adjustment problems lent themselves to group consultation. His mathematics and English teacher, art and music teacher, physical education teacher, and school counselor described Tom as wanting to prove that "no one can make me do anything I don't want to." For example, a specific problem described by his mathematics and English teacher involved Tom's frequent roaming from his desk while the class was assigned to in-seat work and independent study. The teacher mentioned that after telling Tom to return to his desk, the two of them inevitably found themselves embroiled in an argument. During the involvement stage of the group consultation, other consultees acknowledged that they also had found themselves involved in power struggles with Tom, and their disclosures seemed to help everyone feel less isolated in their frustrations thus increasing group cohesiveness.

During the second and third consultative meetings, when the group had moved into the problem solving stage, the decision was reached to side-step power struggles by having Tom enter a time-out room whenever he roamed away from his desk. Then the mathematics and English teacher demonstrated the use of the time-out room during a role play, in which the school counselor assumed Tom's role. During the role play, prior to placing Tom in time-out, the consultee scolded him for his inappropriate behavior. Consultees recognized from observing the role play that a more appropriate behavior would be to simply point to the time-out room rather than trying to talk with Tom in the heat of an argument. Consultees also were concerned that Tom might fail to respond to the non-verbal cue. The school counselor commented that Tom had previously talked with her about wanting to improve his relationship with teachers and thought she could inform Tom of how the time-out procedure would be non-verbally cued, in order to assist him in staying seated at his desk and to prevent arguments from erupting.

At the two week follow-up session, the consultees agreed that the number of power struggles with Tom had decreased. The consultant inquired whether procedures for rewarding appropriate behaviors, or even slightly improved behaviors, were being utilized. Positive reinforcement procedures were discussed by the group and the consultant provided a brief theory input on "letters of encouragement" (Asselin, Nelson, & Platt, 1975) that could be sent to Tom's parents. The letters were to be written by consultees and addressed to Tom's parents indicating that, as concerned and interested parents, the consultee was certain they would want to hear about the appropriate behavior and progress their son was making in school. The rationale for the letter of encouragement was based on the hypothesis that the parents would, in-turn, compliment their son and, thus, again reinforce appropriate school behavior. Finally, the school counselor noted that in the past Tom had been critical of other boys in school who wore glasses, and suggested that part of Tom's inattentiveness to in-seat work may have been associated with feelings of awkwardness relative to wearing a new pair of glasses. Other consultees were surprised and commented on how they thought the glasses made Tom look more mature than most boys his age. Consequently, the group recommended that this perception be shared with Tom in order to "win him over" and to lower his resistance to wearing glasses. At the time group consultation terminated, the consultees reported an improved relationship with Tom and a noticeable decrease in the frequency of his out-of-seat roaming. Six group consultation sessions were held, the latter three essentially acted as follow-ups to interventions that had been developed during the earlier meetings.

Again, Kirby's developmental phases of consultation can be used to place our comments in perspective. Once the consultant and consultee have developed an educational or therapeutic intervention, Case Consultation can be conceptualized as having moved through Stage 5 of the Facilitative-Directive Process Model (Kirby, Chapter 1). That is, explicit steps in delivering the intervention have been clarified and the stage ends with an agreement to implement the intervention, observe the outcome, and report back at an agreed upon follow-up time. The follow-up sessions frequently are scheduled biweekly and are considered to be an essential part of Case Consultation.

Following-Up the Case Consultation

Kirby's Stage 6 of the consultative process is designed as a follow-up to the planned intervention. Relative to a follow-up interview, the consultant reconsiders the *working agreement,* and with the participation of the consultee, summarizes the problem that has been addressed during consultation, restates the goal toward which consultation has been directed, and reviews the *jointly* constituted intervention procedure.

If the consultee reports that the goal has been attained, then the consultant and the consultee will recognize that the consultative relationship is nearing termination. After noting the consultee's new level of confidence and competence, the consultant can mention that the consultee has developed an educational or therapeutic intervention which can be activated should similar concerns arise in the future. Frequently, the consultant and the consultee need to decide whether the intervention should remain in place or gradually be phased out. The consultant, however, wants to emphasize that the consultee has been actively involved in developing and implementing the consultative intervention. Indicating that the consultee has remained responsible for the progress during the consultation decreases the possible sense of dependency on the consultant. The consultee then is informed that the consultant has enjoyed developing the collaborative working agreement, and the consultee is encouraged to contact a member of the consultation team should additional concerns arise in the future.

Also, if a review of the working agreement indicates that the goal for Case Consultation has only been partially achieved, the consultant needs to evaluate whether the intervention has been implemented as intended. A partial attainment of the consultative goal often suggests that a minor alteration in administering the intervention is required or that a supplementary intervention needs to be added to the planned procedure. The following probes may be used to help the consultant decide whether the plan was implemented as intended.

1. When the intervention plan was administered, what was happening to suggest that this was an appropriate time or context in which to implement the intervention?

2. How often was the intervention implemented; that is, each time the client's inappropriate or appropriate behavior occurred?

3. What portion of the intervention did the consultee believe was implemented appropriately?

4. What portion of the intervention did the consultee have difficulty in implementing?

5. What was the client's response to the intervention?

6. How did the consultee react to the client's response?

7. How did the interactional sequence between the consultee and client end?

Information obtained from these questions may suggest that with a limited amount of additional knowledge and instruction, or with a short period of practice, the consultee's finesse in implementing a particular intervention can be increased. In such a situation, the follow-up permits the consultant to review the consultee's perspective on the case as well as the consultee's understanding of the recommended intervention procedure.

If the intervention appears to have been implemented appropriately and if the consultee reports that the presenting problem is not being resolved, the consultant may suggest that the consultee's disappointment and frustration are signaling a need to review how the presenting problem has been defined and how the consultative goal has been stated. Furthermore, the consultant will need to indicate that the appropriateness of the planned intervention needs to be reviewed. If the consultee agrees to such a review, various questions, including the following, should be addressed.

1. Have the consultant and the consultee clearly defined the client behavior they wish to increase or decrease?

2. Have the consultant and the consultee clearly defined the goal they are working to achieve?

3. Have the consultant and consultee defined when, or under what conditions, the consultee expects the client to behave differently?

4. Has the client agreed that the behavior problem is one which needs to be reconciled and that the goal is one worth working toward?

5. Can the present problem be broken into smaller units?

Occasionally it becomes clear that an important aspect of the presenting problem has not been considered when the educational or therapeutic intervention was being developed and changes in the intervention procedure become necessary. For example, if the problem consisted of the client "interrupting" during class discussions, the consultative goal may have become a reduction in "interruptions." If the intervention plan is limited to ignoring the interruptions, a lengthy treatment period may result. Perhaps the consultant and the consultee decide to establish a second consultative goal; that is, to increase the frequency with which the client "waits her/his turn" prior to responding. "Waiting for a turn" might be operationally defined as raising a hand to be recognized before responding. Establishing the second goal allows a behavior to be rewarded that is incompatible with the presenting problem and, consequently, the second goal helps to accelerate the pace at which the inappropriate behavior is extinguished. That is, the consultee may ignore a client's interruptions and increase pro-social behavior by providing verbal reinforcement when the client raises her/his hand to speak.

If a review of the *working agreement* does not delineate a need for alterations in the definition of the presenting problem, the stated goal, or the planned intervention, the consultant may recommend that the consultee continue to implement the planned intervention and mention that the follow-up findings will be presented at the consultants' "weekly review" in order to gain additional perspectives on the case.

A scenario for the "weekly review" follows:

> The CMHC team members decide that the problem and objectives have been clearly defined but that the planned intervention may need to be altered to more directly address the consultative problem. Moreover, the team agrees that additional assessments are required to better understand the factors which are inhibiting the case from reaching a successful conclusion. As a result of the recommendation for further assessments, the agency counselor suggests that a home visit would make available additional information, the special educator maintains that a classroom visit could provide supplemental data, and the psychologist proposes having the client respond to a sentence completion questionnaire. As a follow-up to these recommendations, the special educator makes a classroom observation. During the visit, the team member notes that the consultee is ignoring inappropriate client behavior and providing verbal reinforcement for prosocial behavior, but minimal progress occurs in reaching the consultative goal. The consultant also observes a limited response from the client at the time the consultee administers a verbal reinforcer and, consequently, hypothesizes that a new type of reinforcement needs to be selected, such as combining verbal and tactile reinforcers.

This scenario portrays what we believe to be a benefit of the consulting team's "weekly review." That is, an interdisciplinary approach to consultation increases the probabilities of the presenting problem and goal being adequately described and, also, increases the likelihood of a successful intervention being developed. We believe that the interdisciplinary effort by the team members helps to ensure the most effective resolution of the consultative problem in the briefest amount of time.

The Case Consultation process often requires two or three interviews in which the presenting problem and goal are clarified, along with the development of a planned intervention. While the first three consultative interviews occur at weekly intervals, follow-ups are often held biweekly. Upon terminating a particular Case Consultation, the consultant adds final entries to the *working agreement*. For example, one entry may describe problems resolved and goals attained, while another entry may describe problems and goals that remain unresolved. Additional services that lie outside of the consultative relationship also may be specified. We do not schedule "check-up" interviews as suggested in Kirby's *Stage 7* of the consultative process. Rather, we hold to Case Consultation as a brief problem solving experience and, consequently, the consultative partnership is terminated once the *working agreement* is completed.

TAKING STOCK OF THE
CONSULTATIVE PARTNERSHIP

When the consulting team is "taking stock" of their partnership with the school system, Weiss (1972) has suggested that outcomes can be framed by answering the question, "How well does the program work?" (p. 4). In our case, the "program" refers to Case Consultation. Light (1982), in his discussion of children's programs, offered a more expansive description of evaluation and recommended "describing how programs interact with and change the broader social environment in which a child grows . . . documenting the services received by children . . . and describing the transaction between clients and program staff" (p. xii). We believe that at the end of each semester or school year the *working agreements* can be reviewed and a cumulative *evaluation report* written that addresses the following questions:

1. Who were the consultees receiving services: classroom teachers, special education teachers, school counselors, etc.?

2. Who were the clients receiving consideration during Case Consultation: sex, grade level, ethnic group, etc.?

3. With what frequency was *client-centered case consultation* utilized?

4. With what frequency was *consultee-centered case consultation* utilized?

5. With what frequency are commonalities among the various presenting problems identified: teacher-student relationships, peer relationship, academic concerns, etc.?

6. With what frequency were specific assessments conducted; e.g., WISC-R, classroom observation, home visitation, etc.?

7. With what frequency were specific types of information incorporated into the educational or therapeutic interventions: information relative to multi-cultural education, information relative to normal and atypical cognitive development, information relative to normal and atypical psychosocial development, etc.?

8. With what frequency were specific skills incorporated into the educational or therapeutic interventions: sequencing learning tasks from simple to complex in order to attain mastery, utilizing classroom councils to facilitate self-discipline, acknowledging meta feelings while counseling with a reluctant client, etc.?

9. What presenting problems were recorded as "resolved" in the working agreements and how frequently were they recorded?

10. With what clarity can a description of the cost analysis be presented: cost for client-centered case consultation, cost for consultee-centered case consultation, cost for materials, etc.?

Answers to these questions can form the basis for a semester or annual evaluation report. The report lists data in a nomothetic manner thereby safeguarding the anonymity of the consultees and clients. Not only should the evaluation report assist with decisions relative to continuation of consultative services, but also, should assist with planning aimed at stimulating professional growth and development. For example, in the report can be suggested relevant areas in which the school system can provide in-service training or continuing education. Naturally, the evaluation report needs to be modified to answer specific questions posed by a variety of possible target audiences such as the school system, the mental health center, the Community Planning Council, and so forth. However, the report can be viewed as a vehicle for providing these audiences with tangible evidence concerning accomplishments accrued from Case Consultation. As a result, staff morale in the school system and in the community mental health center can be bolstered through a substantive professional activity, and the community-at-large can "see" for themselves the positive outcomes which have resulted from using local resources to resolve meaningful concerns. In the end, pride is stimulated through a recognition that locality relevant programs have provided substantial benefits to the community.

REFERENCES

Asselin, C., Nelson, T., & Platt, J. (1975). *Teacher study group leader's manual.* Chicago, IL: Alfred Adler Institute.

Blake, R. R., & Mouton, J. S. (1976). *Consultation.* Reading, MA: Addison-Wesley.

Blake, R. R., & Mouton, J. S. (1978). Toward a general theory of consultation. *Personnel and Guidance Journal, 56,* 328-330.

Bloom, B. L. (1975). *Community mental health: A general introduction.* Monterey, CA: Brooks/Cole.

Caplan, G. (1970). *The theory and practice of mental health consultation.* New York: Basic Books.

Dobson, L., & Kurpius, D. (1977). *Family counseling: A systems approach.* Muncie, IN: Accelerated Development.

Gil, E., & Lucchesi, E. (1979). Citizen participation in planning. In F. So., L. Stollman, F. Beal, & D. Arnold (Eds.). *The practice of local government planning,* (pp. 552-575). Washington, DC: International City Management Association.

Jencks, C. (1973). Inequality in retrospect. *Harvard Educational Review,* 43, 138-164.

Kaufman, H. F., & Wilkinson, K. P. (1967). *Community structure and leadership: An international perspective in the study of community.* State College, MS: The Social Science Research Center of Mississippi State University.

Kevin, D. (1963). Use of the group method in consultation. In L. Rapport (Ed.). *Consultation in social work practice.* New York: National Association of Social Workers.

Lewis, J., & Lewis, M. (1977). *Community counseling: A human services approach.* New York: John Wiley.

Light, R. J. (1982). In J. R. Travers & R. J. Light (Eds.). *Learning from experience: Evaluating early childhood demonstration programs.* Washington, D.C.: National Academy Press.

Lightfoot, S. L. (1973). Politics and reasoning: Through the eyes of teachers and children. *Harvard Educational Review, 43,* 197-244.

Mann, P. A. (1978). Mental health consultation in school settings. *Personnel and Guidance Journal, 56,* 369-373.

Nisbet, R. A. (1953). *The quest for community: A study in the ethics of order and freedom.* New York: Oxford University Press.

Schein, E. H. (1978). The role of the consultant: Content expert or process facilitator? *Personnel and Guidance Journal, 56,* 339-343.

So, F., Stollman, L., Beal, F., & Arnold, E. (Eds.). (1979). *The practice of local government planning.* Washington, D.C.: International City Management Association.

Stum, D. L. (1982). DIRECT—A consultation skills training model. *Personnel and Guidance Journal, 60,* 296-302.

Tyler, R. (1969). Introduction. R. W. Tyler (Ed.). *Educational evaluation: New roles, new means.* Chicago: National Society for the Study of Education.

Weiss, C. H. (1972). Evaluating education and social action programs: A treeful of owls. In C. H. Weiss (Ed.). *Evaluating action programs: Readings in social action and education.* Boston, MA: Allyn and Bacon.

Werner, J. L. (1978). Community mental health consultation with agencies. *Personnel and Guidance Journal, 56* (6), 364-368.

CHAPTER 7

ORGANIZATIONAL CONSULTATION A CASE STUDY

William H. Culp, Ph.D.

William H. Culp, Ph.D.

Dr. Culp is professor of Counseling at Indiana University of Pennsylvania where he teaches counseling and consultative theory and supervises the practicum and intern experiences. This position, which he has held since 1975, has afforded him the opportunity to develop experiential learning activities which apply theory to practice.

From 1979 to 1982 Dr. Culp participated in a TORI program under the direction of Dr. Jack R. Gibb. Through his experience Bill's emphasis in consultation shifted from primarily educational settings to business, industry, and government. He has used his experiences with various organizations to identify the human services skills needed to help the organization make desired changes.

Dr. Culp has taught in several universities where he has established a record of creating community outreach programs that utilize skills of different agencies. One of these programs, GIVE, was a three-year funded program that provided educators experiences in working with community agencies to coordinate and combine industrial, governmental, and educational resources of Erie County, PA.

Dr. Culp is a licensed psychologist and has worked in schools, correctional institutions, industrial employee assistance progams, mental hospitals, governmental agencies (particularly in the Department of Employment Security), out-patient treatment centers, human resource development programs, and other community and industrial agencies. He is a member of the American Society for Training and Development, the American Psychological Association, the American Association for Counseling and Development, and the Association of Humanistic Psychologists.

ORGANIZATIONAL CONSULTATION A CASE STUDY

William H. Culp, Ph.D.

Human resource development is receiving more attention in a growing number of business enterprises in the United States as work values and expectations change. The trend is toward abandoning the central power mode of management and adopting a human potential catalystic model. The emphasis is shifting from the "learned managers to learning managers. The latter is the real need of today and the future" (Terry & Franklin, 1982, p. 397). In making this transition, business is beginning to look at human development models which were developed in education and psychology. Individuals trained in these disciplines are likely to possess skills that can be effectively used to develop quality human services in industry and governmental agencies.

Historically, human resource development has been viewed as primarily the responsibility of schools. Educational specialists, such as teachers, counselors, and administrators, apply various individual intervention strategies and group techniques to reach their desired goals. The practitioner who is trained and skilled in working in the educational arena should be able to adapt one's methods to make them applicable to the industrial setting.

The successful educator has *the ability to hear, not tell; support, not criticize; liberate, not manipulate; and foster cooperation, not competition.* Compare these skills with those identified as traits of the successful humanistically oriented manager. "A trusting attitude, concern for the personal fulfillment of the employees, a lack of ego, willingness to listen to subordinates, risk-taking innovation, high expectations, collaboration, and the ability to integrate ideas," are the characteristics reported by Ferguson (1980, p. 348). The central element appears to be a focus on the process of learning and discovering more than on goals. Similarly, in consulting, the process is more important than the consulting goal.

Smith (1983) and Hansen (1984) discussed the human resource development specialist in industry. Hansen defined the human resource professional as the person who is

> primarily engaged in attracting to the work place and fostering human resources, providing for their training, education and development in the work place..., and facilitating the management and utilization of these resources in such a way that both their own goals and the goals of the organization are achieved to the maximum extent possible. (p. 72)

The areas of human resource development that have similarity to education are Training and Development (T & D), Organizational Development (OD), Employee Assistance Program, Career Planning and Development, Recruitment, Human Resource Planning, and Performance Appraisal (Hansen, 1984, p. 75). A consultant may be asked to assist in developing programs in many of these areas.

Several reasons exist as to why individuals trained in education are reluctant to enter business and industry as consultants. One is the attitude that skills they have developed are appropriate only in an educational setting. A second is an unfamiliarity with the business world and its vocabulary. And, a final (and probably most important) is an unclear picture of consulting skills and process. In this chapter a case study from business is, therefore, presented to help the reader gain a perspective of the industrial and organizational setting and ways consulting skills can be applied.

In this study of a consulting experience with a small organization, the Facilitative-Directive Process Model (Kirby, Chapter 1) is used to illustrate the power of adhering to a *rational* consultative plan. This model allows one to apply strategies that encourage exploration for data gathering, moving to a new way of looking at and understanding data better, and developing and implementing an appropriate action plan based on the new perceptions of the issues. Example excerpts of the case, from the initial contact through termination, are presented to demonstrate the application of the model in an organizational setting. The reader may find it helpful to pretend to be the consultant at certain points in this case and decide on appropriate action strategies *before* reading the author's account. For this reason, Reader Involvement Activities are included to encourage imaginative participation.

TORI: A CONSULTANT'S PERSONAL PREPARATION

The author has been deeply influenced personally and has developed many consulting strategies while completing three years of training in the TORI Intern Program with Jack Gibb (1978). TORI is an acronym formed from the first letter of the four Discovery processes: *Trusting, Opening, Realizing, and Interdepending.* In a high trust environment an individual or organization creates one's being or identity through interweaving these processes. The four discovery processes are self-rewarding and self-generating. Completion of one process triggers movement to the next successive process in a manner similar to the following:

> "I trust myself, therefore, I am free to discover my uniqueness and be who I am. Then I am capable of *opening* to others by revealing myself and having a genuine communication with them. In the opening process I begin to *realize* my emerging self, my uniqueness, my similarities, and my special role in life. As I realize my uniqueness, I begin to value the uniqueness of others thus the process of *interdepending* begins to develop. When these processes interweave, I create with another a relationship that is built on combining our strengths and discovering new ways of being and working together."

In Table 7.1, "The TORI Discovering Processes," is shown how movement through the TORI developmental stages facilitates the process of becoming more and more receptive to others, thus, strengthening the interactive relationship and creating synergistic growth and individual energy which accelerates group development.

The TORI process is very important for the beginning (or for that matter advanced) consultant. But, unfortunately, to communicate this significance in a written description is difficult. Experiential learning is necessary to fully understanding the personal impact the TORI processes can make on the practitioner. Thus, writing about TORI is somewhat like writing a book on the theory of electricity and trying to convey the feeling of an electrical shock. A reader may understand the concept, but the sense of the shock and responses it produces are not known until the shock is experienced. In an attempt to overcome this problem the author has tried to involve the reader as experientially as possible by including Reader Involvement Activities. Completing these activities when they are presented will involve the reader in the consulting and help make the consultative process clearer.

The first element of the TORI process is *TRUST: self-trust.* The opposite of trust is fear. Self-fear is destructive and is learned very early in life. What happened to Humpty Dumpty? Can he ever be put back together again? Not according to the rhyme, and it is that belief that makes one so afraid to take action and risk failure.

The first element of the TORI process is the most important one for the beginning consultant. In this context, it is important to remember that trust means trusting oneself and one's ability. A simple example may help. We have all experienced mornings when we knew our day is going to go well. On such a day one feels good about starting work, knowing—or more accurately, trusting—that everything is going to go fine and, then not being at all surprised when one has a great day. The good feelings were precipitated by high trust and thus a "great day" resulted.

Reader Involvement Activity 7.1 was designed to assist the reader in recalling the feeling of high trust.

READER INVOLVEMENT ACTIVITY 7.1: Trusting

1. Think back to a time when you trusted yourself, and experience again the feelings of that moment. Avoid the trap of criticizing yourself for being naive. Also, avoid saying, "but,

Table 7.1 The TORI Discovering Process

Discovering processes	Orientation of the person	Proactive energy focused on:	Personal wants
TRUSTING- (T) BEING Personing Centering Accepting Warming	*Being me* — discovering who I am How do I create me? What is my uniqueness?	*Accepting self and others* Trusting Expressing warmth Seeing differences	*Love* — giving and receiving love
OPENING- (O) SHOWING Letting in Listening Disclosing Empathizing	*Showing me* — discovering how to reveal myself to others How to let you in and share our space? How to show you how I feel and see?	*Spontaneity* Impulsivity Rapport Tuning in	*Intimacy* — giving and receiving intimacy and communication in depth
REALIZING- (R) ACTUALIZING Asserting Exploring Evolving Wanting	*Doing what I want* — discovering my wants and how to realize them What matters to me? What is my life for?	*Searching* Fulfillment Life enrichment Allowing Achievement	*Fulfillment* — giving and receiving personal fulfillment
INTERDEPENDING- (I) INTERBEING Integrating Joining Sharing Synergizing	*Being with others* - discovering how to live and work with others How do I create my freedom? How do we transcend our own beings?	*Interacting* Participating Cooperating Giving and getting freedom	*Freedom* — giving and receiving freedom

NOTE. From *Trust: A New View of Personal and Organizational Development* (p. 21) by Jack R. Gibb, 1978. Los Angeles, CA: Guild of Tutors Press. Copyright 1978 by Guild of Tutors Press. Reprinted by permission.

if I only knew this and that, I would have done this and that." Hindsight is excellent, but unfortunately experience is not a part of the present. For the moment, recall, visualize in your mind, your period of high trust and enjoy the accompanying feeling without being critical or evaluating yourself. Do you have the image clear in your mind?

2. *Now take a deep breath, inhale deeply and exhale completely. This is an excellent way of relaxing. Repeat the breathing but this time inhale more deeply and exhale more completely. And, while you are doing this, remember the period of high trust which you have visualized.*

3. *You may want to combine this with a positive affirmation about yourself. A simple one would be, "I am relaxed and trust myself." Create an affirmation which you like and which works for you.*

4. *You will probably profit from repeating this exercise for several days. Long practice periods are not necessary but frequent practice will help. Use the time when you have nothing else to do, like when you are waiting for a red light to change. Breathe deeply while repeating a positive affirmation.*

5. *Devote sufficient time to this exercise so you will be able to do it automatically when you feel yourself becoming tense and fearful.*

Everyone has experienced fear. Fear prepares one for **fight** *or* **flight** *and unfortunately neither of these are appropriate responses for the effective consultant. In a state of fear questions race through the mind, "Can I do it? Will people like me?" Questions such as these induce distrust and self-criticism.*

When one is fearful, one transmits this fear to others and they reciprocate with distrust. Fear reactions are the common precipitators of defensive reactions. Defensive reactions limit interaction and make others uncomfortable. Fear restricts freedom. Fear serves as blinders, thus, a fearful person develops tunnel vision where only one solution seems possible and that is usually the solution that the consultant has previously used and found somewhat effective. Fear causes one to restructure the world in accordance to one's fearful perception of it.

*Defensive behavior is fear induced. This seems contradictory since the term "defensive behavior" seems to imply that this behavior **defends** a person and is, therefore, valuable. Nothing could be further from the truth. The effect is fear induced habitual responses that results in denial or distortion of information. Thus, data collection and understanding are blocked and an action plan developed on these data will not be productive because it is not directed at the real problem area.*

A fearful consultant blocks information that is available in the consulting environment, and since information is filtered out, the consultant responds not to the consulting situation but to a distorted view of it. Defense reactions hamper the ability to receive pertinent information and they are, therefore, a barrier that makes effective communication impossible. In Figure 7.1 fear in communication is illustrated.

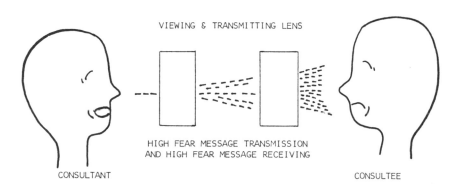

THE DISTORTION PROCESS

VIEWING & TRANSMITTING LENS

HIGH FEAR MESSAGE TRANSMISSION
AND HIGH FEAR MESSAGE RECEIVING

CONSULTANT

CONSULTEE

Figure 7.1 The distortion process in high fear message transmission.

The consultant on the left sends a message which is distorted by the high fear (thick) transmitting lens. The consultant's message is further distorted by the thick (high fear) defensive lens of the consultee. Both the sending and receiving is distorted in both directions.

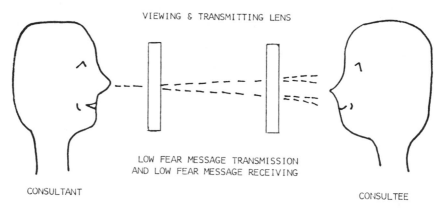

THE DISTORTION PROCESS

VIEWING & TRANSMITTING LENS

LOW FEAR MESSAGE TRANSMISSION
AND LOW FEAR MESSAGE RECEIVING

CONSULTANT

CONSULTEE

Figure 7.2 The distortion process in low fear message transmission.

Figure 7.2 represents message transmission and viewing under low fear where less distortion of the messages occurs and the consultant can receive and validate information. Conceptually, if the consultant has accepted the consultee with respect and genuineness, the consultee will be in a low-fear low-defensive attitude and will be able to accept the validation process without feeling threatened.

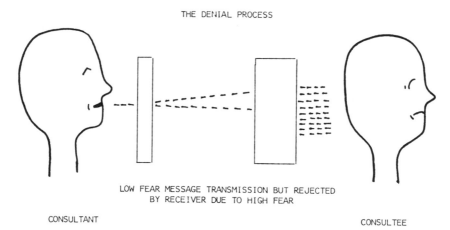

THE DENIAL PROCESS

LOW FEAR MESSAGE TRANSMISSION BUT REJECTED
BY RECEIVER DUE TO HIGH FEAR

CONSULTANT

CONSULTEE

Figure 7.3 The denial process with low fear message transmission and high fear on part of receiver.

In Figure 7.3 the consultee is denying the message of the consultant. This involves ignoring the message and pretending it does not exist. The consultee is disregarding and paying no attention to the message. The message is not considered by the consultee and the response which follows is constructed in a way which indicates this.

Reader Involvement Activity 7.1 is probably the most important exercise in this chapter. If the consultant is open to information, the consultee is encouraged to explore the problem so effective change can be planned. This point is being emphasized because some consultants put the responsibility for providing information on the consultee, not realizing that it is the consultant's responsibility to provide an environment *that is relaxing, thus facilitating the consultee to higher levels of trust and openness.*

The importance of the consultant developing the ability to approach situations in a trusting and relaxed state are by now obvious. During data gathering stage, the consultant must remain open to the information that is being presented. Fear and the accompanying defenses will block exploration and data generating and will cause the consultees to become closed and defensive. **Probably the most important factor in completing the initial step in the consultative process is a confident, trusting consultant.**

Functionally, trust opens the consultant to ideas, beliefs, feelings, experiences, and styles of thinking as presented. Trust allows uniqueness to be appreciated and individual perceptions to be accommodated. The trusting consultant has little difficulty applying effective leadership strategies. Trusting others, a prerequisite for the effective application of the Facilitative-Directive Process Model, is grounded in self **trust, openness** *to one's own experiences, self* **realization** *and feelings of* **interdependence**—*these are the conditions comprising TORI.*

The elements of the TORI process transfers to the consultee a developing self-awareness, acceptance of self and realization of personal uniqueness. And, interdependence with the consultant is precipitated. In this environment, objective understanding develops and direction evolves. When this occurs, the consultee is ready to plan an action program which will help construct the person or situation one has envisioned. Moving from the individual to a group perspective, a similar phenomenon occurs: as group members explore their collective behavior, they begin to understand themselves and the unique identity of their group. The group then begins to develop a consensus of what they would like to become. At this point they can identify an action plan which will enable them to achieve goals they have set for themselves.

ILLUSTRATIVE CASE STUDY
CONSULTING IN A BUSINESS CORPORATION

The case study of the C.C. Corporation (CCC), presented in this chapter illustrates the unfolding of the organizational consulting process. The CCC participants began by exploring their present functioning so they could understand it, and then they developed a plan for becoming something different. The account of consulting experiences with CCC that follows is presented developmentally as a first person story. This approach is used to help the reader identify with the changing feelings, perceptions, and reactions of the consultant as they occurred.

Case Study: Complete Care Corporation (CCC)

Mr. Smith, owner and manager of CCC, was aware of this writer's consulting activities and his involvement in the TORI Intern Program. Also, both the writer and Mr. Smith were active in American Society for Training and Development (ASTD). In a small group at a ASTD business meeting, Mr. Smith casually mentioned that he was thinking about hiring an organizational development specialist to do some consulting work for his company. At this point, I had no idea that Mr. Smith was interested in my consulting services. He had expressed his intent but I had not understood that he was directing it to me. I was surprised when Mr. Smith called several days later to inquire about securing consultative services concerning "personality problems" in the office. He wanted advice on what, if anything could be done to make his small company operate more effectively. Over the telephone he was very vague about his concerns and I was unable to get him to be more concrete about the "situation" to which he constantly referred. The telephone contact ended with an agreed upon time and place to meet to discuss his problem.

PLANNING FOR INITIAL CONTACT

In the initial contact it is common for the consultee to express vague concerns. The general idea is that something is wrong and something needs to be done about it. But the consultee does not have a clear understanding of the dynamics of the "situation." The initial contact is difficult for both the consultee and the consultant. The consultant recognizes the distress which the consultee is experiencing and wants to do something to relieve the problem. The novice consultant must guard against falling into the trap of being an "expert" with a quick diagnostic-prescriptive "fix" and offer a simple solution. To resolve fear and tension in this way is not effective.

A consultant is sometimes tempted to suggest ideas or training that the consultant has found effective in other seemingly similar situations. And, again this is usually not effective. By definition in the consultative relationship the problem belongs to the consultee therefore the resolution must reside with the consultee. The most appropriate approach is the consultant and consultee working together, using a process model, to determine an appropriate course of action for the consultee. *One of the most important goals of consultation is to leave the consultee with problem-solving and decision-making skills that they can apply to new problems.*

The recommended approach at this point is to open the discussion to gather information about the problem situation. The consultant naturally will need to be trusting and receive information as the consultee presents it. During the time the problem is being explored the skills of reflective listening and empathetic responding are most important. Using effective communication skills the consultant can (1) clarify so that correct information is received; (2) demonstrate caring through listening attentively and letting the consultee know what was heard by using restatements; (3) encourage the consultee to further explore the problem thus generating additional data with which to work; and (4) build a constructive relationship with the consultee.

READER INVOLVEMENT ACTIVITY 7.2: Preparation for the Meeting with Mr. Smith

> *1. How would you plan for the meeting with Mr. Smith?*

2. *What do you consider to be most important information that Mr. Smith has provided?*

3. *Now imagine yourself preparing to go to the meeting. Go through the entire process: What will you wear? What material will you take with you?*

> *Note: The most important consideration here is to establish a working relationship with Mr. Smith. Anything you can do to make yourself feel comfortable will be effective. You have been trained in empathetic responding and this is a powerful data gathering technique. You will use it extensively in your interview.*

DEVELOPING THE CONSULTANT-CONSULTEE CONTRACT

A contract needs to be developed so that assurance can be given that all have common expectations—consultant, consultee(s), and participants. To develop the contract will necessitate data gathering including interview with consultee(s).

The contract serves as a basis for determining at the end of the consultation whether or not goals were achieved. Consultant and consultee can use the contract in developing a plan of action for the consultation which will need to be shared with participants.

Consultant-Consultee Contact at CCC

Upon arriving at the appointed place Ms. Finch, Mr. Smith's secretary, recognized me as the individual who was "here for the ten o'clock meeting" and she quickly and politely ushered me into Mr. Smith's office. She, Ms. Finch, appeared to be a woman in her late thirties or early forties, was neatly dressed in a blue suit and contrasting blouse and presented herself as a person who had control of herself and the office procedures.

Mr. Smith was warm and greeted me enthusiastically with a hearty handshake. His office had once served as the living room of an affluent family home which is now part of the business district of the city. The room was attractively furnished but still looked somewhat like a living room being used as an office. It had an oversized desk at one end and a large table (probably used for conferences) at the other.

Mr. Smith motioned for me to sit in one of the fireside chairs and he took his seat in a chair opposite me. He asked if I wanted coffee or tea, and when I indicated that I did not he dismissed Ms. Finch. I felt warm and comfortable as our meeting was about to begin.

Mr. Smith talked eagerly and I listened intently. He became quite involved in the process of exploring the concern he had about his business. Briefly he shared the following information about himself and his company.

Mr. Smith began as an insurance salesman 24 years ago. About fifteen years later when he became a broker, Ms. Finch began working as his full-time secretary. Seven years ago, as an independent agent, Mr. Smith developed and began marketing a new health insurance program which was designed to compete (in service and cost) with the larger medical insurance carriers. The marketing of the program grew at a rapid pace and he found it necessary to hire additional staff members to assist him in marketing as well as support personnel for the new staff. Presently CCC is composed of eleven employees in addition to Mr. Smith.

Several months ago Mr. Smith purchased an older home which he has enthusiastically converted into an office building for the company. Most of Mr. Smith's recent efforts have gone into designing the type of office he wants and redesigning the building. Therefore, he has been leaving the marketing and development functions to Ms. Finch and five salesmen. Product development has been neglected in the expansion process and now Mr. Smith is concerned about the long-term effect of some of his choices. Presently he is searching for an associate to help him develop new products. Mr. Smith's present plans call for the development of an employee assistance plan and a preventative medical service which he believes will strengthen and supplement his health care program.

Mr. Smith expressed concern about the high employee turnover particularly with secretaries and shared an uneasiness about low morale. To him these problems seemed contradictory: he had had high expectations that the move to the new office would be a source of pride and new energy, but this has not happened. Instead he feels that he has lost control of what is happening with his employees and is not in touch with them personally. In Mr. Smith's words "Things just aren't the way they should be" and he wants them to be different. By "different" he specifically wants a cohesive close knit group who is enthusiastic and energetic about the product they are marketing. He believes the positive feelings of CCC Personnel will be translated into sales efforts and communication styles with clients or customers.

Organizing Data

In whatever fashion is reasonable the consultee presents data to the consultant. The consultant has the responsibility to validate, clarify, and summarize. By analyzing "themes" and expectations of the consultee, the consultant can begin to combine important data so the problem can be viewed from a more objective or different point.

This consultant was in a unique situation at this juncture because of the role expectation of the consultee. Services of the consultant were secured because the consultee thought the consultant had the ability to understand the problem. In this case, for example, Mr. Smith was focusing on problems and could not see the relationship between problems and his dream for the company. The consultant, being an outsider, was able to "hear" the direction the data themes suggested and help Mr. Smith make problem and goal statements. Mr. Smith was able to see the goal as a challenge that offered hope; whereas, these problems had been seen as barriers which drained energies through nonspecific attention.

A consultant facilitates a consultee's understanding by combining data elements and presenting these to the consultee in a summarizing statement. The consultee is then in a position to move to an understanding of the problem or to correct the consultant's summary, thus helping both the consultant and the consultee to better comprehend the problem and data.

READER INVOLVEMENT ACTIVITY 7.3: Understanding Data

Problem Presented

Goal Statement

> *1. Write problem statements in the left column. Use the data provided by Mr. Smith in the initial interview.*

2. *Write goal statements for each problem in the right hand column.*

3. *Now make a summary statement that combines the information in goal statement column. Make the summary statement one that the consultant can use in formulating a consultative agreement with Mr. Smith.*

The chart (Figure 7.4) that follows presents the data elements which Mr. Smith developed with the consultant. The goal statements were developed by the consultant and verified by Mr. Smith. Finally, a summary goal statement, combining the individual goal statements, was developed and expressed. Figure 7.4 displays the information that was generated during the initial consultative contact.

Problem Statement	Goal Statement
"develop new products"	want to develop new products
"develop employee assistant program"	
"high employee turnover"	want to attract employees and have them stay at CCC
"low morale"	want employees to feel like "family"
"lost control of what is happening with employees"	want to have more control over what is happening
"not in touch with his employees"	wants to be involved in a personal way
"wants (things) to be different"	wants to make some changes
"wants cohesive close knit group with enthusiasm"	wants employees to like being a part of CCC

Summary Goal:

You would like to have a closer working relationship with your employees and you want them to work with you to develop plans for your company.

Figure 7.4. Consultant-Consultee's problem analysis and goal statement for CCC.

Misunderstanding of Data

The consultant will sometimes combine data or respond inappropriately to data which the consultee has presented. However, when the consultant clearly presents the statement of understanding as shown in Figure 7.4, the consultee will correct the error. This happened in the consulting work with Mr. Smith.

Misunderstanding Data at CCC

At one point I thought Mr. Smith wanted me to assist him in developing an employee assistant program. I clearly stated the goal as I saw it at that point: *You would like me to assist you in developing an employee assistance program.* Mr. Smith indicated that this was not his intent and then proceeded to present additional data which lead to a clear statement of his intended goal. When the new data were combined into a summarizing statement that accurately reflected Mr. Smith's underlying desires, he quickly verified the stated goal: *You would like me to assist you in developing a closer working relationship with your employees so they can help you develop plans for your company.*

Action Plan

When the consultant and consultee have a clear statement of the goal which both accept, an action strategy can be developed. The consultant must be certain, however, that the consultee is ready to make a commitment to work on the action plan. The commitment is usually expressed as the consultee's acceptance and endorsement of the goal statement. Solid commitment results in enthusiasm for the potential outcomes of working together in the consultative process.

Even though the goals may seem clear to the consultant a "contract" is still needed to prevent any misunderstanding of either the content or process. The consultant will want to obtain either a verbal or written (usually preferred) agreement to work together on the problem. In an individual contact it may seem sensible and more expedient to use a verbal agreement, however, the agreement should be restated in a letter to the consultee. Data used to arrive at the goal statement should also be included in the letter.

Changing Consultant-Consultee Role at CCC

Mr. Smith accepted the goal statement as presented and clearly indicated that this was the area in which he wanted the consultant to work. Possible action strategies were explored and discussed. Individual interviews with CCC employees were considered but dismissed because Mr. Smith felt this would not produce the group cohesion which he wanted.

Other action strategies were likewise dismissed until a Group Development Strategy (GDS) seminar series was proposed. The Group Development Strategy appeared to be an efficient and effective method of working toward the stated objective and it was consistent with Mr. Smith's values. Mr. Smith needed to feel comfortable with the action plan because he more than anyone else knew the problem situation and the environment for which the intervention strategy was being planned. He could, therefore, evaluate the strategy and determine its potential effectiveness. Also his support for the process was the "critical element" in the eventual outcome.

In the individual contact Mr. Smith and I had moved through the consulting process of exploring and collecting data about the problem, combining data to develop an understanding of the problem, constructing a goal statement based on the understanding of the problem, and finally developing an action strategy based on the goal statement. At this point, individual consulting with the consultee terminated. The Facilitative Phase (Stages 1 through 3) of the Facilitative-Directive Process Model (Chapter 1) was applied in working with the consultee. The proposed group work will be initiated by beginning again at Stage one of the process model but will continue only if agreement is reached with the group to work together in a consultative relationship.

In moving from the individual work with Mr. Smith to the group approach whereby I would work with all employees, I made my role transition clear. Additionally, Mr. Smith accepted the concept that the group would *become the consultees*. Mr. Smith's role would change to the Initiator (see Chapter 1), and he would relinquish control of the process by giving control to the group. Because this working relationship was agreeable, I, as the consultant was ready to plan for the group's involvement.

Working with groups involves some additional problems which the consultant can anticipate. As with individuals, the development of trust within the group is important. When individuals comprising the group trust themselves, they will trust the consultant and the group. The group, therefore, can meet and solve problems as they develop. Initial activities that build trust are the suggested approach at this point.

READER INVOLVEMENT ACTIVITY 7.4: Planning Activities

1. *Think about the following questions:*

   - *What group activities would you like to use with CCC?*

   - *What are the objectives in using these activities?*

   - *What are some problems which you might anticipate?*

   - *How can you design your activities to avoid the problems?*

2. *To effectively plan a training program for a company is not easy even when you have the support of the owner, have small enough number of people (12) that you can do the training yourself, and have all company personnel involved. If you will recall Reader Involvement Activity 7.1, you clearly will understand a major concern and avoid increasing fear during your training program. Introduce the program and select your program activities to be incremental, thus avoiding overwhelming your group with high expectations which they might not be able to meet. Mr. Smith, your initiator, can be very helpful in judging the level of stress which each activity will cause in the group.*

3. *After designing your program, discuss it carefully and in detail with the Initiator.*

4. *Plan, modify, redesign, and restructure until you are both sure about and comfortable with the plan.*

Group Plan at CCC

After several meetings with Mr. Smith an intervention plan was developed and strategies were planned. During these meetings Mr. Smith was very helpful in selecting and developing activities. He was the expert on operations of his company and he was skilled at anticipating participants reactions when working through activities. His influence and suggestions are reflected in the planning decisions that were made.

First, the title of the training should clearly reflect the intent of the Initiator and the trainer. Honesty was to be one of our major goals. Employee involvement is easier to obtain if the GDS plan and goals are obvious to everyone. Hidden agendas are not appropriate. The title of the training and development series, "Build for Tomorrow—Dream and Plan," will clearly represent Mr. Smith's expectations.

Second, the decision was that terms used would be those with which people in the company were most familiar and not terms from psychology and counseling. We, therefore, called our group meetings Group Training seminars (GTS) rather than group counseling or some other psychological term. In a similar spirit we decided to refer to our program as "training." The term Quality Circles was used to describe the group because in industry the term implies a group which is formed to increase productivity and contain cost (Yeager, 1980, 1981, 1983).

Third, the final consideration was that the training should be fun. Mr. Smith wanted to develop the friendly good-natured camaraderie in the group. He felt that if we could develop a playful, harmonious relationship, we would tap the creative ability of each participant. The synergistic creativity of the group would develop a plan which would be accepted and implemented by CCC.

With these decisions made, an agenda was written for distribution at the first meeting of the group. The agenda was as explicit as possible as is illustrated in Figure 7.5.

MEETING 1—GETTING ACQUAINTED

Initial Contact with Group

At the first meeting of a group the consultant needs to share and explain a proposed agenda so participants (and the consultant) have a clear picture of what is expected. For group development openly address the

AGENDA
"BUILD FOR TOMORROW—DREAM AND PLAN"

DATE	ACTIVITY
JANUARY 4	GETTING ACQUAINTED
JANUARY 11	GATHERING INFORMATION: WANT-THINK-FEEL-DO
JANUARY 18	WRITING NEWSPAPER ARTICLE
JANUARY 25	STORYBOARDING FOR 2001 NEWSPAPER ARTICLE
FEBRUARY 1	PLANNING, IMPLEMENTATION, AND ACTION
MARCH 1	EVALUATING ACTION

Coffee and donuts will be available during breaks in the outer hallway area. Please finish before returning to the training area.

No smoking during training sessions. Please use outer hallway area for smoking.

Figure 7.5. Agenda used with CCC at initial group meeting.

purpose of group meetings and many smaller issues such as eating, smoking during meetings, attendance, promptness for training, and other behavior which might affect the group. Some issues should be resolved by group consensus; others may be decided on an individual basis because of health or some other critical reason. If a standard is set before the training begins, the decision should be presented and not discussed. If, for example, the decision not to smoke has been made, the rule should be stated or even included on the agenda as it was in Figure 7.5.

As the working rules are being developed with the group, various forms of resistance and ambivalence are to be expected. This is true for all groups and is identified as the consultees orientation at Stage 1 of the Facilitative-Directive Process Model. Resistance is usually a result of fearful expectations of the training, therefore the consultant needs to communicate clearly *goals* of the training and *methods* that will be used to reach those goals. Recognizing the participants' fear and communicating directly to the meaning of that fear are important.

For the group leader to communicate a respect for each participant during the initial meeting is a necessity. The trainer can demonstrate respect by being open, genuine, and honest with the group and responding without judgement to each individual. Selecting an activity or method that will enable the trainer to learn participants' names and connect some personal information with each name is an effective way to demonstrate respect.

During the initial meeting the consultant models the desired sharing behaviors, thus establishing group norms that encourage participation. The main goal of the first meeting is to obtain an agreement to participate in the training. The consultant also will begin gathering data about group participants and the organization. This should be communicated on the agenda.

The consultant also should model effective communication skills, verbal and nonverbal, throughout the groups' work time together. If the leader responds to information that is presented with acceptance, the group quickly will move into self-exploration by emulating the listening and responding attitudes of the consultant. If these behaviors are accepted as the norm in the orientation stage, the impact of the conflict stage of group development will be kept to a minimum and the group can reach the work stage in an efficient manner. This seems especially important when working with consultees from the business sector because of the value they place on production and the production measures they use for success.

First Meeting with CCC Group

Mr. Smith had scheduled the first group meeting with the company's personnel (including planning and marketing, secretarial, and janitorial) for Wednesday morning beginning at 9:30 a.m. and ending at noon. The group of eleven (or twelve counting Mr. Smith) was scheduled to meet for five consecutive Wednesdays with the follow-up meeting to take place one month later. The meeting was held in a large room on the third floor of the building. The furnishings included two large tables and two dozen chairs. No telephones were in the room and incoming calls were to be taken by an answering machine on the first floor.

When the group gathered, Mr. Smith introduced me briefly and then joined the group. First, I explained the purpose of the "training sessions" and goals which we would be working toward. I referred to several articles published in *Training and Development Journal, Personnel Development Journal, Personnel Administration,* and *Trust* (Gibb,

1978). All of these materials and other relevant information were placed on a table in the meeting room and participants were invited to browse and read them at their convenience.

At this point the Agenda was distributed (see Figure 7.5). An open discussion of the program, the role of the consultant, and expectation for participants were addressed. Questions were encouraged and answers were given honestly and genuinely.

Consistent with the first stage of the Facilitative-Directive Process Model being applied, the trainer's role was discussed briefly and goals for the group were stated. Relationship behaviors were reinforced by the trainer as the group discussed organization and procedures such as time, attendance, length of breaks, and availability of coffee and donuts. Interaction was encouraged and sufficient time was spent for the group to reach consensus about values of the group training and express understanding of the role of the trainer and goals of training.

A verbal agreement to work with the consultant on the topic and within the structure outlined was obtained. The group was informed that they had the option of attending training sessions or performing their usual work duties at CCC instead of training. They were given until the end of the mid-morning break to decide but once they had made the decision they were expected to participate for the entire program. Prior to the break, the following items were made clear to the group:

1. The goal of the training is to help the group develop into a cohesive working unit that encourages individuals to be active participants in decisions of the company.

2. Participants will be paid for attending but attendance is voluntary (with no coersion on any individual to remain) but returning for the second half of the first session signified an agreement to complete the training.

3. The consultant will function outside the CCC structural hierarchy; he will make no evaluation comments about any employee.

4. The consultant's expertise is not in the field of insurance but rather in his ability to assist organizations to explore and understand where they are and plan the direction in which they would like to develop.

5. The consultant is trained to listen and assist individuals and groups in expressing their ideas so that they can develop an action plan they can use.

6. The consultant will assist the group in their discovery process and will *not* offer answers or a "cure" for them to implement.

At this point the group was given a half-hour break during which coffee and donuts were served. The group was not too talkative and spent much of the time browsing and looking over the reading material that had been mentioned earlier. All members of the group returned promptly at the end of the break and seemed ready and eager to begin. This was interpreted as willingness to begin the training process.

Building a Working Relationship

When the group agrees to work with the consultant, the consultant is ready to begin the data gathering process. An activity which provides participants the opportunity to present themselves individually to the group (and the consultant) as they want to be seen by others is an effective method to begin the process of trusting and opening. The consultant will encourage this process by empathetically responding to each individual. Respect for the individual is effectively communicated when the consultant can connect names with faces and with important personal data about the individual. People tend to place considerable importance on their names, therefore it is very important that trainers identify names with faces as quickly as possible. The consultant's credibility increases dramatically with the group when "first name friendship" has been accomplished.

The beginning training activity also should provide the consultant an opportunity to model role expectations by accepting information from the group and placing responsibility for sharing information with the participants. As the group moves into the exploration process, sharing becomes very important. Consultees Activity 7.1 was designed to accomplish the twin goals of identifying names and modeling the consultant's expectation for the group.

CONSULTEES ACTIVITY 7.1: Getting Acquainted

1. *Have participants write their names and position with the company on 3x5 cards.*

2. *Give a brief (spontaneous) talk about the way individuals are viewed, and comment on each person's importance in the group. The talk presented below is a suggestion but it would not be appropriate to use it verbatim. The talk should communicate the leader's real feelings. Trusting oneself and opening to the group in the initial phase of the relationship is important to group development.*

> *"The world is a stage and your life is like a play. Each of you has a part in your play, like the once popular television show, the play could be called 'This is Your Life.' Add your name after the word life in the statement 'THIS IS YOUR LIFE. . . . . .'"*

> *"You know your life script well because you are the one who has been living and developing it for many years. You know your part and you are the star because it is your show. The other people in this room are the supporting cast to you in your starring role. The better we know your role the more effective we will be in our supportive roles with you. Today I would like you to write about your starring role and tell the group about your roles so we can work together in developing our parts."*

3. *Ask the participants to write phrases from their life scripts that they consider important.*

4. *Form dyads and try to pair individuals who do not know each other well. Structure the activity by giving your goal. "Get to know the person who is your partner. Get to know him/her so you can introduce your partner to the group." Partners can share as much of the information which they have developed as they choose.*

5. *After about ten minutes, interrupt the dyads and bring them back to the larger group. Now ask the group participants to introduce their partners to the group.*

6. Listen as each group member is introduced. The leader needs to note the name and what that person "wants," "thinks," "feels," and "does" for use later (see Consultees Activity 7.2 for the application of this idea). At the end of each introduction the leader needs to acknowledge the person introduced and the person who does the introduction but be especially careful not to use "That's good" as this is often interpreted as evaluation.

7. After everyone has been introduced, ask partners to get together again and this time each person tells one's partner a little more about oneself. Assign roles to partners: one is to be a listener, the other the talker. At the end of five minutes, interrupt the pair and change roles so that the talker becomes the listener.

8. Repeat 5 and 6.

The CCC group was somewhat reluctant to pair off for this activity, so they were placed into the dyads. There was a slight hesitation about introducing partners, but when they became involved in the activity they appeared to enjoy it. Most of the reporting in the first round involved names, high school, and factual data about the person.

When the dyads were formed a second time and when they were asked to report "a little more about their partners," reporters were able to provide the group with a more personal and complete introduction. The want-think-feel-do (see Consultees Activity 7.2) statements that were noted by the consultant during the introduction were used in acknowledging the introductions when possible. Most of these statements involved their activity at CCC and this was encouraged because that was to be the focus of the group's work.

The nonverbal and verbal behavior of the CCC group indicated that as they participated in the introductions they gained in their acceptance of their individual uniqueness (Trusting) and became more disclosing of themselves to others (Opening) as they became more familiar with the activity. From this the consultant inferred that goals for the session were achieved. Data were gathered, uniquenesses were recognized, and the consultative process was initiated. All members of the group agreed to continue working with the consultant.

What elements worked effectively to enhance the consultant's effectiveness during the session? Basically the consultant demonstrated respect for individuals and the group. The group was able to start the interactions and transactions of the group, describe the role of the consultant, and become involved in the process. Individually and collectively they agreed to work with the consultant for the specified length of time. They expressed optimism about and dedication to the task. Stage 2 of the Facilitative-Directive Process Model was completed with these agreements being reached.

READER INVOLVEMENT ACTIVITY 7.5: Testing Group Activity

Test the Group Activity you developed in Reader Involvement Activity 7.4. Did it increase participants' trust? Is it honest and does it clearly work toward your stated goal? Are your terms familiar to your intended audience? Does the activity reflect values of the group?

*The consultant needs to enter the group at the **level at which the group is operating.** Selecting an effective activity is important but what is probably more important is for the consultant to honor every member of the group and to assure that all contributions are valued equally.*

MEETING 2—GATHERING INFORMATION
WANT-THINK-FEEL-DO

Group Data Gathering

Data gathering activities that strengthen trust and further help foster the opening and disclosing process while moving toward realizing uniqueness and interdepending are appropriate at this point in the development of the group. The consultant can facilitate the process by accepting individuals and the group as they choose to present themselves. The skill of responding empathetically to the individual and about data as it is presented will be a positive factor in developing trust.

When the group is at the stage characterized by group identification, the individual is seen as unique and the group is viewed as special. From the group process perspective this is a very important stage because at this point work norms are established, data offered by the group are systematically reinforced and data are organized by the consultant. In terms of the consultative process, Stage 3 of the Facilitative-Directive model is being applied.

Activity 7.2 offers a procedure that helps a group generate data and relate personal information to the functioning of the group and the organization. These data are first separated into elements WANT-THINK-FEEL-DO and then these elements are combined in a later activity (Lazarus, 1976, 1981).

CONSULTEES ACTIVITY 7.2: WANT-THINK-FEEL-DO

1. *Divide the group into triads. For better interaction form triads using people who do not know each other well and/or have the least contact with each other in the work setting.*

2. *Designate members of each triad by letters A, B, and C to be used later to structure the sequence of talker, listener, and responder. Individuals will share information with their respective groups.*

3. *Present the concept of WANT-THINK-FEEL-DO, give examples, and structure the work time for triads. Begin with WANT statements.*

4. *Discuss WANTS (put "WANT" on Display Board or newsprint). Ideas that might be used in the presentation of the concept follow:*

   "WANTS are what we desire. Dreams, goals, aspiration and images are wants. Wants, dreams, and goals turn our attention and our energy in a direction. An illustration would be a motorist driving from New York to San Francisco. San Francisco is the goal! That is where the motorist wants to be. Other want examples one frequently hears are:
   > *I would like to be rich.*
   > *I think being independent is important.*
   > *I would like to have a new car.*
   > *I want to be a good salesman.*

I want to do what is expected in the group.
I want others to like me.
I want to get to know people in the office better.''

5. *Ask the triads to share individually their WANT statements with A talking, B listening, and C observing. Allow about 3 minutes for the talker and about 2 minutes for observer feedback.*

6. *Repeat Step 5 until all have taken a turn at talking.*

7. *Ask the triad to share wanting statements with the larger group.*

8. *Write on newsprint or display board want statements developed during Step 7.*

9. *Move to THINK statements. Discuss THINK as was done with WANTS. Display the word THINK on the board. Ideas that might be presented follow:*

"The THINKING process is our interpretation of data we receive. Thoughts we have about ourselves, others, and our external world are important to us and make us unique. Interpretation and different meanings are given to our experiences based on our thinking process.

People sometimes present thinking statements using the word **feeling***. I feel it is good to complete my assignments, is really a thinking statement and not a feeling statement. To change this to a feeling statement it could be restated as I feel good (about myself) when I complete my assignments. To use it as a thinking statement restate it as I think it is good to complete my assignments. Other examples are:*

I think I am learning something.
I think this is fun.
I think I can finish this today.
I think Sam is a nice person.
I think I am important.''

10. *Repeat Steps 5, 6, 7, and 8 for THINKING.*

11. *Ask the group to move to FEEL statements.*

12. *Discuss FEEL and display the word FEEL on the board. Ideas that might be presented follow:*

> *"Your FEELINGS are responses you make based on your interpretation (Thinking) and your expectations (Wants). They can be happy or sad, joyful or depressed, calm or confused, satisfied or uncomfortable, elated or angry, or any other emotion. Although your feelings are internal states, they all have external signs. You know the difference between when someone is happy or sad. Examples of feeling statements are*
>
>> *I am happy when I am with others.*
>> *I enjoy sports.*
>> *I feel great when I am with my friends.*
>> *I feel good about the group.*
>> *I feel uncomfortable doing these exercise steps of the activity.*
>> *I feel rushed."*

13. *Repeat Steps 5, 6, 7, and 8 for FEELING.*

14. *Ask the group to move to DO statements.*

15. *Discuss DO and display the word DO on the board. Ideas that might be presented to explain the concept of DO statements follow:*

> *"A DOING statement is an action which is sometimes expressed verbally but which quite often is expressed nonverbally. Examples of doing statements are*
>
>> *I run around a lot.*
>> *I sit doing nothing.*
>> *I scratch my head when I don't know the answer.*
>> *I talk alot in this group.*
>> *I drink too much coffee during breaks."*

Participants may want to help each other identify some personal DOING statements, both verbal and nonverbal DOING statements.

16. Repeat steps 5, 6, 7 and 8 for DOING statements.

17. At this point, help the group members make summary statements. Ask them to combine the information from the four elements to develop a personal goal statement. An example for each of the four elements is

I WANT (to be a better salesman and make more money.)

I FEEL (good about my work.)

I THINK (I am a good salesperson.)

I DO (work hard.)

A summary example of the above elements is

I think I am a good salesman, but I want to be even better so I can make more money and feel good about what I have done.

READER INVOLVEMENT ACTIVITY 7.6:
Data Gathering Using
WANT-THINK-FEEL-DO

1. Think about yourself and answer these questions:

What do you WANT?
What do you THINK?
How do you FEEL?
What do you DO?

2. Form dyads and ask partners to share your ideas with another person. Try to respond to these four parts of your partner.

3. *After 10 minutes, ask each dyad to consider the following:*

   a. *Did you enjoy talking with your partners?*
   b. *Did your partner enjoy talking with you?*

4. *Ask each dyad to write a summary statement that integrates the information from the four elements.*

5. *Have dyads to share summary statements with the group.*

WANT-THINK-FEEL-DO Development with CCC Group

The CCC group moved into Consultees Activity 7.2 enthusiastically. From the agenda (see Figure 7.5) they understood that this was a technique for gathering information about individual participants and that the information would be used to develop a portrait of the CCC group at the January 18th meeting. Interestingly, the initial WANT statements reflected company wants and gave very few cues about individual and personal wants. Two example statements that were used illustrate this point:

1. I want CCC to become a large company.
2. I want Mr. Smith to be happy with my work.

By using these statements and helping personalize them during the discussion of the activity, the consultees began to generate statements of personal wants. Thus "I want CCC to become a large company," because "I want to work in a large company." And, "I want Mr. Smith to be happy with my work" becomes "I want to do my work the way Mr. Smith wants it done."

This activity provided the group with a way of gathering data about themselves in their work setting so they could better understand themselves. This process strengthened individuals' trust to the group. In the process of making personal statements about themselves the individuals began to discover and realize what they WANT-THINK-FEEL-DO.

At this point the consultant has introduced the group to their responsibility for presenting information and through this experience they have learned that their ideas will be accepted as valid and important.

Thus norms for the group have been established to include high-trust, high-participation, and openness. Developmentally the group has moved into the "Work" stage in which relationships are relaxed and interdependent. A very important point is for the consultant to continue to nurture these attitudes.

MEETING 3—WRITING NEWSPAPER ARTICLE

Feature Article

Consultees Activity 7.3 moves the group from the individual perspective to the group perspective. In this activity participants describe the company in terms of WANT-THINK-FEEL-DO statements and use these elements to express the way the company presently functions. The procedure requires individuals to combine ideas and function as a group as they collaborate to write an article that will tell the public about the company: what they want, what they think, what they feel, and what they do. Experience has shown that the group is likely to use this activity to write about how they would like others to see them rather than depict the organization as it presently functions. If this occurs, the consultant should accept the "article" as valid and use the information to help the group move in the direction of the goals they set for themselves as this is the next step in the consultative process.

CONSULTEES ACTIVITY 7.3: Feature Article

> *1. Present the following idea:*
>
> > *Today we will develop a verbal portrait of our company—what we WANT-THINK-FEEL-DO. We will do this by writing a feature article that tells others about us. We can use the information we generated during the last session to write this article. First we will work as a group, then we will work individually.*
>
> *2. Review WANT-THINK-FEEL-DO statements developed by the group that referred to the organization. Relate organizational needs to personal needs.*

3. Have the group list consensus statements on the board that relate to the four elements: *WANT-THINK-FEEL-DO*. Leave displayed throughout the session.

4. Assign *"Feature Article."* Each person writes an article. Read the following instructions (In most cases these instructions should also be written and distributed.):

Instructions: Pretend you are writing a feature article...

In writing your article feel free to use any method you want to present your wants, thoughts, feelings, and doing statements.

These wants, thoughts, feelings, and doing statements may be consistent with the group as a whole or may be unique and personal. (It helps to use the name of the group, or if the group does not have an identity, you may want to develop one before beginning the activity.) Write a catchy title. Present your ideas in any way you choose. Consider illustrating your work with drawings, pictures, cartoons from other sources, and funny paper cutouts. Use anything you choose to present your group effectively to someone who has no knowledge of you and your work. You will have thirty minutes to work.

5. After thirty minutes, reconvene into a large group. All members share their articles. Debrief the exercise by reviewing and summarizing the important points that were presented.

6. After a break, reconvene into small work groups. This time the work groups will each write a feature article that will reflect the thinking of the group.

7. After work groups report, have the group as a whole to develop an article. If time is a factor, a representative, chosen by the group may collect the work group reports and write an article for the group.

8. If possible, have the article distributed to the group so they will have time to look at it before the next meeting.

READER INVOLVEMENT ACTIVITY 7.7: Your Newspaper Article

1. *Write a newspaper article about yourself, building on what you have said about yourself in Reader Involvement Activity 7.6. Try to describe yourself where you are now. Sell yourself by describing your assets. Give the article a catchy title.*

2. *Allow some time to pass. Choose a time when you feel really good about yourself and rewrite the article. This time really emphasize your strengths.*

3. *Next, shorten the article as much as possible to prepare it for publication. (If you don't shorten it, the editor will and it may not say what you want it to say!)*

4. *Share your article with someone else. Ask for their reaction.*

Newspaper Article Development by CCC Group

The CCC group decided to tell their story so that it could be used as a photo feature in the magazine and television section of the Sunday paper. One group spent considerable time planning the photo layout, captions, title, and story. An abbreviated version is included as Figure 7.6.

Figure 7.6 Feature article written by CCC group.

The article written by the CCC group offers both powerful pictorial messages and verbal messages.

READER INVOLVEMENT ACTIVITY 7.8: Critiquing Newspaper Article

1. *Critique the CCC News Release which is given in Figure 7.6 by including the following questions:*

   What verbal messages are included?
   What nonverbal messages are there?
   How does the company operate?
   What changes would I implement if this were my company?

2. *Compare your critique with what was obtained in the actual situation which is as follows:*

The verbal messages are that the company has a new address, they want you to visit them, they have several divisions which Mr. Smith directs, and they want to visit you and plan your insurance needs. The nonverbal messages show that information and decisions follow administrative lines of responsibility and then they are presented to the staff.

The article shows the power of Ms. Finch. She has been Mr. Smith's secretary for many years and in many ways the company is still operating on that model. The company is divided: Smith and Finch are seen as the company and everyone else is seen as workers. The group illustrated this both verbally and nonverbally and rather surprisingly the group accepted the portrait as an accurate representation of the way the office operates.

By remaining emotionally detached from the decisions of the consultees, the consultant can assist the group in the process of presenting operational procedures so the group can gain a larger, more objective picture of what is happening and thus move toward understanding it better. Once understanding is achieved the group is ready to design operational procedures which will meet more effectively needs and goals of their organization of the employee group and individual employees. Although the overall consulting goal sounds somewhat overwhelming, it is really simple if one focuses on group strength.

By empathically responding to participants and providing a system designed to assist individuals in presenting themselves to the group i.e., WANT-THINK-FEEL-DO, the consultant has encouraged participation and valued the uniqueness of participants. The group has systematically combined the individual perspectives into a larger picture that portrays the company as it now functions. A deeper understanding of the organization has been achieved in this way. A summary of this (see Figure 7.6) is presented to the group so they can evaluate it.

GROWING FOR YOU
THE STORY
OF THE
COMPLETE CARE CORPORATION

MR. SMITH AT HIS NEW
OFFICE AT 2 PARK AVENUE.

THE COMPLETE CARE CORPORATION IN THEIR NEW LOCATION AT 2 PARK AVENUE IS AWARE OF YOUR INSURANCE NEEDS AND IS DEVELOPING TO MEET THESE NEEDS. MR. SMITH HAS DESIGNED THE NEW OFFICES TO REFLECT THE COMPANY'S GOAL-INSURANCE FOR THE PEOPLE.

THE SECRETARIAL STAFF &
MS. FINCH IN THEIR NEW
OFFICE.

MR. SMITH & MS. FINCH
DISCUSS NEW OFFICE
PROCEDURES FOR IMPROVED
CUSTOMER SERVICE.

THE MARKETING, DEVELOPMENT, AND SALES STAFF IS WORKING WITH MR. SMITH IN PLANNING EXPANSION IN ACCORD WITH GROWING NEEDS OF THE AREA AND IS IN THE PROCESS OF VISITING AREA BUSINESSES TO EXPLORE THEIR PROGRAMS AND IDENTIFY EXPANSION PLANS AND GOALS.

MS. SMITH MEETS WITH
MARKETING STAFF TO DIS-
CUSS DEVELOPMENT.

MS. FINCH DISCUSSES
OFFICE PROCEDURE WITH
THE OFFICE STAFF.

THE SECRETARIAL STAFF IS HEADED BY MS. FINCH WHO SUPERVISES THE OFFICE AND ASSURES THAT ALL INSURANCE PROCESSING IS HANDLED EFFICIENTLY AND QUICKLY.

JIM BROWN FROM THE MARKET
& DEVELOPMENT DIVISION
WITH MR. BROWN WHO IS
PRESIDENT OF ELECTRICAL
PROCESS COMPANY.

ON SUNDAY

FROM 1:00 PM TO 4:00 PM

COMPLETE CARE CORPORATION

WILL HOST AN OPEN HOUSE & TOUR

OF THEIR NEW OFFICE BUILDING.

PLEASE VISIT THEM.

THE
COMPLETE CARE CORPORATION
AT THEIR NEW HEADQUARTERS.

Figure 7.6. Feature article written by CCC group.

At this point the consultative process has moved the group from a collection of individuals to a synergetic group who are combining and in some ways minimizing individual needs as a group identity develops. Focusing on the task of combining ideas captures the essence of the group and produces a group which lives and works well together.

Obstacles for the Consultant

Remember that some individuals may not be ready to make this shift to a group identity. In moving toward a group identity some people fear that they will lose their individual identity. Holding this assumption inhibits the individual from spontaneous participation in group activities.

Another problem may begin to develop at this point. Activities which the consultant has been using with the group facilitate self-exploration and self-understanding (Egan, 1982) in individual participants. Individuals will occasionally become preoccupied with the individual process and will, therefore, not be ready for full participation in the group. This happened with the CCC group and presented the consultant with a dilemma.

Consultant's Dilemma at CCC

At the break during the third training session Ms. Finch asked if she could talk with me individually about something that was important to her. I gave her my card and told her to call to make arrangements. She called the next day and an appointment was scheduled.

During the individual contact she expressed concerns about her personal life and a general dissatisfaction with herself and her situation. Additionally, she said she began working for Mr. Smith when she was seventeen and had enjoyed her work very much from the beginning. When she was 21, she married but the marriage did not work as she had hoped. She has been divorced for three years. She has one daughter, 11 years of age, who lives with her.

Her time is spent at work, with her daughter, and at several singles bars where she has met a lot of people but no one who is really interesting. She indicated a "slight" concern with her drinking. She expressed a "frustration with life" combined with an inability to do anything to improve her situation. Weekends were especially difficult with the drinking because she was lonely and bored.

Ms. Finch indicated she would like to be more than a "secretary" and would like to "improve herself." She enjoys her work but would like to have more responsibility. She wanted some suggestions and perhaps assurance from the consultant.

READER INVOLVEMENT ACTIVITY 7.9: Consultant's Relationship

> *1. Before reading Step 2, try answering the following questions:*
>
> > *What would you do with Ms. Finch?*
> > *Would you schedule her for individual counseling?*
> > *What type of treatment do you think she needs?*
> > *Should the consultant become a counselor?*
>
> *2. After answering questions in Step 1, review what occurred in the actual situation.*

Given the concerns of Ms. Finch, counseling seemed suggested. As a consultant for CCC, I felt it would not be appropriate for me to work with Ms. Finch as a counselor.

Combining the consulting and counseling role is confusing to the consultant and also confusing to those with whom the consultant is interacting. A consultant can develop easily a vested interest in decisions a consultee makes when several different relationships are involved. The consultant's role does involve helping but to simultaneously relate to the group as a consultant and an individual group member as a counselor is not professionally sound and in practice if done will place the consultant in a position of conflict of interests. In the case of Ms. Finch, the consulting relationship had precipitated an environment where she had identified a peripheral problem, but the consultative relationship had to be maintained; therefore, referral was the chosen procedure.

MEETING 4—STORYBOARDING FOR 2001
NEWSPAPER ARTICLE

Futures Building

The CCC group understands and accepts where they are from the process which they have now completed. Based on this understanding they are prepared to begin the process of planning to become something different. The consultant's role is to assist the group in forming their ideas of the future based on data they have presented. Creating an image of the place they would like to go (goal) is the first step in this process.

The group must have an idea of what they want to become so they can progress toward the action stage in the consultative process. With the CCC group the consultant has orchestrated a process that has enabled them to see more clearly where they are and they understand this objectively. But without a plan for the future they lack direction.

To use the analogy of the orchestra, the consultant combines individual strengths and uniqueness (instruments) to develop harmonious melody. The consultant-conductor does not play the oboe but instead encourages performers who are playing that instrument to sound their notes clearly and loudly so all can hear and appreciate the unique contributions which they make to the music. In a similar fashion the consultant helps the group understand how their individual uniqueness blends, harmonizes, and produces what each is working toward in their individual way.

Unfortunately at this point some consultants begin to identify with the performing rather than the conducting role. They try to play all of the instruments; they rush around blowing a horn, fiddling, plucking a string, and beating a drum. They wear themselves out and anger others with their impetuous enthusiasm. And when they leave, everything (and everyone) returns to the way things were before because participants have not been trained to combine efforts in a directed way.

In order to guide the group in developing their own ideas, the Storyboard technique (Consultees Activity 7.4) was used to generate ideas creatively which could be used to create an image for the future (Grossman, 1984).

CONSULTEES ACTIVITY 7.4: Storyboard

1. *Obtain a large corkboard, a stack of 3 x 5 cards for statements, and tacks, all of which will be needed to create the storyboard. Everything must be movable and changeable so the leader can reflect accurately the flow of the group's ideas.*

2. *Use a procedure in developing the group's statements which is similar to that used in Consultees Activities 7.2 and 7.3 except in this 7.4 Activity the group is dealing with what they would like to "BECOME." Again the title of the story should receive careful attention. Do not rush this activity. Play with the idea. As related statements are proposed, try to synthesize information and use subheadings to include all aspects of a statement and to generate new ideas. Ask each person to write his/her own statement so the consultant can place it under the appropriate category.*

3. *Put each statement on a separate card. Generate as many statements as possible. Strive for quantity not quality. Do not evaluate.*

4. *When the storyboard is completed and the group has no additional ideas, distribute a supply of stick-on-dots to everyone to use in "voting." (Seals, stars, or almost anything could be used, but dots all the same color seem to work best.) Have each participant put a dot on statements they like. Individuals may vote for any card; it does not have to be their idea and they can vote for as many ideas as they like.*

5. *Rearrange the storyboard asking the group's permission before discarding any ideas. The group may want to generate creatively new ideas by building on a card—encourage this.*

6. *If appropriate, assign individuals or sub-groups to work on refining ideas.*

7. *If time permits, divide into work groups to begin clarifying, developing, and refining idea statements which will be used.*

8. *As a follow-up, reproduce the storyboard content and distribute it to participants before the next meeting.*

The goal for this step in the consulting process is to help the group generate ideas for a plan that they can put into operation to achieve the image. The storyboarding technique selected for this activity has two advantages. First it is fluid-changeable-developing. It can change and go in any direction the group chooses. Because the cards are only pinned to the wall (or board), they can be moved easily or discarded totally. Nothing is fixed and nothing is permanent. Changes are constantly made with new ideas being built on those stated previously and with those ideas serving as a catalyst for new ideas.

Second, this technique has the advantage that by its design information used comes from the group. The consultant's role here is pinning and not judging. The consultant develops and sustains the creative spirit of the group so they can generate and record their ideas. The storyboard is created in an hour or so and it is unique and different every time it is created. It is a powerful technique and the potency of this process can only be appreciated after it has been tried.

Storyboarding at CCC

An abbreviated storyboard produced by CCC is included as Figure 7.7. Notice how the ideas are developed. Although an idea might not have been accepted on the first voting it often was used by another individual to build a new idea. The group was energetic and creative on this activity and they generated ideas quickly. The consultant took their ideas which they had presented and pinned them on the board according to their direction.

The idea of voting was enthusiastically accepted. The group rearranged, discarded, and modified their storyboard until they were satisfied with it. Group consensus was achieved quickly and the activity ended with a cohesive working group. The group was now ready to write scenarios that project their future.

Scenario writing, which is the writing of a proposed series of events which one imagines as a possibility for the future, has become quite popular (Brubaker, 1978). The company or consultee has a future. The doomsday scenario would have the company bankrupt and no longer in existence. Of course this is possible and unfortunately some organizations operate as though this was their scenario for the future.

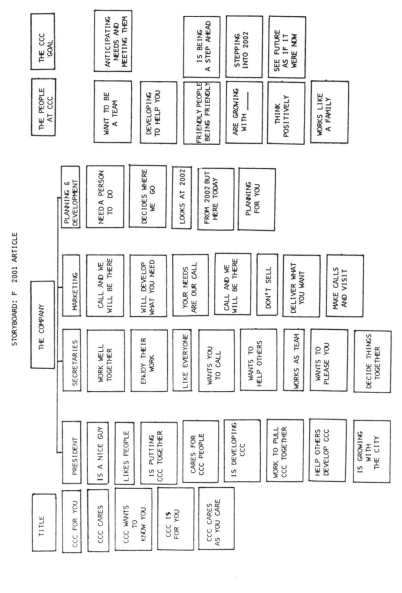

Figure 7.7 CCC Storyboard for 2002 article.

The traditionalist scenario would have the consultee survive with no changes. The company in the future would be identical to the company today. Concentrated energy is often used to perpetuate this idea. Organizations often have well developed groups who are committed to developing this scenario. Examples include Labor unions, faculty committees, bureaucratic policies, licensure laws, and professional membership. These can be used to block change and provide a sanctuary for the frightened. Unfortunately, such groups suffer the disease of all who are fearful—distortion and denial.

In creative scenario writing the assumption is that the future will be different. Although the consultant and the consultee have no way of knowing what tomorrow holds, a plan can be developed. By clearly imagining a future the consultee can develop expectations and a plan to use to guide the company toward the future. Writing a future Scenario is really an expansion of the wishing process and the consultee is now very familiar with this concept.

2001 Newspaper Article Developed by CCC Group

The 2001 Newspaper Article was written by the CCC group to concretely develop the ideas generated in the storyboard. The group moved from idea generation to idea development, from divergent thinking to convergent thinking. The need to move to a task-oriented activity where a concrete product is produced is important in moving toward an action plan.

The CCC group moved quickly into this activity. They decided quickly that they did not want to use "2001" which I had suggested, but preferred to plan for "2002" instead. The idea seemed to have the support in the group. Why? That was "what they wanted."

Now, with the group in control they quickly developed ideas from those shown on the storyboard. Ideas came quickly with spirited participation from everyone in the group. An abbreviated version of the future article is given in Figure 7.8.

READER INVOLVEMENT ACTIVITY 7.10: Comparing Now With Future

1. Compare Figure 7.8 with Figure 7.6.

2. What differences do you see?

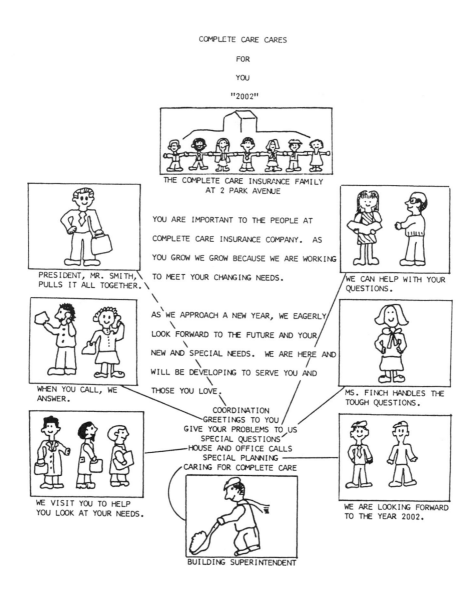

Figure 7.8 Future scenario developed by CCC group.

In this case the consultant has assisted the CCC group in construct-ing a portrait of the organization which represents the company as the group wants it to be. The plan is based on an understanding developed in the consulting process but the plan is concrete and definite. The image is clearly communicated and defined.

MEETING 5—PLANNING, IMPLEMENTATION, AND ACTION

Consultants may sometimes be divided into two groups: the consul-tant who enjoys the process of exploring to better understand the con-sultee and the consultant who enjoys planning action with the consultee. The effective consultant knows that action can not be planned if an understanding has not been developed. Also the consultant recognizes and hopefully participants realize that an action plan is necessary if con-structive change is to take place.

With the completion of the futures article the CCC group was ready for a plan of action with commitments to complete the steps necessary to finish the plan. At this point the consultant wants written plans which in-clude each step needed to achieve the goal and an individual identified and committed to complete each identified goal.

To accomplish the written plan, Consultees Activity 7.5, was used.

CONSULTEES ACTIVITY 7.5: Planning Action—Individual and Group

> *1. Distribute two copies of the contract forms (see Figure 7.9).*
>
> *2. State the overall goal, i.e., what the group wants to become.*
>
> *3. List activities the group (individually and collectively) must do to achieve their goal.*
>
> *4. Now list activities that they must do to achieve the goals listed in a second column.*

5. *Examine each goal and activity in terms of resources which will be needed to complete it: time, money, skills, and cooperation from others. Include these needed resources under comments.*

6. *Have individuals who will be taking responsibility to write the "to become goal" on their Contract Sheet and indicate the action for which they will take responsibility in the "activity to complete" column.*

7. *If it seems appropriate, go through the resources needed for each activity with each individual or with work groups.*

8. *Have the individual commit to the action by completing the "date to be completed" column.*

9. *Have each individual complete two copies of the Contract: one should be returned to the consultant and the other should be retained by the individual as a worksheet.*

A sample of action plans developed by CCC is included as Figure 7.9. An individual contract format was used, and the plan was signed. The form also allowed the individual to enter dates actions were completed. If more than one person was responsible, the action was included on each person's Contract. For example, five people were responsible for completing 5 x 7 data cards for clients therefore this action was included on five Contracts. The date to be completed and the date completed may be (and was) different on all contracts.

MEETING 6—EVALUATING ACTION PLAN

The final and follow-up activity, that of evaluating the action plan, is very important. Accountability procedures require that after an individual (or group) is committed to a goal, a supervisor has the management responsibility of assessing the individual and supervising the progress toward accomplishing the goal. This procedure is referred to as management by objectives and is effective only if the individual's work is assessed.

ABBREVIATED CONTRACTS

To Become Goal	Activity to Complete	Comments	Date to be Completed	Date completed
To involve employees in appropriate decision making and seek information from them	Weekly meetings with agendas		Begin February 1	February 1
	Open door policy when door is open, employees welcome to stop and talk		February 1	February 1
To share insurance expertise with office personnel	Secretary assigned to handle all special areas of insurance		January 28	January 28
To express friendly personal greetings on all client calls	Personal data about client on 5 x 7 cards	Completed by all sales and marketing personnel	February 15	February 20

Figure 7.9. Action plan for CCC group.

The final interview also is very important for the consultant. It provides an opportunity to test the effect the intervention strategy has had. In some cases, it may be necessary to do additional consulting or to develop a new plan. The consultant should carefully evaluate the change in the consultee using these goals (or objectives) which were agreed upon during the initial contact.

READER INVOLVEMENT ACTIVITY 7.11: Completing Goals

> *1. Reread goals which were developed during the initial individual interview with Mr. Smith.*
>
> *2. Answer the following questions:*
>
>> *Have the initial goals been completed?*
>> *Have you established a personal goal for yourself?*
>> *At what stage are you in completing it?*

Final Meeting With CCC Group

The CCC group was cheerful and eager to discuss the progress which they had made since we last met as a group. With group support, Mr. Smith had hired a full time employee for planning and product development. This individual also was made responsible for coordinating employee input. In reality, the consulting function was now the responsibility of this CCC employee.

The 2002 Story which was developed (and presented as Figure 7.9) was revised several times and in the modified form was used as a paid advertisement in the Sunday paper. New advertisements using a graphic technique developed by the group were being planned.

The consultant's contractual agreement had been completed and a final meeting designed to evaluate the progress which the consultee had made concluded the consultation. During the meeting the consultant mentally compared the consultee's present functioning behavior with the behavior when consulting was initiated to determine the effect of the intervention strategies. In addition, the consultant evaluated the consulting services provided to improve consulting skills.

EVALUATING CONSULTING PROCESS

At the conclusion of consulting an important procedure is for the consultant to evaluate carefully the effect of the interventions made. Kirkpatrick (1983) suggested four areas to consider: "Reaction, learning behavior, and results" (p. 19). It will probably be helpful to evaluate the consulting with CCC using these criteria.

What was the reaction of the consultee to the consulting? CCC was so pleased with the training program that they hired a full time employee to continue the program. A review of the case will reveal other examples of satisfaction.

What attitude change and learning were achieved during the consulting? The learning at CCC is concretely demonstrated by noting the changes which have taken place. CCC has a plan for the future and they are working toward that future as a cohesive group. This is in contrast to the fragmented, uncoordinated individual efforts which were present when consulting began.

What behavior changes took place as a result of the consulting? The behavioral changes as planned were completed (as illustrated in Figure 7.9).

What were the results of the consulting? This is a very important but difficult question to answer. Is productivity increased? Is the quality of the work relationship improved? Is there a reduction in cost combined with an improvement in employee morale? Questions such as these should be asked to effectively answer the question.

The consultee can be very helpful in evaluating effects of the consultant's intervention. Mr. Smith answered questions such as those posed above and was pleased that the consultant had taken the time to ask them. A satisfied client is therefore developed through careful evaluation.

Other evaluation methods also could be used appropriately but the important factor is the consultant must evaluate the consulting. The evaluation method is less important than an honest desire on the part of the consultant to effectively evaluate (and improve the quality) of consulting services.

PLANNING TO ENTER ORGANIZATIONAL CONSULTING

The service provider who is interested in working as a consultant in industry may be looking for skills which can be used to enter this professional field. Several suggestions will be given to assist the interested reader in making the transition from a student of consulting to an industrial consultant.

Become familiar with the literature in the field. The ASTD Press distributes and publishes books and materials which they consider the most significant books available for the human resource development professional. One may write for a copy of current listings. The pamphlet *Careers in Training and Development* which is available from the America Society for Training and Development will be especially helpful to the entering professional. Dipado and Patterson (1983) discussed training for becoming a trainer.

The entering professional person also will need to become familiar with training practices used in government and industry. Ferrara (1983) discussed the use of the quality of work project at Fairchild Industries and LaVan, Mathys, and Drehmer (1983) looked at the career counseling practices of major corporations.

Become professionally associated with one of the organizations interested in the consultation area. Read their publications and attend their meetings. Local chapters of these organizations are located in major cities and they usually meet monthly. A regional (several states) and a national meeting usually are held annually. The two major professional organizations are

> American Society for Training and Development
> 600 Maryland Avenue S.W.
> Suite 305
> Washington, D.C. 20024

> American Society for Personnel Administration
> 30 Park Drive
> Berea, Ohio 44017

BIBLIOGRAPHY

Brubaker, J. (1978). Future consultation: Designing desirable futures. *The Personnel and Guidance Journal, 56,* 428-431.

DiPaolo, A. J., & Patterson, A. G. (1983). Selecting a training program for new trainers. *Training and Development Journal, 37,* 96-101.

Egan, G. (1982). *The skilled helper.* Monterey, CA: Brooks/Cole.

Ferguson, M. (1980). *The aquarian conspiracy.* Los Angeles, CA: J. P. Tarcher.

Ferrara, J. V. (1983). Fairchild's OWL program improves performance. *Personnel Administrator, 29,* 64-67.

Gibb, J. R. (1978). *Trust: A new view of personal and organizational development.* Los Angeles, CA: Guild of Tutors Press.

Grossman, S. R. (1984). Brainstorming updated. *Training and Development Journal, 38,* 84-87.

Hansen, G. B. (1984). Professional education for careers in human resource administration. *Personnel Administrator, 29,* 69-96.

Kirkpatrick, P., & Donald, L. (1983). Four steps to measuring training effectiveness. *Personnel Administrator, 28,* 19-25.

LaVan, H., Mathys, N., & Drehmer, D. (1983). A look at the counseling practices of major U.S. corporations. *Personnel Administrator, 28,* 76-81.

Lazarus, A. A. (1976). *Multi-modal behavior therapy.* New York: McGraw-Hill.

Lazarus, A. A. (1981). *The practice of multi-modal therapy.* New York: McGraw-Hill.

Smith, R. L. (1983). The development of Human Resources: HRD as a growing field. *Caps Capsule, 4,* 2-5.

Terry, G. R., & Franklin, S. G. (1982). *Principles of management.* Homewood, IL: Richard D. Irving.

Yeager, E. G. (1980). Quality Circle: A tool for the 80s. *Training and Development Journal, 35,* 60-62.

Yeager, E. G. (1981). The quality control circle explosion. *Training and Development Journal, 35,* 98-105.

Yeager, E. G. (1983). *Careers in training and development.* Washington, DC: American Society for Training and Development.

CHAPTER 8

CONSULTANT: THE PRACTITIONER

Jonell H. Kirby, Ed.D.

CONSULTANT: THE PRACTITIONER

Jonell H. Kirby, Ed.D.

This chapter focuses on the practitioner—the person who implements the consultative role—and contains suggestions for training. Consultation may be performed within or outside the context of one's place of employment. In either case, the personal characteristics and the professional competencies of the practitioner will weigh more heavily and influence the outcomes of the consultative contact than the model(s) or strategies used. In other words, successful practitioners may vary greatly in their ways of *thinking* about the consultative process, but they inevitably approach the consultative relationship with *objectivity, confident* in their ability to bring about needed and desired changes, and self-assuredly armed with a *repertoire of techniques* that can be appropriately applied to facilitate movement in the desired direction. Unsuccessful practitioners, on the other hand, may lack objectivity and get embroiled in the emotional reactions and behavioral responses of their consultees, or they may not have the self-confidence needed to intervene in a decisive and convincing fashion, or they may simply be unsuccessful in applying an appropriate technique because their response repertoire is barren.

The practice of consultation and the training of a consultant involve three separate, albeit related, component parts. These are

1. *Affection*—the way the consultant *feels* about the role of consultation and the issues being addressed;

2. *Cognition*—the way the consultant *thinks* about the dynamics of the interactions and the process while consultation is being experienced and later upon reflection; and

3. *Reaction*—the personal and professional *behavior* the consultant displays in the interactive process.

These three components can be used to examine the personal characteristics of the practitioner. They also might be used to articulate training competencies, or to identify those professional competencies that closely align with the practice of consultation. In Figure 8.1 are displayed these three elements and specifics regarding major competencies that make up each element.

THE SELF OF THE PRACTITIONER

Regardless of professional training or identity, a professional practitioner is first a person. As is true for all professional and personal/social role functions, a consultant brings one's own history and experience,

1. Affection

    a. Displays objectivity—separates personal needs from the diagnosis of the consultee's needs and system of interaction.
    b. Accepts and has feeling for uniqueness of self and others.
    c. Cares about and has empathy for feelings of consultee.
    d. Feels good about own values and "owns" personal feelings.
    e. Emotionally able to hear and respond appropriately to criticisms and confrontations of consultees.

2. Cognition

    a. Thinks about the dynamics of the interaction between consultant and consultee(s) and among participants as relevant to the consultative process.
    b. Explains individual behavior and group dynamics in conceptual terms using models and theoretical constructs.
    c. Identifies themes and underlying messages in verbal and interactional messages.
    d. Understands relationship between group process development and task completion.
    e. Predicts impact of intervention strategies on goal-seeking behavior.

3. Action

    a. Listens attentively and actively; hears the message of the individual and group and responds appropriately.
    b. Applies intervention strategies that are congruent with the consultative model being implemented.
    c. Uses relationship needs of individuals and group to facilitate task resolution.
    d. Makes consultees' reference point the focus for explanations, changes, and motivations.
    e. Responds to changes in the consultative process and shifts in individual/group interactions.

Figure 8.1 Components of consultative practice and training.

beliefs and values, knowledge and thoughts, and interpretations of these to the consultative situation. The practitioner, then, not only is dealing with the perceptions of the consultee, but also is dealing with the very real perceptions he/she brings to the consultative relationship.

The viewpoint or personal perspective of the consultant can enhance or retard goal-seeking efforts of the consultee. A consultant's perspective can be a problem, of course, inasmuch as one may not be sensitive to one's own bias and prejudices: one may not know one has lost objectivity and become immersed in issues and dynamics of the process, and one may not recognize that one is dealing with one's own unresolved problems as a part of issues presented by the consultee.

In spite of potential problems, the very human characteristics of *identity* and *caring* can have a positive effect when they help bridge the gap between "me" to "you" (i.e., from "expert" to "novice"), and become "us;" when they help identify feelings represented in verbal and nonverbal messages, and when enough common experience exists that similarity is communicated and commonality is experienced.

A consultant as a professional helper is expected to possess the requisite attitudes for helping. Positive regard and appreciation for individual uniqueness (for self and others) are cornerstones upon which successful consultation is built. This posture of acceptance and openness can be expressed as skill statements; therefore, the behavioral manifestations can be learned and systematically taught.

Consultation is appropriately implemented by those whose philosophical bent might be identified as humanistic. Humanists are concerned about others in an objective but caring way. Humanistic people have the personal qualities that allow them to view the world from the reference point of the other person, the consultee. Therefore, they are open to the consultee's viewpoint and they communicate warmth and friendliness. These are qualities of people who themselves have positive self-concepts, and because they see themselves as adequate they are not easily threatened by external references and pressures. How one perceives others is primarily a projection of one's self-image. Becoming self-confident about oneself and sensitive to one's perceptions, then, becomes the first order of business in becoming a consultant. Culp (Chapter 7) talked about the importance of high trust of oneself as the most important element in consultation. A consultant cannot be open to others and accepting of their human qualities until one's own humanness is owned and apreciated.

Humanistic interactions are person-centered with the focus of transactions being on understanding the other person and facilitating dialogue. West and Berkeley in their chapter on case consultation (see Chapter 6) demonstrated consultants can probe and clarify in a humanistic fashion. Their probes are in stark contrast to the less person-centered consultant who uses questions and remarks to impart their sense of appropriateness and knowledge. Asking "good" questions presents a real difficulty for consultants. Questions that on the surface appear to solicit information, may be used to control the consultee and/or communicate superiority. Five types of controlling questions are as follows:

1. *Binding question:* "People who are lazy and are ill prepared hate change—isn't that true?"

2. *Soliciting agreement questions:* "That is the best way to cure the problem, isn't it?"

3. *Forced choice question:* "Do you want to rework this report or do you want me to pass this on to your supervisor as is?"

4. *Double bind question:* "Have you stopped resisting work on the report?"

5. *"Why" questions:* "Why don't you require attention to detail?"

An analysis of questions asked by the consultant may be used to assess the consultant's level of openness and acceptance.

THE ROLE OF STRUCTURE IN PRACTICE & TRAINING

Interestingly, a humanistic orientation is not equated with lack of structure. As West and Berkeley (Chapter 6) implied, structure helps set the twin goals of "task orientation" and "task completion." Husson (Chapter 3) detailed how structured procedures can be a source of power that helps ensure successful consultation, especially for the internal consultant. This writer has found that structure, in the form of a plan, allows her to function as a consultant with an ease and efficiency that is not otherwise possible. Bubenzer (Chapter 4) imposed structure on data representation at each step in the process model so that the next level of specification is suggested. Evidently consultees perceive a structured process as objective and goal specific rather than subjective and relationships specific. Training components for potential consultees can also be structured and tightly planned to meet desired outcomes.

The Train-the-Trainer Model offered by Childers (Chapter 5) articulates a structured program designed to teach human relationships and communication skills to health care givers. This program has been highly successful with hospital workers, but the model, as well as the process and procedures, are easily adapted to the training of consultants. Essentially, the model proposed by Childers substitutes reflective statements for questions and, thus, avoids many of the pitfalls discussed earlier. Reflecting content is much more person-centered and much less controlling than questions. Helping the potential consultant make a transition from questioning behavior to reflecting behavior usually requires an intermediate step to create sensitivity to one's personal agenda and style. A structured "empathy workshop," suggested in the next section, may be a useful addendum to effective communication training (using Childers,plan as a model).

Empathy Workshop for Consultee Trainers

A structured plan called an Empathy Workshop can be used to develop sensitivity to others and awareness of one's comfort-discomfort dimensions within the interactional process. Even though an empathy workshop is carefully designed to meet specific goals, it does not need to be long nor should it be designed to bring about personality changes, a la therapy. The focus of an empathy workshop is to help the consultant-trainee develop sensitivity to the impact of one's attitudes on personal interactions, to assess individual strengths and weaknesses, and to develop a plan to change those aspects of self that have the potential for damaging a consultative relationship. A brief, but effective, approach to this training competency is provided in the workshop.

The purpose of the empathy workshop for consultee trainers is to help consultant-trainees experience focused listening, observing, and sharing. The following four activities and related materials will provide the content and format for the workshop.

ACTIVITY 8.1: Attending

> *1. Pair off. Allow two minutes for the couple to interact. The instructions are*
>
> > *a. "Spend one minute describing everything you observe (and your impressions) of your partner?*

(Partners do not respond). "Begin each sentence with "I see..." or 'My impression is..."

b. *"When time is called, the* **observed** *becomes the* **observer** *and you have one minute to share your observations. Use the same words to begin each sentence 'I see' or 'My impression is.'"*

c. *"Listen and try to remember what your partner tells you."*

2. *Repeat Step 1 with new partners until base of "recognizing" and "owning" observations is established. The consultant-trainee will begin to distinguish between "me"—my projections and observations about you—and "you."*

ACTIVITY 8.2: Sharing Feelings

Pair off (new partners). This time the consultant-trainees are asked to "tell about yourself." This time begin each sentence with "I," "I am...," "I like...," "I wish...," etc.

ACTIVITY 8.3: Clarifying

Large group discussion: "How did you feel about that experience?" Raise such questions as the following:

1. *Was it easier to share your observations of others or about self?*
2. *Was listening easy or difficult?*
3. *How did you feel when others told you what they observed about you?*
4. *How did you feel when others told you about themselves?*

(Use round-robin techniques to assure each person a chance to share his/her feelings.)

ACTIVITY 8.4: Developing an Index of Helpfulness (IH)

1. *Ask the group to close their eyes and:*

a. *"Think about a problem you have had—a very bad problem." (Pause)*

b. *"Think about the person you would go to if you were to seek help."* (Pause)

c. *"Open your eyes. List the characteristics of the person you choose as the person you would go to for help with your problem."* (Scratch paper)

2. *Make a composite list of the characteristics on the chalkboard. Include all characteristics, but discuss what they mean to the individual and the group. After all characteristics are listed, review them and ask the group if they see these characteristics, individually and as a composite list, as representing the characteristics of someone whom they would go to for help (or a "helpful" person).*

3. *Hand out worksheet (Figure 8.2, Index of Helpfulness—IH) and offer the following instructions:*

a. *"Using your worksheet, list the characteristics of a helper we have on the chalkboard."*

b. *"Next, on the scale beside the characteristic you have listed (from 1 to 9) estimate the degree you feel you possess that characteristic. For example, suppose you listed "good listener" and you feel you are about average as a listener—then you would place an X on the 5 on the scale for that characteristic."*

c. *"Add your scores and divide by the number of characteristics you listed. This will give you an "Index of Helpfulness." Write this index on "Worksheet I—(Index of Helpfulness) at the bottom of the page."*

4. *Hand out Worksheet II (Figure 8.3, My Plan). Raise questions to help consultees-trainees make plans for improving their helping skills. Indicate that they can examine their IH for strengths and weaknesses. Suggest places they may be able to secure more training in communication, human relations, group dynamics, or related areas relevant to their plans for improvement.*

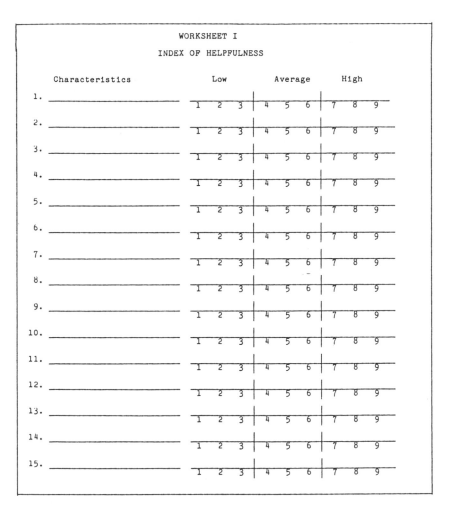

WORKSHEET I

INDEX OF HELPFULNESS

| Characteristics | Low | Average | High |

1. _____ 1 2 3 | 4 5 6 | 7 8 9

2. _____ 1 2 3 | 4 5 6 | 7 8 9

3. _____ 1 2 3 | 4 5 6 | 7 8 9

4. _____ 1 2 3 | 4 5 6 | 7 8 9

5. _____ 1 2 3 | 4 5 6 | 7 8 9

6. _____ 1 2 3 | 4 5 6 | 7 8 9

7. _____ 1 2 3 | 4 5 6 | 7 8 9

8. _____ 1 2 3 | 4 5 6 | 7 8 9

9. _____ 1 2 3 | 4 5 6 | 7 8 9

10. _____ 1 2 3 | 4 5 6 | 7 8 9

11. _____ 1 2 3 | 4 5 6 | 7 8 9

12. _____ 1 2 3 | 4 5 6 | 7 8 9

13. _____ 1 2 3 | 4 5 6 | 7 8 9

14. _____ 1 2 3 | 4 5 6 | 7 8 9

15. _____ 1 2 3 | 4 5 6 | 7 8 9

INSTRUCTIONS:

    a. On the scale list characteristics of Helper.
    b. Rate each Scale for "how much" this is like you.
    c. Add scales and divide by number of characteristics you listed. This gives you an average for "Index of Helpfulness." Record your average below.

INDEX OF HELPFULNESS _____

HIGHEST POSSIBLE SCORE _____

YOUR NAME _____

Figure 8.2. Worksheet I, Index of Helpfulness.

WORKSHEET II
MY PLAN

NAME_____

DATE _____

PERSONAL PROGRESS AND PLAN

In order to be a better consultant I need to

_____

_____

I believe my major strengths are

1._____

2._____

3._____

My major weaknesses are

1._____

2._____

3._____

The next steps I will take in becoming a more helpful (facilitative) consultant are

What I will do	How will I do it	When will I do it
1.		
2.		
3.		

Figure 8.3. Worksheet II, my plan.

Monitoring and Reassessment of One's Behavior

Any plan to improve one's behavior needs monitoring and reassessment at reasonable intervals until competency is achieved. One way to encourage progress and improvement is to establish a procedure for systematic observation of skills under consideration. If the consultant-trainee is being observed by the trainer, as Childers suggested, Worksheet III, Parts A and B, might be used to obtain data and provide feedback to the trainee. If the consultant is working independently, Worksheet III, Parts A and B, might be used by a peer or colleague if possible, or as a self observation device. Self observations have many weaknesses and certainly should not be the exclusive procedure for monitoring one's behavior and style.

A worksheet (Worksheet IV, Figure 8.5) to be used as a rating scale for self or trainees is suggested as an observation form that might be applied in the consultant training program, especially in role-playing situations. The trainer might apply this instrument as a part of training follow-up at regular intervals in order to capture the range of behaviors (positive and negative) used by the trainee and/or by the consultant.

Helping Consultees Structure Interventions

The point has been made that the consultant uses structure to manage the process of the relationship between consultant and consultee. Similarly, at times the most useful consultative help one can provide is to help the consultee *structure a plan* to implement a desired intervention with his/her clients (referred to in Chapter 1 as "primary client). Developing a structured plan and role-playing example situations to be used with that structure are useful training approaches. An example of a structured plan useful for helping children is offered as Worksheet V (Figure 8.6). An example application of the plan is provided as Figure 8.7. This example pertains to a teacher's intervention with a child to bring about a desired change. The assumption here is that the teacher, as a professional, has the basic understanding needed to intervene effectively. The teacher's problem has occurred because of some failure in the process: to articulate the desired outcomes clearly; to listen and accept the perceptions of the child; to establish conditions of reward and feedback; and so forth. With help in structuring the process, the consultee can communicate to the primary client, i.e., child, more clearly. The approach has an added advantage, the teacher can monitor his/her own behavior in the process.

WORKSHEET III: RELATIONSHIP INTERVENTIONS

PART A: OBSERVATION FORM

FREQUENCY & TIME STUDY	CONSULTANT'S RESPONSES	CONSULTANT'S BEHAVIOR	OUTCOME
EXAMPLE: 10:00-10:05 10:15-10:17	Active Listening	Nodding, "uh-huh," eye contact; made repeat	Consultee explored idea
	Active Listening		
	Reflects feeling (empathy)		
	Questioning to explore consultee's ideas (open-ended probes)		
	Asked a "closed" or "why" question		
	Restatement for clarification		
	Clarifying through translating (or judging)		
	Responded with an interpretation and analysis		
	Supporting (concentrates on action not actor)		
	Confronting (pointing out conflicting information offered by consultee)		
	Feedback (self-disclosure shares personal feeling with the consultee		
	Explanations (subject related)		
	Suggesting (tentative in tone)		
	Silence (active attending)		
	Summarizing		
	Irrelevant comments		
	Lecturing		
	Correcting (disciplining)		
	Used sarcasm		

Figure 8.4. Worksheet III, relationship interventions.

PART B: SUMMARY

A. Most frequent behaviors were:

B. Behaviors which produced positive outcomes:

C. Behaviors which produced negative outcomes:

D. Suggested changes:

E. Plan for making changes (to be developed with trainee):

Figure 8.4. Continued.

WORKSHEET IV: COMMUNICATING
(RATING SCALE FOR SELF OR TRAINEES)

	RATINGS				
A. Listening & Responding (communicating, caring, & respect)	LOW		AVER-AGE	HIGH	
	1	2	3	4	5
1. Eye contact with client (undivided attention)					
2. Restates client's message to insure understanding					
3. Language and feeling tone corresponds to level and intensity of client.					
4. Helps client expand and clarify by reflecting (in tentative fashion) content and implied messages (verbal and nonverbal)					
5. Voice tone warm and moderated but genuine and spontaneous.					
6. Physical distance and position open and inviting (example: client does not have to "look up to" nor "over desk")					
B. Clarifying and Defining (Communicating Help and Expertise)					
7. Responds to the personal meaning of what the client is saying.					
8. Probes for specific instances and details.					
9. Responds with "I" statement (feedback)					
10. Asks open-ended questions (Humanistic probes)					
11. Reflects and clarifies when the client gives conflicting information: verbal and nonverbal (confrontation)					

Figure 8.5. Worksheet IV, Communicating: Rating scale for self or trainees.

	RATINGS				
	LOW		AVER-AGE	HIGH	
	1	2	3	4	5
12. Moves from general questions to more and more specific questions (helps define/ clarify)					
13. Helps interpret experiences in terms of meaning for the present (why is this important now).					
14. Initiates action through defining problem, suggesting possible directions summarizing, and so forth					

SUMMARY:

Areas of strength

Areas of weakness

Figure 8.5. Continued.

WORKSHEET V
Structured Intervention Plan

---

1. *Specify the Problem.* What behavior do you want your client to change?

2. *Confer with the Client.* Explain, Listen, Accept, Specify.

3. *Develop a Plan.*

      a. What behaviors will be changed (from what to what)?

      b. What changes will you (helper) make?

      c. How long will the plan be tried?

4. *Follow-up Plan.*

   Daily: Positive reinforcers

   Consequences suffered:

5. *Assess progress as specified.*

      a. What happened?

      b. Make new plans—offer new suggestions.

      c. Set new goals.

6. *Thank the Client.* Hold conference to express appreciation and how new behaviors has made life different.

Figure 8.6. Worksheet V, structured interview plan.

NOTE. Adapted from "Six Steps to Behavioral Change" by J. Kirby, *Second Marriage,* Muncie, IN: Accelerated Development, 1979, pp. 123-124. Reprinted by permission.

1. *Specify the Problem.*

   Billy hit and tripped two boys several times during the past week.

2. *Confer with Child* (consultee's notes are shown below).

   I tell Billy what behavior I find disruptive—why and how I want him to change.

   He tells me he is "picked on" because he is "little" and he feels I am "unfair."

   I accept Billy's feelings and perceptions.

   We discuss the purpose of his behavior and other ways he might react to achieve his goals. We explore things he enjoys doing and people he enjoys being with.

3. *Develop a Plan.*

       a. Billy stated behaviors causing disruptions (hitting and tripping) and agreed to refrain from this for *one week*. If he forgets he will remove himself from the group and work on a specified activity.

       b. I will reassign Billy to work groups with students he enjoys being with, and I will observe Billy more closely to assess precipitating events and, if appropriate, take other actions.

       c. He will follow this plan *one week*.

4. *Follow-up Plan.*

   Check with Billy concerning his relationships with the new group to which he is assigned; comment on *my* feeling about the work of his group and enjoying seeing him happy with this group.

5. *Assess Progress as Specified.* Hold follow-up conference (one week as agreed). Assess successes and problems with plan. If appropriate, develop a new plan.

6. *Thank the Child.*

   Express appreciation to Billy for his cooperation and helpful attitude. Let him know my pleasure at seeing him happy, etc.

Figure 8.7. Helping a child make behavioral changes. (An applied case study using Worksheet V, Structured Intervention Plan, Figure 8.6.)

PERSPECTIVE TAKING

A consultant needs to know how to take the role of others, to gain the perspective of the other person with whom one works, and to try to comprehend the perspective of the consultee's client (i.e., "primary client"). Earlier chapters have discussed ways to develop empathy and work from the reference of the consultee.

Two other models, not already discussed, that are highly recommended for this purpose are Kohlberg's "moral decision making" (Lande & Slade, 1979) and Harrison and Bramson's (1982) "styles of thinking." The first is suggested because Kohlberg's model helps us understand the individual's cognitive processes and formulate verbal responses that can be understood by that individual. Kohlberg helps us understand why some responses go unheeded. The latter model, "styles of thinking," also is directed at understanding the individual's preferred thinking styles, but the important factor for the consultant, especially when using group consultation, is the potential for enriching the output of the group by tapping into the strengths of their several styles. A discussion of the use of these models in training consultants follows.

KOHLBERG'S MORAL DEVELOPMENT MODEL

Kohlberg (1966) offered a model of moral development which focuses on *reasoning* (cognition) as opposed to behavior. Popularization of psychology perhaps accounts for a rather vague but general awareness of Kohlberg's idea or "stages" of moral development. Only a brief description of Kohlberg's theory and related research are presented herein, and these are chosen to focus on issues most appropriate to the *practice* of consultation and the skills this writer believes to be most useful to the *practitioner*. The discussion that follows is concerned with applying Kohlberg's model to consultation.

Notes on Theory: Moral Reasoning and Stage Progression

Kohlberg indicated that moral reasoning is developmental and hierarchial. Every person begins at stage one and progression to the next higher stage is a function of both time (cognitive development) and experience (information gathering and gaining of social perspectives). Before one moves successively to higher stages one must explore cognitive conflicts involving moral issues and be able to take the social perspective of others who hold significantly different views.

Ten moral issues are viewed as universal:

1. punishment
2. property
3. roles and concerns of affection
4. roles and concerns of authority
5. law
6. life
7. liberty
8. distributive justice
9. truth
10. sex (Pietrofesa, Bernstein, Minor & Stanford, 1980, p. 399).

The idea of development as a function of *time* and *learning* when we consider some aspects of human behavior seems logical and obvious. For example, when we speak of language maturity, one easily conceptualizes a development sequence that is dependent upon the individual's cognitive experiences which is limited, but not fixed, by age. For example, a four year old child would not have had time to develop full language maturity. Time is so important at the earliest stages of language development that growth is measured by months, but differences begin to fade out about age 16 when more and more people peak or drop out of the learning process. A hypothetical relationship between language and age is depicted in Figure 8.8 to demonstrate the concept of a developmental process.

Moral reasoning as a developmental process is more difficult to conceptualize. First, many people do not separate reasoning from behavior when talking about guiding moral growth. Thus, the idea is new and scary for them. Others have difficulty with the idea because they see little practical value in making the distinction. Then numerous other people

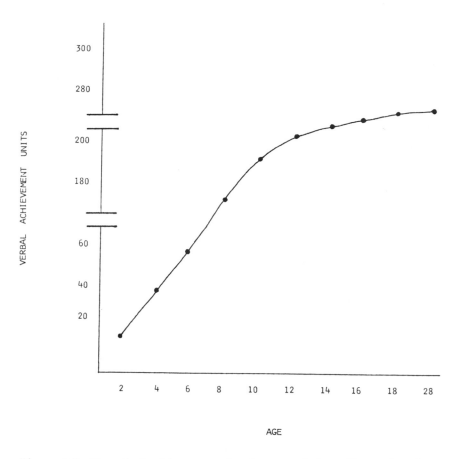

Figure 8.8. Hypothetical language developmental chart illustrating that as the child progresses in age/experience, language growth occurs.

view morality as an issue which is primarily a religious one and not an appropriate concern for parents, teachers, or others in the secular segment of society except insofar as the parent chooses to encourage or teach a religious dogma. One public school, for instance, reportedly offers moral education under the label of "civic" education as an effort to minimize negative reactions of fearful parents who believe moral education does not belong in their school (Bennett, 1978).

This writer perceives Kohlberg's model as very useful for consultants who are concerned with helping consultees make choices. This model neither presupposes a religious belief nor is religion viewed as antithetical to moral development. Believers, agnostics, and atheists are found at all stages of moral reasoning. Adults may stabilize at any stage, even at stage one, and never progress to the higher levels. While Kohlberg did not necessarily assume that people who reasoned at higher stages are better, he did assume that higher levels of reasoning approached superior decision-making criteria of universality, objectivity, and consistency (Gazda, 1978).

Kohlberg's Stages: An Explanation

The concept of stages as employed by Kohlberg's model has its roots in the theory by Piaget. "Piaget's main argument, like that of other 'stage' theorists, is that the development of moral thinking involves a progression through a sequence of stages: each of Piaget's steps is characterized by thinking of a particular 'quality'" (Graham, 1972, p. 192). Stages of development imply something of gradual change and cumulative growth. Stages indicate a new integration of that accumulated change which results in a quantitatively different mode of operation; nevertheless, a new stage does not mean discontinuity of development. In Piaget's concept, progression to the next stage meant the individual increasingly made "use of mode of functioning characteristic of that stage and gradually less use of the more 'primitive' modes of functioning, though these may still be retained and used on occasion" (Graham, 1972, p. 10).

Practically, the application of stage theory to helping tells us that the same material or information will be interpreted in different ways at different stages. This has broad implication for consultants and other helpers. Some suggested uses gleaned from a review of the literature include

1. responding to a consultee, student, child, etc. using reasoning at a cognitive level which the individual can comprehend (Duska & Whelan, 1975);

2. providing the necessary conditions whereby an individual can move to the next higher cognitive steps (Staub, 1975);

3. understanding and working with delinquent youths and reluctant clients (Samby & Tamminen, 1979);

4. facilitating decision-making in family groups (Englund, 1980);

5. developing and implementing a comprehensive counseling program (Gazda, 1978);

6. guiding socially responsible behavior through the exploration of alternatives and potential outcomes (Hersch, Paolitto, & Reimer, 1979); and

7. offering the individual concerned with religious and "belief" content a structural system for working in the "faith" dimension (Wilcox, 1979).

In addition to these specific suggestions, moral development theory and practice seem to have a broader application. Professionals who seek to help others are more effective if they operate from higher stages of moral reasoning. Research findings (Wilcox, 1979; Graham, 1972) support the notion that *persons cannot understand reasoning about moral issues at a stage higher than one level above the one at which they generally function.* If one believes this, then one begins to approach others by viewing the world through their lenses. When one takes another's perspective, one develops empathy for that person, and becomes quite approachable. To use Ginott's (1972) term, we establish a "minute-to-minute humanness" in which we are open to others (p. 54). This seems to be a necessary characteristic for consultants.

As contradictory as it seems at first blush, this writer agrees with Englund's view that the "use of Kohlberg's moral developmental framework satisfies the educator's desire for wanting to provide direction without moralizing" (Englund, 1980, p. 7). One might also substitute the word consultant for educator in the last sentence. Englund went on to explain that moral development provides a means for examining questions involving moral conflict, and as such, it is "not so much a matter of endorsing the 'right' behaviors as it is of knowing for oneself the logic of one's choice" (p. 54). This approach helps the consultant offer help without judgment and with respect for differences and uniqueness.

Kohlberg's Social Perspective Taking and Decision-Making Criteria

Kohlberg's ideas were influenced by Piaget but as Graham (1972) pointed out, Kohlberg "has greatly elaborated" Piaget's theory in a number of ways. Kohlberg delineates three levels of social perspective taking and then identifies two stages of moral reasoning associated with each level. The social perspective taking levels are generalized approaches to problems while stages are differentiated by the criteria used by individuals in making moral choices (Hersch, Paolitto, & Reimer, 1979). These levels and stages are shown in Figure 8.9.

Stabilization (Adult Stages)

Kohlberg's theory conceptualizes sequential stages of development, but it is not meant to imply that everyone progresses from level one through all stages to level six. As one can understand easily, stabilization at any level is possible, and certainly does occur. Age related cognitive development is a necessary but insufficient condition for moving up to the next higher level of moral judgement. For example, Samby and Tamminen (1979) stated that they have found, "most hostile, belligerent youngsters in trouble with the law" are youngsters operating at Stage 1. A typical approach to relationships with others is "What will you do to me if I don't do as you say?" (p. 507). Similarly, Lande and Slade (1979) noted that "criminal offenders are remarkably lower in moral judgement development than non-offenders (p. 29). They go on to point out that 75 percent of noncriminal adolescents and young adults are at Stage 3 or 4 while delinquents and offenders are at Stages 1 and 2. The position of Kohlberg is that the central tendency of judgement moves up with increasing age although not everyone passes through the whole sequence (Graham, 1972). Eventually a "moral stabilization" for the majority of adults occurs at the conformity Level II of social perspective with most women basing decision on Stage 3 (conformity) criteria and men at Stage 4 (law and order) criteria. Graham (1972) quoting from Kohlberg and Kramer summarized this view: "Stage 3 personal concordance morality is a functional morality for housewives and mothers; it is not for businessmen and professionals. Adult moral stabilization, then, appears to be more a matter of increased congruence between belief and social role than of novel integration of experience" (p. 233).

LEVEL	SOCIAL PERSPECTIVE	STAGE	CRITERIA USED FOR MAKING MORAL JUDGMENT
I	Pre-conventional or Premoral.	1.	Good is doing what adults say; action is based on "not" getting caught.
		2.	Good is what benefits self and others; action is based on trading favors or reciprocity.
II	Conventional or role conformity	3.	Good is pleasing one's friends or social group, showing concern, loyalty, respect; action is based on gaining and keeping approval of significant others.
		4.	Good is maintaining authority and keeping the social order; action is based upon obligation to society (as a whole).
III	Post-conventional or self-accepted principles	5.	Good is respect for democratic principles of fairness, freedom, personal worth; action is based on obligation to one's social-legal contracts.
		6.	Good is what is consistent with ethical standards reflecting unconditional regard for human worth; action is based on universal moral principles.

Figure 8.9. Kohlberg's conceptualization of levels (social perspectives) and stages (criteria).

Stabilization at a given stage seems to be associated with a pervasive feeling one has about self (self-concept). While not articulated by Kohlberg as part of his theory, for this writer for each stage of moral reasoning others have an accompanying perception about the motivation of the individual. In Figure 8.10 is displayed this relationship. This paradigm could prove to be a useful diagnostic tool for consultants concerned with identifying the purpose of individual behavior. If I view another's behavior as primarily DEFENSIVE, for example, I can asume that person feels HELPLESS and I have a clue about the kind of helpful responses to make. In this instance I would know I will have to recognize and accept his/her feelings of helplessness (be empathetic) and offer cognitive reasoning at a social perspective of Level I, Stages 1 and 2.

LEVEL	STAGE	FEELS ABOUT SELF	PERCEIVED BY OTHERS
I	1	Helpless	Defensive
	2	Isolated	Opportunistic
II	3	Powerless	Manipulative
	4	Powerful	Controlling
III	5	Responsible	Democratic
	6	Competent	Altruistic

Figure 8.10. Perceptions and feelings associated with preferred stages of moral development—a proposed tool for consultants.

Decision Making and Developmental Stages

A consultant's goal is to facilitate growth to the highest level of an individual's potential because each successive cognitive developmental stage allows for more adequate and satisfying decision-making. They are more satisfying because more options are considered, outcomes are realistically assessed, and choices are made which are realistic and socially, as well as personally, satisfying. The adult's level of stabilization is reflected in kinds and amount of data examined and used in decision-making.

People who feel helpless and isolated (operating at Level I, see Figure 8.10) for example, view their environment in a very limited way. This viewpoint affects their decision-making behavior. This is true for people operating at each of the developmental levels. Each level produces its own problem-solving behaviors. The relationship of developmental levels (and accompanying stages) and the problem-solving behaviors are summarized in the next three paragraphs. Problem solving behaviors for each level are listed.

Level I (Stages 1 and 2) *Failure to Consider Options.* The adult who is stabilized at this level does not consider nor perceive very many alternatives. Basically Level I people are reactive. Since a person at this level feels helpless, the individual is motivated to avoid punishment (at Stage 1) or to seek what is pleasurable (at Stage 2). Therefore, most options are not considered.

Level II *Failure to Predict Outcomes.* Adults stabilized at this level make choices based on their view of what is appropriate for their social group: accepting and supporting the status quo. Feeling powerless (usually women, Stage 3) or powerful (usually men, Stage 4) they behave in stereotypical ways (i.e., manipulative and controlling). Outcomes are unrealistically assumed to be viewed as acceptable or unacceptable, leaving little room for exploration and experimentation.

Level III *Logical and Responsible Choice.* At this level the individual sees many possible alternative actions to a given situation. Each option is examined against personally held or objective standards and the potential outcomes of each course of action is assessed adequately and realistically. Based upon this personal analysis, the individual makes a clear and seemingly good choice and is willing to assume responsibility for the outcome. Feeling responsible (at Stage 5) and competent (at Stage

6) the decision is socially satisfying either in a democratic sense or in an altruistic sense.

MORAL DEVELOPMENT WORKSHOP
FOR CONSULTANT-TRAINEE

This section presents a structured workshop that might be used to help consultant-trainees understand and apply moral development theory and practice as a consultative strategy.

Training individuals to apply Kohlberg's model in the consultative process can be effectively accomplished in a tightly defined structured workshop of about two or three days duration. The outline provided in this section contains a Procedural Approach for the training of consultants in the use of the strategies suggested by Kohlberg and others for understanding arguments and criteria used in making value laden and moral choices. Activities that are included may be used by the trainer as presented but the primary intention of these examples is to provide suggested kinds of materials with the view of stimulating the workshop planner to develop workshop-specific materials that focus on the personal orientations and work environments of the consultant-trainee. Additionally, the level of educational sophistication and openness of the consultant-trainees will determine the pace of the workshop and the amount of redundancy that needs to be included.

WORKSHOP
MORAL DEVELOPMENT TRAINING FOR
CONSULTANTS

In this section are presented the workshop outline and sample materials for moral development training for consultants. The outline is in step-by-step procedure with accompanying materials.

1. Set the Atmosphere for the Workshop

The outline presented in Chapter 7 on initial meeting with the group (consultant and participants) is suggested as a format. The major components are as follows:

    a. Introduce leader
    b. Help consultants-in-training to become acquainted and begin to function together with group identity
    c. Explain purposes/goals for the workshop
    d. Outline commitment to participate in the workshop

2. Utilize the Dilemma Technique

    a. Recognize purposes for using the dilemma technique

       • Will serve as a preassessment device

       • Provides personal application of the experience that contributes to motivation to learn the model, and

       • offers a common group experience that allows participants to consider the model in the context of decision making.

    b. Present Margie's Dilemma

       Kerri steals a pair of sunglasses from a store and gets away but a security guard detains her friend, Margie, and tells her she will be in trouble unless she reveals the thief's identity. What should Margie do?

    c. Ask each participant to

       • Decide *what* you would do if you were Margie.

       • Write your reaction and the *reason* for your choice.

       • (Action)_____

• (Reason)_____

3. Present the Moral Development Model as conceptualized by Kohlberg.

    a. Use Figure 8.9 either as a handout or display as a chart while explaining Levels and Stages of development.

    b. List the participants' responses to Margie's dilemma: Give both "Action" and "Reason."

    c. Compare their responses with the Levels and Stages depicted on Figure 8.9.

    d. Explain the meaning a dilemma has for an individual and help participants see that the Level/Stage can *not* be determined by the *action*. Only the "thinking" component is used to judge the Level of moral development. A suggested statement for explaining use of dilemmas follows:

> "A dilemma is a situation in which there are at least two and usually more logical and reasonable choices or alternatives. Values come into conflict for the individual who is caught in a dilemma and must choose a course of action. The choice an individual makes in such a conflict situation will be based upon that person's ideas of right and wrong. The basis of moral judgment is primarily cognitive—even though feelings are involved—and one's actions may or may not be consistent with one's beliefs about what 'should be' or what is 'right.' In other words, higher levels of moral reasoning do not always result in more altruistic or just behavior. Also, one's action does not always reveal the justification for that action. Therefore, the moral development stage at which a person is functioning can be determined only by knowing the criteria used by the individual to arrive at the judgment."

e. Work through the Levels and Stages of moral development for "Margie" demonstrating to the group how the *action* may be either for Margie "to tell" or "not tell" at any level. Figure 8.11 is a suggested chart to use with the dilemma of Margie.

4. Practice the Model.

   a. Announce to the participants that they will use another dilemma to practice the model.

   b. Ask each participant (individually or in small groups) to attempt to come up with arguments that represent thinking at each Level and Stage of moral development and to record them on a worksheet as shown in Figure 8.12.

   c. Present Wanda's Dilemma

      Wanda, a freshman at college, became pregnant when she entered a sexual relationship which she nor her partner expected (nor wanted) to be permanent. She is an ambitious student with better than average grades. Her parents do not even suspect that she is sexually active and indeed they assumed that her religious upbringing would prohibit such behavior. Wanda, like her parents, is of the Catholic faith, and abortion to her is a dreadful if not an unforgiveable sin.

      What should Wanda do?

   d. Upon completion of the individual or small group work, make a composite chart of representative thinking for each level and stage of moral development.

COL. I	COL. II	COL. III	COL. IV
REASONS	ACTIONS	VALUE CONCEPT	STAGE
She might get punished if she does not tell.	a. Tell on Kerri	Amoral:	
The item was of too small a value to be worthwhile for the security guard to do anything about it.	b. Do not tell on Kerri	Punishment-/Reward	1
Because Kerri walked out on her to "face the music" alone.	a. Tell on Kerri	Trade off:	
She is not responsible for the store—they never did anything for her.	b. Do not tell on Kerri	Expedient	2
Because others will not approve of her if she doesn't.	a. Tell on Kerri	Conformity:	
All of her friends will stick together, no matter what.	b. Do not tell on Kerri	Nice girl; good boy	3
To help enforce laws on stealing and teach Kerri responsibility.	a. Tell on Kerri	Authority:	
Society is built on trust and capitalism would fail if we reported all misdeeds.	b. Do not tell on Kerri	Law & Order	4
The cost of theft is passed on to every consumer and creates hardship for all.	a. Tell on Kerri	Rational Altruistic:	
The economic system has to suffer some as people learn to deal with the structure of society.	b. Do not tell on Kerri	Protect rights of others	5
To support the notion that we are independent and we rely on each person to perform their roles.	a. Tell on Kerri	Universal Human Rights	
The security guard will not suffer any ill effects—and Kerri can be served better through support of a friend.	b. Do not tell on Kerri		6

Figure 8.11. Chart for Margie's Dilemma to illustrate Kohlberg's Moral Development Model. (Arguments or reasons offered to support recommendations for *action* are the basis of judging developmental level.)

STAGES	VALUE CONCEPT	ACTION	REASON
1			
2			
3			
4			
5			
6			

Figure 8.12. Worksheet for recording reasoning for each stage of moral development.

5. Focus on Expanding Options and Points-of-View

a. Present Bill's dilemma.

Bill purchased a beautiful antique chest from an elderly couple who lived on an isolated farm. The couple told Bill they were "selling out" because they were moving into a retirement home and they had no children and no one they could leave their antiques to with the feeling that they would be treasured. They agreed that whoever bought the chest would want it, so they were happy that Bill had wanted it enough to pay their rather handsome, but realistic, asking price. Bill's dilemma occurred when he was cleaning the piece before presenting it to his wife—as her birthday present. Inside, tucked into a smaller drawer, was an envelope containing two $50.00 bills—a third of the cost of the chest. No one knew about the the money and it was likely that the previous owners even remembered that they had tucked it there.

What should Bill do?

b. Instruct the group as follows: "Think of as many arguments as you can. Identify the values each idea implies and decide what development stage this implies. For each of your arguments try to think of a counter argument. Be as comprehensive as possible."

c. Record answers on worksheets constructed in the manner suggested in Figure 8.13.

ARGUMENTS	VALUE	STAGE

Figure 8.13. Worksheet for recording responses from Bill's Dilemma.

6. Cause Age Perspective Taking (Role-playing Activity)

    a. Assign each participant to one of 5 age categories as indicated

        Group A—Assumes Betty's age to be 5-7 years
        Group B—Assumes Betty's age to be 8-10 years
        Group C—Assumes Betty's age to be 11-13 years
        Group D—Assumes Betty's age to be 14-16 years
        Group E—Assumes Betty's age to be 17-Adult

    b. Provide the groups with copies of the story of Betty's dilemma.

        Betty was in the cloak room when Sara came into the adjoining classroom and took a sandwich from Mary's desk. Betty saw Sara give half the sandwich to her sister and eat the other half herself.

        Later, the teacher tried to learn who took the sandwich. She asked everyone individually and collectively. Finally, she said, "Unless someone confesses, or someone reports someone else, all of you will have to stay in at recess."

        What should Betty do? Why?

    c. Ask each person to identify their group assignment (A to E) and to assume a specific age within that range. For example, ask several people: "What age are you?" This helps get the people into the frame of reference for the role taking they are asked to perform.

    d. Have the groups read the story of Betty's dilemma. Ask a recorder for each group (1) to keep track of *all* of the arguments advanced by the group and (2) to develop a *consensus* statement for the group telling:

- The *Action* Betty should take, and

- The *arguments* supporting that action. To insure accurate note taking, a recorders sheet with space under each two items might be provided each group. A model is suggested in Figure 8.14.

e. Form a panel comprised of a spokesperson from each sub-group.

Have the members of the panel share the arguments they generated and their consensus decision.

Open the discussion to allow audience participation.

Ask the group how they felt playing their assumed roles.

Story of Betty   Age Perspective _____

(Recorder's Report)   Number in Group _____

ITEM A: Arguments and rebutals offered by Betty and her peers. Record
         Arguments here:

_____

_____

_____

_____

_____

ITEM B: What is the group consensus? Decide what action Betty should take and
         the reasons and record here:

_____

_____

_____

_____

_____

Figure 8.14. Worksheet for recording responses from Betty's dilemma.

f. Using Figure 8.15 construct an age related developmental chart from the data generated by each group showing Betty's arguments at each age, her values and the accompanying developmental stages.

Developmental Stages—Arguments and Values

Work Groups	Age Perspectives	BEHAVIOR & REASONING (Consensus statements from sub-groups)	Value Concepts	Stages
A	5-7			
B	8-10			
C	11-13			
D	14-16			
E	17			

Create a developmental chart showing Betty's moral reasoning and comparing values and stages. Use the information generated by the use of Recorder's Report sheet to complete this activity.

Figure 8.15. Worksheet for recording Betty's age related moral reasoning.

7. Apply Reasoning to Communication Style

a. Present a rationale as follows:

"Reasoning expressed in verbal exchanges represent one's values and stage of moral development. You, as consultants, are in the position of wanting to influence the behaviors and attitudes of your clients but you have to work from the client's perspective in order to be understood. This exercise is concerned with communicating effectively.''

"The purpose of this exercise is

• to develop an awareness of the way normal reasoning is expressed in day-to-day dialogue; and

• to examine how differences in moral reasoning create communication problems.''

b. Divide participants into dyads.

c. Present Figures 8.16 and 8.17 as worksheets to be worked on in pairs.

d. After the trainees have identified the Stages of moral development represented by each statement, ask some of the following questions:

• In what ways could communication be improved? (Remember that an individual can comprehend reasoning *no more* than one level above the one at which he/she is functioning.)

• What happens when the teacher (Scene A) or the parent (Scene B) uses reasoning inconsistent with the level of moral reasoning used by the student and daughter?

• Whose responsibility is it in each situation (Scene A and Scene B) to identify values which are implied and respond to those values? Why?

• How could the teacher (and parent) respond so that the student (and daughter) would know they were heard and valued as an individual?

• What values are communicated by teacher? By father?

SCENE A
Teacher and Sam

INSTRUCTION: Read the dialogue. Identify moral Stage for each response.

TEACHER:

Sit up Sam. Pay attention to your homework assignment—I won't repeat it.

(Stage)

SAM:

I can't do the work anyway. I'll just get an "F" even if I try.

(Stage)

TEACHER:

If you want to get promoted and stay with your friends you had better start paying attention.

(Stage)

SAM:

Why do I need this anyway?

(Stage)

TEACHER:

Math is a universal concept. We wouldn't be competitive as individuals or as a nation if we didn't have math.

(Stage)

Figure 8.16. Dialogue between teacher (Helper) and student (Helpee).

SCENE B
Dad and Mary

INSTRUCTIONS: Read dialogue. Identify moral Stage for each response.

MARY:

Dad, can I have 15 dollars for my trip to the fair?

(Stage)

DAD:

Mary, you have your allowance and you knew you would want to go to the fair. You should have saved.

(Stage)

MARY:

If you'll give me 15 dollars, I'll really be good—I'll not ask for any more money—and I will help you clean the yard Saturday. Please, Dad!

DAD:

Mary, our budget just won't tolerate stretching it like that. You know we agreed to purchase this house and all we get has to go into repaying the down payment.

(Stage)

MARY:

Everyone else gets to go to the fair and they have at least 20 dollars to spend. I only want 15 dollars. All my friends will have more than that.

(Stage)

Figure 8.17. Dialogue between father (Helper) and daughter (Helpee).

e. Use statements of Sam as stimulus statements to practice responding at the speaker's level of moral development.

- Ask one person to assume the role of Sam and another the role of teacher.

- Ask the two persons to dialogue the situation.

- Ask the group to observe dialogue and assesses the "teacher's" ability to respond appropriately to Sam.

- Ask Sam to share with the group the feelings he experienced during the dialogue.

f. Use the statement of Mary as stimulus statements and repeat the exercise outlined in Step 7.e.

8. Using Moral Development Model as a Communication Tool.

a. Introduce the following concepts:
- Individuals can comprehend reasoning at *only one* stage higher than that which is usually used in formulating choices;

- Individuals prefer higher, rather than lower, stages of reasoning;

- Growth in moral reasoning is encouraged when the service provider acknowledges the client's stage of reasoning (by reflecting content) and then suggests content from the next highest stage.

b. Provide practice in responding to people with information they can understand.
- Introduce Figure 8.18 as a worksheet for this purpose. Have the group work in pairs to practice stating and responding. The service provider is to frame responses that incorporate the

"essence" of the speaker's arguments (Acknowledge Speaker's Reasoning—ASR) and then add an idea that introduces the next highest stage (INS).

• Review Figure 8.19 which is provided for the trainer as an example worksheet for Figure 8.18. In some instances a helpful procedure is to go over this example with the consultant-trainees and then use new statements for them to work through.

9. Provide Additional Practice

a. Form triads (a service provider, a client, and an observer) to role play communicating with individuals using the speaker's stage of moral reasoning as the critical factor in formulating a helpful response. Statements may be generated within the group and recorded on a worksheet as shown in Figure 8.20.

b. Initiate the discussion in the triads by introducing several statements that may be used for practice. The following are illustrative:

• Man to Friend: "Dad doesn't think my wife should work—he wanted to know if I couldn't support her myself. Do you think I should let her work?"

• Female to Friend: "If I don't have dinner ready when Jim gets home, he gets mad and won't talk to me. I have to get home before 3:00."

• Student to Teacher: "Billy doesn't dress out in gym. Why should I have to if I don't want to?"

• Delinquent to Counselor: "What will you do to me if I don't do what you say?"

WORKSHEET: FACILITATING MORAL GROWTH

Directions: Write a growth producing response: first give the speaker an acknowledging comment (basically paraphrasing and then add reasoning from the next higher level (additive).

SPEAKER'S STATEMENT	MORAL DEVELOPMENT STAGE	STIMULATING RESPONSES
"I would not go to the Army if I thought I could get away with giving some excuse."	———	ASR INS
"I don't mind going to the Army if Uncle Sam will send me to medical school when I get out."	———	ASR INS
"If I'm drafted I will serve—that should be expected of everybody!"	———	ASR INS
"I guess we need more men in the Army, I just hope those draft dodgers get what is due them!"	———	ASR INS
"I appreciate the need for an Army and my parents' position, but I think they are wrong and I refuse to be drafted into the Army."	———	ASR INS
"I realize this move will be a hardship on me and my family but the people in that remote land need my skills in order to survive. Therefore, I feel I must go."	———	ASR INS

ASR—Acknowledge Speaker's Reasoning (an answer that contains the essence of speaker's response)

INS—Introduces the Next Highest Stage

Figure 8.18. Worksheet to practice communication for facilitating moral growth.

ANSWER SHEET FOR WORKSHEET VIII
(SAMPLE RESPONSES)
FACILITATING MORAL GROWTH

SPEAKER'S STATEMENT	IDENTIFY MORAL DEVELOPMENT STAGE	ACKNOWLEDGE SPEAKER'S REASONING (ASR) AND INTRODUCE NEXT STAGE (INS)
"I would not go to the Army if I thought I could get away with giving some excuse."	1	ASR: If drafted you don't seem to have much choice, but INS: there might be some benefits for you from being in the service as a veteran
"I don't mind going to the Army if Uncle Sam will send me to medical school when I get out."	2	ASR: If the Army can help finance your training, serving won't be so bad and INS: you will be making your contribution to our way of life.
"If I'm drafted I will serve—that should be expected of everybody!"	3	ASR: It's tough to be caught in the draft age call up—but it's your duty to serve, also, INS: a strong Army assures a strong country.
"I guess we need more men in the Army, I just hope those draft dodgers get what is due them!"	4	ASR: If drafted, you feel you should serve with pride, but INS: there might also be other ways to serve the country and at the same time be helpful.
"I appreciate the need for an Army and my parents' position, but I think they are wrong and I refuse to be drafted into the Army."	5	ASR: You refuse to serve in the army on moral grounds, but INS: there are other ways to fight for truth and freedom.
"I realize this move will be a hardship on me and my family but the people in that remote land need my skills in order to survive. Therefore, I feel I must go."	6	ASR: Your choices are not always easy to live with but they seem just and reasonable.

Figure 8.19. Sample response that might be made in response to statements shown in Figure 8.18.

Directions: On the lefthand side of the page write statements you have heard recently which communicate one of the developmental stages. To the right indicate a growth facilitating response to that statement.

STATEMENTS	STAGE	GROWTH—STIMULATING RESPONSES
	1	ASR INS
	2	ASR INS
	3	ASR INS
	4	ASR INS
	5	ASR INS
	6	ASR INS

ASR—Acknowledge Speaker's Reasoning (an answer that contains the essence of speaker's response)

INS—Introduces the Next Highest Stage

Figure 8.20. Developing practice communication exercises from actual statements.

10. Perform Follow-up Observations

   a. Assign follow-up work. An effective approach is to suggest that the consultant-trainees use the observation form provided as Figure 8.21 to record behavior/choices under real conditions. The assignment might be as follows:

   > "Observe individuals at each age indicated on the observation form. Record the behavior (what choices were made) by the individual and context situation of the behavior. Observe at least one male and one female in each age category. Observations for an individual should extend over several hours and include several different settings."

   b. Use the observations collected as suggested in the above assignment to develop appropriate stories for discussion and dilemmas to be resolved. The dilemmas might be developed around the question, What should ...(*person's name*)... do?"

   c. Use the dilemmas developed in the Step 10b in interviews with others to examine their stages of moral reasoning. The trainer might suggest that the consultant-trainees interview individuals in several age categories represented in dilemmas they developed. Use the dilemma appropriate to the age of the interviewee and where possible, interview both males and females.

   d. Share among consultant-trainees experiences in observing and interviewing. Statements gleaned from the interviews and observations might be used for additional practice.

BEHAVIOR/CHOICE OBSERVATIONS

AGES	BEHAVIOR (What choices were made?)	SITUATION
5-7		
8-10		
11-13		
14-16		
17-Adult		

Figure 8.21. Form for recording behavior and choices of individuals (male and female) in different age categories.

STYLES OF THINKING

Preceding the title page of their book on *Styles of Thinking,* Harrison and Bramson (1982) devoted a page to an apt quote from George H. Kelly: "All thinking is based in part, on prior convictions." This message impresses us with the complexity of human interactions and it helps us understand the polarization around ideas and positions that seem to belie logic. If thinking is based on prior conviction, a successful consultant needs to grasp the essence of that conviction for individuals being served. Through personal conviction or perspective the consultee will address problems, interpret data, and search for alternatives.

"Styles" offers a model that helps the consultant examine issues from the perspective of the consultee. By becoming cognizant of ways people approach problems and values those approaches or styles imply, the consultant can anticipate both questions and decision-making strategies that are likely to be employed by the consultee. Additionally, for the consultant working within the group context, strengths and liabilities of each style can be expected and accommodated. Also, divergent thinking styles can be used in the consultative process for broadening ranges of options available to the group. A variety of thinking strategies decreases the potential for the very real problem of "group think" (Janis & Mann, 1977), in both data search and estimating potential results of possible outcomes.

Notes on Theory: Styles of Thinking

Harrison and Bramson (1982) postulated that each individual has a belief about a "right" way to think about things. That is, individuals employ a limited set of strategies when thinking about an issue or problem. Each individual's preferred strategy has its strengths and weaknesses. Problems for the individual arise when a strategy is overworked or used inappropriately, and when strategies of others are ignored, disregarded, or considered to be "wrong."

Most people, according to Harrison and Bramson (1977), have a strong preference for one or two of the five following strategies for solving problems:

"Style"	"General Characteristics"
1. The Synthesist	challenging; sees data as meaningless without interpretation; integrative process oriented
2. The Idealist	receptive; seeks ideal solutions; assimilative goal-oriented
3. The Pragamist	adaptive; "whatever works," incremental payoff
4. The Analyst	prescriptive; seeks "one best way;" logical method oriented
5. The Realist	empirical; relies on "facts" and objective data; objective task-oriented

The impact of preferred strategies of solving problems is expressed in

• kinds of *questions* the individual is likely to ask in the decision-making process,

• kinds of *data* to which they are likely to pay attention,

- *strategies* they are likely to employ in problem resolution, and

- *alternatives* they are likely to accept (Harrison & Bramson, 1977).

Helping consultant-trainees use the "Styles of Thinking" model as a consultative tool means (1) helping them understand the model; (2) acquainting them with the Inquiry Style Questionnaire (InQ)(Harrison & Bramson, 1983) as a diagnostic instrument; and (3) providing concrete examples and practice in the application of the concept of the InQ instrument with their clients.

Authors of *Styles of Thinking* suggested an outline for training individuals to use the InQ (Harrison & Bramson, 1977), and of course the book, *Styles of Thinking* (Harrison & Bramson, 1983), might be used as a training resource or as a text in a credit or non-credit course. This writer offers a structured workshop outline that she has found to be effective in consultant-trainee situations, and the content and procedures have received highly favorable comments from the trainees.

"STYLES OF THINKING" WORKSHOP

1. Set the Atmosphere for the Workshop

The outline presented in Chapter 7 on initial meeting with the group (consultee and participants) is suggested as a format. The major components are as follows:

a. Introduce leader

b. Help consultants-in-training to become acquainted and begin to function together with group identity

c. Explain purposes/goals for the workshop

d. Obtain commitment to participate in the workshop

2. Administer InQ as a pre-test. Theory is to be presented after pre-test.

(The InQ is included in the book, *Styles of Thinking*)

3. Score individual InQ test (Test is self-scoring)

   a. discuss scores

   b. participants compare scores
      - within group
      - with general population

   c. Refer to chart, p. 190 in *Styles of Thinking* and discuss characteristics, strengths, and liabilities of each style. Have individuals who scored high on each style to react to descriptions.

   d. Turn to pages 98-99 in *Styles of Thinking,* "Behavioral Clues" chart. Read and discuss with focus especially being on "what to look and listen for" aspects of each style. Allow individuals with high/low scores to react to descriptions.

4. Compare descriptions and summarize information

   a. Divide training group into subgroups based on similarities of scores. For small training groups highest scores may be used; whereas, for fairly large training groups the scores may be further differentiated using "one preference," "two-pronged," "three-pronged," and "flat" profiles.

   b. Personalize the information.

      - The subgroup members compare their personal philosophies, likes and dislikes;

      - The groups compare and contrast their individual and group perceptions with the information in the chapters (*Styles of Thinking*) relevant to their respective styles.

- Summary statements are generated that capture the essence of their styles and ways of viewing the world to present to the large group.

c. Present information generated in subgroups to entire group.

- A summary of the chapter examined by each subgroup.

- Personal information from members of the group about their own styles and the match between the way they view the world and what is reported in the book *Styles of Thinking.*

5. Reconvene into subgroups (identified by styles).

a. Provide a problem situation that requires the group to make a decision. NOTE: This writer has used an activity provided her by the authors of the InQ. This activity asks the trainees to evaluate several applicants for the position of Hospital Administrator. However, a situation specific to the interests of the group members has the potential of being more realistic for the trainees.

The important aspect of the assignment is to reach a consensus, and to keep an account of the decision-making strategies (e.g., information sought, values reflected, goals expressed) used by the group in reaching their consensus.

b. Have spokesperson from each small group to share information generated in the small group with the entire group.

c. Process ways decisions were reached, i.e., did the approach used by the group reflect the "style" indictated by the InQ scores?

6. Summarize: theory and model

a. Present theory notes and review purpose of the model.

b. Restate (or have trainees restate) strengths and weaknesses of each style.

c. Review ways consultants can use the model in working with consultees.

d. Discuss application of model in understanding perspective of individuals and in forming groups and managing group dynamics.

7. Give a Follow-up Assignment

a. Suggest that consultant-trainees administer InQ to 6 to 8 members of a work group.

b. Analyze "styles" of individuals and group by

• scoring InQ and identifying strengths and weaknesses of individual styles

• Depicting profiles on a composite graph. Predict potential sources of conflict, supports, etc., within the group; compare with what happens in the group.

c. Share assignment and experience with large group.

CONSULTATION: A PROFESSIONAL ROLE FOR THE PROFESSIONAL HEALTH AND HUMAN SERVICE PROVIDER

An effective practitioner in the Human and Health Services field uses consultation as the preferred method of responding to a wide variety of work related issues. The consultative relationship is short term, therefore, as a helping intervention, it is efficient. Because the consultative contact is problem specific, the motivation of the consultee is maximized and reinforced by the immediacy of the problem. Under these conditions, the probability of a successful intervention is extremely high, especially if the consultant brings appropriate consultative skills to bear on the situation.

Appropriate consultative skills include the application of a rational plan or model that will limit the interaction between the consultant and consultee to the specific problem being addressed. The consultant will also use the model as a guide for choosing strategies that promise to bring about the desired changes for the consultee. Underpinning the professional expertise and technical skills of the consultant, must be a personal philosophy that invites participation and sharing. Obviously, the consultant must be an effective listener in order to respond effectively. One's ability to listen is influenced by one's attitudes toward others. The behavioral manifestations of one's attitudes can be observed and articulated as skills. Thus, behaviors of an effective practitioner can be learned and refined.

Behavioral Characteristics of Competent Consultant

The following ten summary statements describe the behavioral characteristics of the competent consultant:

1. The consultant reflects the feelings and needs of the consultee when stating the concerns and issues to be resolved.

2. The consultant is open to questions from the consultee and invites cooperation through honest dialogue and clearly stating the purpose of the consultative contact and process.

3. The consultant keeps the relationship voluntary by checking out with the consultees their willingness to work on the problem as stated.

4. The consultant and consultees work as professional equals: the consultant is responsible for managing the consultative process; whereas, the consultees are responsible for controlling the content that will be considered pertinent.

5. The consultant keeps attention focused on the situational context of the problem and does not digress or allow others to digress about personal issues.

6. The consultant has no position of authority in the consultative situation and no responsibility for the choices made by the consultees.

7. The consultees are free to choose whether or not to use any or all of the consultant's suggestions and recommendations.

8. The consultant uses materials and shares techniques appropriate to the consultative issues. In other words, the consultant does not have a predetermined body of information that he/she intends to impart.

9. The consultee defines the nature and scope of the issues to be addressed by the consultant.

10. As a result of consultation, consultees learn professional skills and develop understandings that can be applied to similar situations without the help of the consultant.

Consultation Skills

Most of the generic skills needed in consultation are those readily identifiable as skills the Health and Human Service Provider has acquired through training and practice. Nevertheless, the consultative relationship defines the application the practitioner can make of the professional skills and judgments. If the practitioner has a clearly articulated model of consultation as a guide, the choices of strategies and procedures will be simplified. To catalogue all of the potentially useful sets of knowledge and behaviors for the consultant is impossible. However, several categories of information and areas of expertise can be listed as essential for all consultants. These are summarized in this section but their articulation and amplification constitute the content of this book.

Knowledge Base of Competent Consultant

Briefly, the competent consultant works from a knowledge base. Thus the competent consultant knows

1. models of consultation and can differentiate between that professional role and other roles that may be used in the context of providing services to others;

2. organizational theory and understands worker motivations that enhance and impede goal-seeking efforts;

3. how to assess individual and group behavior in the context of the system and how to intervene to bring about predictable changes;

4. procedures for formulating group goals, helping the group reach consensus, resolve conflict, and redirect energies;

5. techniques that prevent crises, but uses disruptions as transition makers that can be used to impel the group toward growth; and

6. sources that can be tapped into for information, specified services and personal help.

Operational Base for an Effective Consultant

The effective consultant must have an operational base so as to be able to

1. relate and communicate in a fashion that helps the consultee express personal and group concerns;

2. validate the consultative contract through verbal exchanges at appropriate points through the consultative process;

3. model positive problem-solving involvement and decision-making strategies as part of the consultative processes;

4. implement group leadership strategies that effectuate goal-setting and goal-seeking behaviors;

5. enter and leave a consultative relationship in a role differentiated and appropriate fashion;

6. impart feelings of hope and encouragement by tapping into the strengths of the consultee and working as an equal;

7. share knowledge and skills as appropriate and needed without becoming invested in the operation of the consultee's work or management of the consultee's client; and

8. interpret data from many sources and help the consultee use the information in formulating problem-solving strategies.

Beliefs Held

To perform effectively the consultant must have basic beliefs. In summary the following statements reflect beliefs held by competent consultants:

1. A belief that the most important element in any consultative process is the individual; thus, the person is viewed as of infinite worth and value.

2. The consultant believes in self, yet accepts the limitations that go with being human without defensiveness or apology.

3. The consultant believes that feedback from each consultee is worthy of attention and is a potential source for growth.

4. The consultant believes that each consultee has the strength to implement and operationalize those aspects of the consultative process that has meaning to him/her.

5. The consultant believes that throughout the consultation he/she will maintain high ethical standards and will use good judgement in making decisions where ethics and value conflicts are involved.

REFERENCES

Bennett, J. (1978). Can education raise morality? *The Pittsburgh Press,* pp. 2-3.

Duska, R., & Whelan, M. (1975). *Moral development: A guide to Piaget and Kohlberg.* New York: Paulist Press.

Englund, C. L. (1980). Using Kohlberg's moral development framework in family life education. *Family Relations: Journal of Applied and Child Studies, 29* (1), 7-13.

Gazda, G. (1978). *Group counseling: A developmental approach, (2nd ed.).* Boston: Allyn & Bacon.

Ginott, H. (1972). *Teachers and child.* New York: MacMillan.

Graham, D. (1972). *Moral learning and development—Theory and research.* New York: Wiley-Interscience, John Wiley.

Harrison, A. F., & Bramson, R. M. (1982). *Styles of thinking.* Garden City, NY: Anchor/Doubleday.

Harrison, A. F., & Bramson, R. M. (1977). *InQ preferences in ways of asking questions and making decisions.* (Administration and Interpretation Manual). Berkeley, CA: Bramson, Parkette, Harrison & Associates.

Hersch, R. J., Paolitto, D. P., & Reimer, J. (1979). *Promoting moral growth from Piaget to Kohlberg.* New York: Longman.

Janis, I. L., & Mann, L. (1977). *Decision making.* New York: Free Press.

Kirby, J. (1979). *Second marriage.* Muncie, IN: Accelerated Development.

Kohlberg, L. (1973). Continuities and discontinuities in childhood and adult moral development revisited. In P. B. Baltes & K. W. Schaie (Eds.), *Lifespan developmental psychology: Personality and socialization,* pp. 180-204. New York: Academic Press.

Kohlberg, L. (1966). Moral education in the schools: A developmental view. *School Review, 74,* 1-30.

Lande, N., & Slade, A. (1979). *Stages (understanding how you make moral decisions).* New York: Harper & Row.

Pietrofesa, J. J., Bernstein, B., Minor, J., & Stanford, S. (1980). *Guidance: An Introduction.* Chicago: Rand McNally.

Samby, M., & Tamminen, A. W. (1979). Can we help belligerent clients? *Personnel & Guidance Journal, 57* (10), 506-512.

Staub, E. (1975). To rear a prosocial child: Reasoning, learning by doing, and learning by teaching others. In D. J. DePalma & J. M. Foley (Eds.), *Moral development: Current theory and research*. New York: John Wiley, pp. 113-135.

Wilcox, M. M. (1979). *Developmental journey (A guide to the development of logical and moral reasoning and social perspective)*. Nashville, TN: Abingdon.

)

INDEX

INDEX

Emergency service providers,
consulting with 77-103
Employee assistance program 238
Englund, C L 312, 347
Evaluation
activities 130-3
effect of treatment 130-3
outcome 130-3
processes 130-3
Evaluation instrument, *Figure* 102
Evaluation report, questions 231-2
Example, teachers concerns about
discipline 51
Expert services, definition 113
Explanation, Kohlberg's stages 311-2
External consultant 4
trainer 27-8

F

Facilitative responding 179-82
Facilitative-directive Process Model
11-2, 19
Figure 14-5
Fact finder 110
role 109
Faculty and staff, meeting 207-10
Fear message transmission
high, *Figure* 243
low, *Figure* 244
Feature article, *Figure* 270
CCC group, *Figure* 272
consultees *Activity* 268-9
Feeling level
accurate 177-9
communicating 177-9
Feeling word, *Figure* 185
surface 177
underlying 178
Feelings, sharing, *Activity* 297
Ferguson, M 238, 287
Ferrara, J V 286, 287
Foley, J M 348
Follow-up, case consultation 227-31
Force-field analysis 120
Franklin, S G 237, 287

Function
Stage 1 13
Stage 2 13
Stage 3 16
Stage 4 17
Stage 5 17
Stage 6 18
Stage 7 18
Function of stages 13, 16, 17, 18

G

Gazda, G M 53, 74, 103, 196, 311,
312, 347
Get acquainted 159
Activity 160
consultees *Activity* 260-2
meeting 1 255-62
Gibb, J 28, 30, 257, 287
Gil, E 202, 233
Ginott, H 312, 347
Global scale
rating communication effectiveness,
Figure 84
Global statement 251
Goal-role statements technique
procedures 55-8
purposes 55
Goals, completing
reader involvement *Activity* 283
Grady Memorial Hospital, Atlanta
154
Graham, D 311, 312, 313, 347
Grossman, S R 275, 287
Group consultation
development 224
phases 224
process model 11
Group development strategy 253
Group meetings 115-6
Group modality 223-7
Group plan, CCC 254-5
Guidelines
anger responses 190-3
consultants in agencies 27-8
responding to anger 190-3

H

Haley, J 120, 144
Hansen, G B 238, 287
Harrison, A F 308, 338, 339, 347
Health care issues 194-5
Helper characteristics, *Activity* 161-2
Helping
  characteristics 161-2
  listening phase 171-2
  person *Activity* 161
  process, first step 162
  resolution phase 174
  skills continuum, *Figure* 171
  understanding phase 173-4
Hersch, C 108, 144
Hersch, R J 312, 313, 347
Home visitation
  observation, *Figure* 217
Hopewell General Hospital staff 97-102
  activities 98
  communication model 100
  opportunity, participants 98
  problem solving 100-1
  reflection 101
Hospital patients, characteristics of
    favorite staff members 150
Hospital staff, categories 151
Human resource planning 238
Humanism 79
Humanists 294
Husson, E C 26, 27, 63, 295

I

Idealist 338
Implementation 281-2
  SSCP 127-39
Index of Helpfulness, developing,
    Activity 297-8
  Figure 299
Information
  gathering 262
  pretest and introductory 159
  request 163-4
Informational experts, role 109

Initiator 5
  definition 6
Integration, strategy techniques 127
Interaction
  humanistic 294
  inappropriate 165-74
Internal consultant, trainer 26-7
Internal consultation team 65
Interpersonal skills 150
Intervention, successful
  factors 110
  training role 110
Interventions
  relationship, *Figure* 302-3
Interventions, structure
  helping consultees 301
Interview 115
  structured, plan 306
Introduction, leader 159
Involvement 169-70
Issues, moral
  universal 309

J

Janis, I L 337, 347
Jencks, C 200, 234
Joint Commission on Mental Illness and
    Health 107
Joint problem solver 112
  role 109

K

Kaufman, H F 201, 234
Kepner, C H 63, 65, 68, 74
Kevin, D 224, 234
Kirby, J 16, 30, 63, 74, 85, 93, 94,
    101, 103, 347
Kirkpatrick, P 284, 287
Knowledge base, competent consultant
    344
Kohlberg, criteria
  moral judgment 314
  stage 314
Kohlberg, L 308, 347
  decision-making criteria 313

O

P

Worksheet, moral growth
    practice communication facilitating,
        Figure 332
Workshop
    moral development 317
    outline for training consultants 317-36
    styles of thinking 339-42

Workshop, empathy
    consultee trainers 296-300
Wrightsman, L S 133, 144

Y

Yeager, E G 255, 287

ABOUT
THE
AUTHOR

ABOUT THE AUTHOR

Dr. Jonell H. Kirby (Ed.D.) is professor of counseling and psychology in the counseling and guidance program at West Virginia College of Graduate Studies in Institute, West Virginia. Dr. Kirby has a long list of professional experiences and interests in family systems, group dynamics, and problem solving. She began her career teaching in public schools in Georgia and has been a visiting professor at Syracuse University, New York, and the University of Georgia, Athens. Dr. Kirby has been director of the Counseling Center at Augusta College, Georgia; director of instruction in Cleveland, Georgia; associate professor at West Virginia University; has worked in the Counseling Program at West Virginia College of Graduate Studies in many capacities and is now Professor. In addition she serves as a consultant, Professional staff for the Scholastic Testing Service. She has served on the editorial board of the *Journal for Specialists in Group Work* and as an advisory editor for *The Individual Psychologist*. Dr. Kirby is a clinical member of the American Association of Marriage and Family Therapists; a certified school counselor; and National Board Certified Counselor. Dr. Kirby has served as a member of the commission on Higher Education of the North Central Accreditation Association; as consultant to overseas workshops in Portugal, Australia, Brazil, Canada, Egypt, New Zealand, Mexico, England, and France; as a member of West Virginia Advisory Council on Professional Development of Educational Personnel; and as a member of the Standing Committee on Continuing Education (State Advisory Council).